Kaleidoscope

Kaleidoscope

Broadening the Palette
in the Art of Spiritual Direction

edited by
INEDA PEARL ADESANYA

CHURCH
PUBLISHING
INCORPORATED

Church Publishing
19 East 34th Street
New York, NY 10016
www.churchpublishing.org

Cover design by Marc Whitaker, MTWdesign
Typeset by John Turnbull

A record of this book is available
from the Library of Congress.

ISBN-13: 978-1-64065-164-7 (paperback)
ISBN-13: 978-1-64065-165-4 (ebook)

Contents

Foreword

The Spiritual Directors of Color Network began forming in March 2008. A classmate, the only other person of color in the Shalem's Winter 2008 Spiritual Guidance Program, and I began to question where other contemplatives of color were. At our first networking opportunity, approximately ten of us, from the United States, Cameroon, South Africa, and Korea, lamented the small number, collectively, of people of color from our various cultures that attended the Spiritual Directors International (SDI) educational event and the spiritual-direction formation programs in which we were enrolled. We instinctively knew that people of color across our cultures were also contemplative. We knew we could not be the only contemplatives of color. Yet we were underrepresented, both in presence and in voice.

At that networking table, we considered writing a book as spiritual directors of color, but after the conference we tabled that idea and went in our separate ways—except for me. I was coming to the end of my eighteen-month spiritual-guidance formation program with the Shalem Institute and I was already considering research on the contemplative spirituality of black people as my final paper. I left that conference in 2008 feeling determined to uncover the contemplative nature of black people and how it intersected with the readings from the almost exclusively European sources used in my formation program. I uncovered twenty additional books exploring the spirituality of black people to help inform my writing—authors like Barbara Holmes, Thea Bowman, Gayraud Wilmore, Peter J. Paris, John Mbiti, Albert Raboteau, and others, and I began imagining a network of spiritual directors of color. I began to reimagine the idea that was expressed at that first networking opportunity to write a book together, an idea that had

been forming unarticulated within me. My final paper, "Black Spirituality and the Art of Spiritual Direction," was written, accepted by Shalem in 2008, and published in SDI's *Presence* journal in December 2009. Our network began to slowly form, with friends and colleagues sending potential new members and supporting the effort themselves, and we continued to gather a networking table at SDI events. We grew slowly from ten conference attendees to more than one hundred spiritual directors of color across the globe.
In March 2014, our first book was published, edited by Sherry Bryant-Johnson, Rosalie Norman-McNaney, and me. *Embodied Spirits: Stories of Spiritual Directors of Color*, was a compilation of the stories of thirteen members on our journeys into contemplation and formation as spiritual directors of color. Barbara Holmes encouraged me to go further with a second volume, which I edited solo, entitled *Ain't Gonna Let Nobody Turn Me Around: Stories of Contemplation and Justice*, which shared stories of the marriage between contemplation and action through a social-justice lens, ranging from prayer and compassion to the ongoing demonstration for peace and healing on Jeju Island in South Korea, to the civil rights of women, written by an Islamic womanist. Its timeliness and efficacy were affirmed as I garnered an Indie Author Legacy Award as author of the year in the area of social awareness in 2018.

The Spiritual Directors of Color Network, Ltd., incorporated in 2014, is served by a board of five members. For this, our third volume, board member Ineda Adesanya was selected as editor. Finally, an effort that was foundational from the beginning to create a curriculum that centered the spirituality of people of color has been realized. In this volume, members of our network present methods of traditional spiritual direction alongside aspects of spirituality particularly evident in the cultures of people of color, but often devalued in the traditional contemplative spirituality of people of European descent.

This volume, like our previous two, breaks new ground—first as a published curriculum of any kind on forming spiritual directors, and even more so as the first publication of its kind to center the contemplative spirituality of people of color. May the Life-giving

Spirit and our souls meet in agreement as we drink more deeply from Wisdom's cup.

THERESE TAYLOR-STINSON
Founding Managing Member
Spiritual Directors of Color Network, Ltd.

Acknowledgments

My formation in spiritual direction began as a student of the Program in Christian Spirituality at San Francisco Theological Seminary. For two and a half years, I studied history, theology, theory, and spiritual formation and spent hours upon hours in a supervised spiritual-direction practicum both in class and in community—this, in addition to my Master of Divinity studies. I am forever grateful for that depth of study and practical immersion.

At this writing, I am in the latter half of my studies toward a PhD in Spirituality and Religious History. In this, the latter half of my earthly years, my intent is to author and edit books toward the expansion and diversification of contemplative studies within the religious academy. I am grateful for this opportunity to provide the first of such literary resources in *Kaleidoscope: Broadening the Palette in the Art of Spiritual Direction*. The challenges of editing *Kaleidoscope* have culminated in one of my most rewarding projects. I thank the Board of Directors of the Spiritual Directors of Color Network, Ltd., for their support, confidence, and encouragement from the conception of this volume into the pangs of the gestation process through the labor and birth of *Kaleidoscope*. I especially thank our Managing Member, Therese Taylor-Stinson, for her vision and commitment to develop a people of color–centered spiritual-direction curriculum.

I extend gratitude to the contributing authors for valiantly offering up both their professional expertise and personal experience toward a text that is both instructional and relatable. Addie L. Walker assisted in providing the glue, in the form of introductions, that would tie together each of the chapters. Diana L. Hayes provided not only the afterword for this volume, lending

her name and influence, but also invaluable guidance and mentor-
ship for me along the way.

I am indebted to my dean and faculty advisor at the Graduate Theological Union for graciously allowing me to extend the
defense of my doctoral comprehensive exams in order to meet the
publishing deadlines for *Kaleidoscope*, thereby honoring its role
in my formation as a scholar. The staff at Church Publishing have
been more than helpful, and I offer special thanks to my publishing editor, Milton Brasher-Cunningham.

Finally, to my family, thank you for enduring my long hours,
locked doors, and "do not disturb" signs. I would be remiss not
to mention by name my daughter, Folasade A. Adesanya. When
my hands refused to type anymore due to flares of rheumatoid
arthritis, Folasade graciously stepped in to receive dictation or to
read my handwritten squiggles and edits to transform them into a
beautifully typewritten manuscript.

Thank you all.

Introduction

Kaleidoscope: Broadening the Palette in the Art of Spiritual Direction is the third volume in a series of liberative and cutting-edge texts from the Spiritual Directors of Color Network, Ltd. *Kaleidoscope* situates spiritual direction in the contemporary world. The art of spiritual direction is blossoming, becoming more accessible—a practice that all can embrace. It is rapidly becoming a mainstream form of spiritual care. There are more than two hundred spiritual-direction training and -formation programs in the United States alone. In its most hegemonic, nondirective, one-to-one form, spiritual direction has been historically practiced most broadly by Roman Catholic priests and white Protestant women, both lay and clerical. The twenty-first century has brought with it a shift in the practice of this spiritual-care art form. Though still a significant minority, people of color (PoC) are increasingly drawing upon the art of spiritual direction as both directors and directees. The formal art and practice of spiritual direction is no longer reserved for middle-class, white, and Roman Catholic–centered persons.

Spiritual direction originated with the desert ammas and abbas of the early centuries who also shaped the monastic traditions and were known to be the first psychologists, exposing themselves to various practices to test their human capacity. Such practices have been documented in the collection of sayings known as the *Apophthegmata Patrum* (Sayings of the Fathers). Among the desert fathers of Gaza, for instance, there was the prominent theme in their ascetical effort toward spiritual vigilance, freedom from anxiety, or the remembrance of God. In medieval times, spiritual direction was most notably present in the Roman Catholic monastic traditions and later extended into Protestant Christianity in the late twentieth century and then into the new millennium.

Moreover, in this global society, this art and practice has become of multireligious value as a spiritual practice expanding beyond ecumenism to include interfaith practice.

Herein you will find a comprehensive curriculum and guidebook that, from a PoC point of reference, offers more inclusive resources and tools appealing to spiritual directors of many faiths and orientations who will accompany people of diverse cultures and traditions. *Kaleidoscope* begins with a brief history of the foundations of spiritual direction, followed by a description of its current presentation and use. In addition to core skills such as deep listening, hospitality, and discernment methods, this book presents up-to-date lessons on internal liberation, knowing the guest, imaginative discovery, and systemic trauma. While spiritual direction is taught by more than two hundred educational institutions and spirituality centers in the United States alone, there is no single textbook that includes the breadth of basic and common elements that originate out of its core and that serve to maintain its authenticity as an art. The typical spiritual-direction curriculum does not generally reflect the current cultural reality and growing diversity of the art and practice. Those two hundred–plus training and formation centers continue to have very little ethnic, racial, or cultural diversity. The perspective of persons of color is largely absent, with some centers incorporating a lecture or optional reading to represent PoC.

The scope of this book is not like our first anthology, *Embodied Spirits: Stories of Spiritual Directors of Color*, where the SDC network sought to share the formative and informative voices of spiritual directors of color from the perspective of both director and directee. Our current purpose is to provide a comprehensive and user-friendly curriculum from experienced spiritual directors of color for all who may train, guide, and accompany PoC. Spiritual Directors International (SDI), the premier educational membership organization for spiritual directors, published the five principles of spiritual-direction training programs as (1) core traditions and orientations; (2) discernment; (3) psychological-social-cultural dimensions; (4) practicum/internship; and (5) supervision. *Kaleidoscope* breaks these principles down into twelve easily digestible chapters covering history, spirit, sacred space, listening, hospitality, discernment, creativity, freedom, healing, self-care, vocation, and supervision.

In lieu of a lengthy preface that includes a summary of each chapter, Addie L. Walker and I have contributed a subject-specific introduction preceding each part and chapter that serves as the cohesive, curricular palette of the fundamental subjects that can or should be found in all spiritual-direction programs. In addition to providing the "nuts and bolts" of the art in the curriculum, each chapter is then customized to present those fundamentals in action from the perspective of a spiritual director of color (SDoC) to include narrative components and opportunities for integration. In creating this bond, the theme of Ubuntu arose as evident in each of the writers' voices. Ubuntu is a spiritual concept found in many cultures and broadly documented in the native cultures of South Africa.

This concept, which is gaining significant popularity around the world, simply means "I in You and You in Me." Christians acknowledge that part of God's greatest commandment is to "love our neighbors as ourselves" and understand this commandment to be one of mutuality and interdependence. Likewise, Ubuntu means that each individual's humanity is ideally expressed in relationship with others.[1]

The art of spiritual direction is in service to relationships. The directee brings to each session multiple relationships—with others, with self, and with the Divine. Together, the chapters bring together an inclusive presentation of clear and authentic examples of the skills, qualities, sensibilities, and sensitivities that are of value in practicing the art of spiritual direction. A host of organizational, practical, and literary resources follows the chapters to round off the comprehensive intent of the work. We present a book that can be used for teaching or training a vast range of people who practice spiritual direction, a textbook for anyone who teaches or studies spiritual direction as both preparation for and deepening of their call.

Kaleidoscope in one text offers a comprehensive introduction to the various components that contribute to the art of spiritual direction. With intentionality, we embrace the core competencies of the practice while acknowledging and confronting the differences and complexities that present in the art of spiritual direction through the lens of the SDoC. As you read, remember that this is an anthology and that each author is sharing from their own perspective, experience, and preference. This indeed is part of the beauty of this work—that we offer you a place to enter and engage authentically in the colorful, healing possibilities that reside within the art of spiritual direction.

Notes

1. Ineda P. Adesanya, "The Ideal Beloved Community: The Perichoretic Nature of the Trinity Reflected in the Communal Nature of African-American Believers as a Qualitative Model for the Ideal Beloved Community," *American Baptist Quarterly* 35, no. 2 (Summer 2016): 140.

Part I: Foundations

This book is divided into four sections, each of which contributes to the overall art, discipline, and study of spiritual direction in the formation of spiritual directors, written from the perspective of directors who are people of color from the global community. In this first section, we begin, fittingly, with history. In the second chapter we move to the critical role of Spirit in spiritual direction. The author addresses the question of human longing for God, or the transcendent, or what may be termed "a Spirit which is committed to dwell with us, guide us, and share our humanly existence."

1

Soul Care
A Brief Historical Overview and Nature of Spiritual Direction

Maurice J. Nutt

TRAINING PRINCIPLE | HISTORY

Laying the foundation of this book in history does two things. First, beginning with history allows us to frame the conversation about spiritual direction within a larger context, helping us to appreciate the past, assess our current place and role in time, and giving us clues for envisioning the future. Though the practice of spiritual direction or spiritual accompaniment is ancient, we have chosen to frame the historical context within the Christian story and its biblical texts. Second, history operates at the heart of doing spiritual direction, helping others to reconnect to their true identity, the story of God, and the story of the community in order to live faithfully.

Engaging history—looking back, reconnecting with foundational stories, knowledge, and ancestors or foremothers and forefathers—is also known as Sankofa, which is a Ghanaian concept that refers to looking back, learning from and reconnecting with the past in order to be present in the now, and to carrying the future within our grasp, gently, carefully. This is relevant not only for understanding the field of spiritual direction, but also the very activity of companioning another in spiritual direction and helping the directee reconnect with their own beginning in God, as one created in the image and likeness of God and for the purposes of God. This ancient concept is complemented by another African concept, Ubuntu, which is best translated as "humanity" (persons) emphasizing social unity (community, oneness), generosity of spirit, and kindness. Ubuntu refers to behaving well toward others, or acting in ways that benefit the community (and all creation) consistent with a shared identity with all other humans, in the One who created all. We can only know our true identity in relationship: with others, with self, with God. The essential goal of spiritual direction is to help us to reconnect with the Source of all being, with the story of God in history, with all creation, with our ancestors, our fathers and mothers in faith, and to come to know our true identity so that we can live freely and grounded in this truth.

Rightly, Maurice Nutt begins with a brief overview of the field that he calls "the science and art of leading Christians toward holiness." He starts by clarifying what the ministry of spiritual direction entails, then moves to chronicle the evolution of this ministry beginning with the Hebrew and Christian scriptures, noting the development and dramatic changes through the ages since, and concludes by highlighting the importance of "discipline, practice, and accountability." The chapter ends with a story of spiritual direction that captures its importance in the author's life today.

Ask advice of every wise person; never
scorn any profitable advice.
Tobit 4:18 (NAB)

Keep your thoughts positive because your thoughts become
your words. Keep your words positive because your words
become your behaviors. Keep your behaviors positive
because your behaviors become your habits. Keep your habits
positive because your habits become your values. Keep your
values positive because your values become your destiny.
An adaptation from Mahatma Gandhi (1869–1948)

Defining Spiritual Direction

Throughout our nation and beyond there is an incessant need to "be all right"—to be affirmed or validated. There have been an incalculable number of books written to satisfy the need of people looking for answers about themselves and their relationship with the divine. People are urgently seeking to find the path of righteousness or holiness. Others categorize themselves as "spiritual" but not "religious." This quest to find a divine connection with God, to become "more spiritual," and to be accompanied on the journey to wholeness and holiness is not a recent phenomenon. What is being sought after is known as spiritual direction. Personal spiritual direction has aptly been defined as the science and art of leading Christians and others of faith toward holiness. It is carried out through guidance offered by a competent spiritual director. Those charismatically gifted by God's spirit with a call to accompany others include men and women, clergy, vowed religious, and laity across Christian denominations.[1] This ministry of "caring for souls" has as its ultimate goal to help people draw closer to Christ by guidance or accompaniment. It is understood as a helping relationship focusing on a person's growth in the spiritual life over a period of time. Many seek spiritual guidance and support in response to the complexities and challenges in life and in a person's faith journey. Through spiritual direction they explore a deeper intimacy with God and discern their responses to this relationship in the daily concerns of life and discipleship. This process unfolds under the continual impulse, inspiration, and action of the Holy Spirit. Spiritual direction, therefore, actually involves three persons: the directee (person seeking direction), the director (the one giving direction), and the Holy Spirit.[2]

Cultivating an awareness of God's transforming presence as foundational for spiritual direction is a common theme in devotional theology. However, one must understand and accept the omnipresence of God: God is present everywhere at the same time. Therefore, when directees within the context of spiritual direction say they are "seeking God," they are expressing an unconsciousness that they are surrounded by the presence of God. We cannot attain the presence of God because we are already totally immersed in the Holy Presence. What's absent is awareness.

The profundity of the simple notion of learning how to experience God's presence is made clear through the observations of Gary W. Moon and David G. Benner, psychologists grounded in Christian formation and ministry. They contend:

> Many in the Christian world have recently reawakened to the truth that wearing the label "Christian" is not synonymous with experiencing the intimate, moment-by-moment relationship with God that souls were designed to enjoy, and these many have begun to place hope in the practice of spiritual direction as a path toward abundant living. Across denominational barriers, there seems to be a tidal wave of interest in learning how to experience intimate friendship with God.[3]

Adding yet another helpful insight in gaining clarity about the presence of God, acclaimed African American Protestant theologian Rev. Dr. Howard Thurman in his book *Deep Is the Hunger* states:

> If God be far away, then He comes to us only on rare occasions and in rare situations. Of course, there is a sense in which this is true; the high moment, the great experience, the supreme challenge, the poignant sense of great contrition, all these may mark a sense of special Presence. But we do not live in such a rarefied atmosphere. What we most want to know about God is whether He is present in the commonplace experiences of ordinary living, available to ordinary people under the most garden variety of circumstances. That God is not far from any one of us is the essence of the Gospel that Jesus proclaimed. "Closer is He than breathing, nearer than hands or feet."[4]

A Disciplined Spiritual Life

Awareness, mindfulness, or focused attention are all about becoming a disciplined and singularly focused individual. That is to say, one does not typically "let life happen to them" or accept unconsciously the unfolding events of daily life; rather, one's focus must be to consciously and fully participate in the life the person is actually living. Coming to a place of openness means to be fully aware. Awareness is also a place of unlimited potential in order to begin the process of learning to perceive the integral nature of all things, events, and experiences. People choose to live life with focused attention, not for its own sake but rather as a beginning in the lifelong journey of becoming whole, healthy, holy, and hopefully spiritually mature. In many spiritual traditions this step is recognized as responding to the invitation of the "Divine Other"—the Holy One, in the Christian tradition. It is understood as becoming cooperative with the grace offered by God.

Spiritual direction helps us to commit to living a truly disciplined life: a life of awareness and focused attention. However, embarking on a spiritual journey does not mean that we suddenly need to expend our energy to root out from our lives negativity, unhealthy distractions, behaviors, or habits. Such changes may evolve organically, especially as we are drawn toward experiences of the sacred and holy. To become intentionally focused on the sacred or holy is to be consciously aware of what we are choosing and to understand the reasons underlying our choices. Distractive behaviors, even those that we might convince ourselves are harmless or even necessary, will become less and less important to us, and we release them as we continue to mature and develop in the spiritual life.

Biblical Foundation

Christian spiritual direction has its roots in both the Hebrew and Christian Testaments of the Bible. We would be hard-pressed to name the chapter and verse illustrating spiritual direction as it is practiced today. However, we certainly find in scripture valuable indications that give a foundation for spiritual guidance and accompaniment as we know it. For example, the book of Sirach recommends that we "have constant recourse to some devout person, whom you know to be a keeper of the commandments, whose soul matches your own, and who, if you go wrong, will be sympathetic" (Sir. 37:12 NAB).

To grasp a better understanding of the foundations of spiritual direction as seen in the Gospels, it is essential to understand the spiritual relationship that Jesus had with the One whom he called Father or Abba. Jesus proclaimed his relationship with the "Divine Other," not with the uninspiring, mundane rhetoric of the scribes and the Pharisees, but with the enthusiasm and dynamism of an intimate relationship. For Jesus, his cherished relationship with Abba was not only possible but was desired by the One who was Father.

As the ministry of Jesus unfolded, he chose not to debate with those who may well have had a different understanding of God. He chose instead to simply share with the people who were willing to listen to his experiences of Abba and his conviction that Abba was never far away from them. Jesus's preaching and teaching inspired the people of Galilee and invited them to imagine and accept the realization that God had not abandoned them but was passionately concerned for them. Jesus conveyed an important message of hope to the people: God was intimately present with them and cared about the circumstances of their lives. This message aligns with the core outcome intended through spiritual direction.

In the Gospel passages, we find the examples of Jesus, the Good Shepherd who has a personal and intimate connection with his sheep, whom he knows individually and calls each one by name; they know him, he knows them, and they listen and follow him (cf. John 10:14–15). Throughout the Gospel texts, we find Jesus in dialogue with his disciples, religious leaders, the sick, suffering, marginalized, those accused as sinners, and Gentiles. Jesus did not construct barriers neither with those with whom he needed to minister or with those who had reason to approach him. These encounters provided opportune times for healing, both physically and spiritually. They were also teachable moments for Jesus to give salient advice, to offer insightful parables, to encourage, and to challenge. For example, the Gospel passages invite us to see Jesus speaking to Nicodemus in a clandestine midnight meeting in order to ease Nicodemus's troubled mind about the meaning of being "born again" (cf. John 3:1–21); they provide insight through the Samaritan woman at the well, who received comfort and peace at the revelation of the "living water" (cf. John 4:4–30); and they offer a compassionate lens as gleaned through the "treetop encounter" with the despised publican Zacchaeus who zealously converted, repented, and was restored (cf. Luke 19:2–10). Were these encounters with Jesus strictly spiritual-direction sessions? Not in our understanding of spiritual-direction sessions as an ongoing discipline that focuses on the living process of communion between individuals under the sanctified grace of the Holy Spirit. The gospel provides clarity that whenever someone in desperate need of healing and wholeness came to Jesus, for whatever he might have imparted to them, they were never rejected or left unaided. Those in need received a prophetic word from Jesus that their condition would not be their conclusion.

Spiritual Direction within Monastic Life

The biblical foundation of spiritual direction also grew up among the desert fathers in Palestine and North Africa during the fourth through sixth centuries and came to be recognized as a special charism of these holy men. We find in early monasticism the first historical testimonies of the process and models of systematic spiritual guidance. The practice of spiritual direction did not develop in a strictly linear fashion but rather in a variety of related spiritual traditions. Included in the diversity of terms used to designate the person whom today we would call a "spiritual director," the most frequent ones were *abba* (father) and *amma* or *imma* (mother), at times followed by the adjective *pneumatikós* (spiritual). Other terms, although used less often, were *didáskalos* (teacher) and *paideutês* (educator).[5] According to José Manuel Martin, the principal quality a "spiritual father" should have is precisely the fact of being "spiritual", in other words, of possessing the Holy Spirit and acting under the impulses of the Paraclete.[6]

The objective of spiritual direction in early monasticism was to understand one's thoughts. The monks believed that what must be manifested in spiritual direction was not one's sins but rather the thoughts that disturb one's peace of mind and soul. It was understood within monasticism that one sought spiritual advice or direction when battling or struggling with internal temptations that brought upon confusion, robbed an individual of peace of mind, and vexed one's spirit. It was advised that before someone came to a spiritual father for spiritual direction, they should first do an examination of conscience to discern the goodness or malfeasance of their thoughts. Likewise, the one providing spiritual counsel should not only be "spiritual" but also possess the gifts of discretion and discernment. The word *discernment* is derived from the Latin word *discernere*, literally meaning "to sever," "to set apart," and has been interpreted to mean "to distinguish." Therefore, it is incumbent upon the spiritual director to have the ability to patiently wait and intently listen for the manifestation of God's will in one's life. It was clear among the monks that a spiritual director could not help others to discern the will of God in their lives if they did not first do so in their own lives.

The Evolution of Spiritual Direction

The notion of spiritual direction evolved out of various diverse spiritual traditions. The broad view of the development of Christian spiritual direction reveals that while there is a common origin, it follows three divergent paths: the Roman Catholic, the Protestant, and the Orthodox.

Within the Catholic tradition, spiritual direction was for centuries strongly directive and associated with the role of confessor. Although spiritual direction and the Sacrament of Reconciliation have two distinctly different functions, it was strongly suggested that one's confessor and spiritual director be the same person—and therefore a priest. The development of spiritual direction within the Roman Catholic context was closely affiliated in practice and structure with certain religious orders. The Benedictines, the Carthusians, the Franciscans, the Dominicans, the Carmelites, the Jesuits, and the Redemptorists all have a distinct aura to the ministry of spiritual direction. The Benedictines (founded 529 CE), for example, emphasize *Lectio Divina* and the primacy of meditating on the Word of God and the centrality of the liturgy in the spiritual life. The Carthusians (founded 1084), who are hermits, stress silence and the value of being still and listening for the voice of

God. The Franciscans (founded 1209) offer the witness of holy simplicity through their identification with poverty. The Dominicans (founded 1215) provide their rich teaching on the theological and cardinal virtues of prudence, temperance, courage, and justice. Prudence is the ability to discern the appropriate course of action to be taken in a given situation. Temperance is the ability to exercise restraint, self-control, abstinence, and moderation in regard to one's appetite. Courage is the ability to confront fear, uncertainty, and intimidation. Justice is the ability to always promote fairness and to be righteous in one's actions. The Carmelites (founded 1190) supply their teaching on mysticism and "the dark night of the soul."[7] They also focus on contemplation but contemplation in the broad sense of encompassing prayer, community, and service. The Jesuits (founded 1540) present their Spiritual Exercises, helping the faithful to appreciate the role of the imagination for spiritual growth and development. The Spiritual Exercises of the founder of the Jesuit order, Ignatius Loyola, help a person discern the will of God for their lives, leading to a personal commitment to follow Jesus whatever the cost. The Redemptorists, founded by Alphonsus Liguori in 1732, are missionaries dedicated to preaching the gospel to the poor and most abandoned. Redemptorists focus on the importance of fundamental conversion and the vital role of unceasing prayer in sustaining the Christian life.

The Eastern Orthodox Church tradition (founded 1054), once in union with the Roman Catholic Church until the East-West Schism triggered by disputes in doctrine and over the authority of the pope, recognized the importance of sacramental reconciliation, but also highlighted the role of the "spiritual father." This experienced spiritual guide was often a monk with a reputation for sanctity who, being knowledgeable in the ways of the heart, could introduce his disciples to the practice of unceasing prayer (1 Thess. 5:17). In more recent years, the Protestant tradition developed and gave legitimacy to the role of the pastoral counselor in the church. Often a nonordained layman or laywoman, the counselor used therapeutic techniques as a way of helping a person to focus on and deal with concrete problems in his or her life. While the pastoral counselor was not a spiritual director in the sense of the word, his or her use of modern psychology in a recognized church ministry paved the way for its eventual integration into spiritual direction and other helping relationships.

The Nature of Spiritual Direction: The Three Disciplines of Henri Nouwen

Among those who made a significant impact on our concept of spiritual direction in the twentieth century within both Protestant and Catholic circles, there is one person who clearly stands out: Henri Nouwen (1932–96). This Dutch Catholic priest, theologian, spiritual writer, and professor initially devoted his life to psychology, pastoral ministry, spirituality, social justice, and community. Near the end of his life, after spending years as a professor in various American academic institutions, he chose to commit his time as a "spiritual father" to those with intellectual and developmental disabilities in Canada. Throughout his life, Nouwen struggled with loneliness, depression, self-doubt, and the need for interpersonal connections. These seemingly unbearable afflictions were transformative and served as inspiration for his spiritual writings and the formulation of his disciplines for spiritual direction. His writing was popular primarily because of his transparency with his personal struggles that were both invaluable and insightful to his readers. He credited his approach to his interest in the daily life of people and to his own Christian journey:

> I wanted to know how we could integrate the life of Christ in our daily concerns. I was always trying to articulate what I was dealing with. I thought that it was very deep, it might also be something that other people were struggling with. It was based on the idea that what is the most personal might be the more universal.[8]

Nouwen believed that "any spiritual direction commitment affords the opportunity for spiritual friendship, and provides the time and structure, wisdom and discipline, to create sacred space in your life in which God can act."[9] He advocated for securing "sacred space"—a part of ourselves that we don't haphazardly give away in the rush of daily life, spiritual "me time" forbidding anything or any-one to infringe upon the space and time that we set aside to com-mune with God. Nouwen even suggested that spiritual direction provided an "address" for the house of our lives so that we could be "addressed" by God in prayer. Spiritual direction for Nouwen was giving ourselves permission to surrender to God's love and grace and letting God heal and restore our lives. This sacred time and space of spiritual direction could be transformative in ways that we could hardly imagine.

Henri Nouwen was unmistakably clear that spiritual direction was about formation and that a spiritual life cannot be formed with-out discipline, practice, and accountability. He posited three classic disciplines or spiritual practices that are beneficial in obtaining the fullness of a spiritual-direction relationship. Following these disci-plines enables us to create space for God within us: (1) the discipline of looking within to the heart; (2) the discipline of looking to God who is present in the Word of God; and (3) the discipline of the church or community of faith. Nouwen contended that adherence to these disciplines offers the structure and practice needed to grow and deepen our experiences of the spiritual life.

Look Within to the Heart

This spiritual discipline requires that the spiritual director must first guide their directee to search their heart. Introspection and contemplative prayer invite us to seek God in our heart. Interior prayer carefully draws us to the One who dwells in the center of our being. Prayer is the pathway to acknowledging God who in-habits our souls. Nouwen asserted, "With practice, we allow God to enter into our heartbeat and our breathing, into our thoughts and emotions, into our hearing, seeing, touching, and tasting, and into every membrane of our being."[10] Through this spiritual discipline of prayer we are awakened to a deeper reality of God's presence within us and we begin increasingly to experience the presence of God in the world around us.

Looking within the heart enables us in prayer to not only listen *to* but also listen *with* our heart. We are both invited and challenged to honestly listen to God's voice and to allow God to speak to us from every corner of our being. The challenge comes in the realization that God knows everything about us and that we cannot hide anything from God in prayer. We stand before God with all that we have, with all that we are not, simply as we are. Nouwen believed that we must be totally transparent with God about who we are: "our fears and anxieties; our guilt and shame; our sexual fantasies; our greed and anger; our joys, successes, aspirations, and hopes; our reflections, dreams, and mental wandering; and most of all our family, friends, and enemies—in short, all that makes us who we are."[11] The difficulty of this discipline within spiritual direction is that human nature causes us to only want to present "our best self," meaning only those things in our lives that we are comfortable sharing or that evoke a positive response. Inhibitions within prayer cause our spiritual life to be shallow and narrow. Openness and seeking God who lives at the center of our hearts promises an abundant spiritual life.

Look to God in the Word of God

Second, Nouwen proposed that it was essential in spiritual direction to look to God in the Book—the word of God. This spiritual discipline is known as *Lectio Divina*, a method of reading the sacred scriptures and other spiritual writings by utilizing meditation as a core component. This is how Nouwen described meditation as a spiritual discipline vital to spiritual direction:

> Meditation means to let the word descend from our minds into our hearts and thus to become enfleshed. Meditation means eating the word, digesting it, and incorporating it concretely into our lives. Meditation is the discipline by which we let the word of God become a word for us and anchor itself in the center of our being, as well as a wellspring of our actions.[12]

A seasoned spiritual director would suggest *Lectio Divina* to a directee because they understand that meditating on sacred texts cultivates in us the ability to seek God in the word and to be formed by God in the word. This spiritual discipline or methodology is capable of transforming our lives, thoughts, and actions as we grow in greater knowledge of Christ and his teachings.

Look to Others in Community

The third discipline fundamental to spiritual direction is the discipline of the church or faith community. While spiritual direction is seemingly an isolated spiritual exercise, in truth no one lives or functions in complete solitude. The spiritual life requires that we fully participate in our faith community and to witness to the life of Christ working within us. This spiritual practice challenges us to be in relationship with the body of Christ, the church. "For where two or three are gathered in my name, I am there among them" (Matt. 18:20). The faith community reminds us continuously of what really is happening in the world and in our lives. A person of faith who worships with a faith community understands that they bring their daily life and experiences to prayer and in communion with others like them who have struggles, sorrows, accomplishments, and contentment and who seek God's blessings and wisdom in the midst of the community.

In this communal discipline of prayer within the context of spiritual direction, Nouwen suggested that the worship experience has value because the liturgical feasts, celebrations, and themes "teach us to know Jesus better and unite us more intimately with the divine life within the community of faith." He further posits, "The more we let the events of Christ's life inform us and form us, the more we will be able to connect our own daily stories with the great story of God's presence in our lives."[13] Therefore, meeting with a spiritual director offers us an opportunity to share how our individual lives are inextricable from the ever unfolding story of God's people.

Integration

An Experience of Spiritual Direction:
In Search of Something Different

As a Roman Catholic priest in the Redemptorist community, I have been a spiritual director for nearly thirty years. I could not continue to accompany people in a spiritual-direction relationship if I were not seeing a spiritual director myself. As I have reflected on the origins and nature of spiritual direction, it has called me to an "examination of conscience" of my own experiences as a directee. I began spiritual direction as a naive thirteen-year-old, a boarder at a high school seminary. Attending spiritual-direction sessions was required of all students. I didn't have a choice. I was assigned to a priest who was my spiritual director. After the first year, I could choose my own spiritual director. Admittedly, during the first few years of spiritual direction, I was trying to find my way. As an African American young man, I vividly remember staring at my spiritual director and wondering if I could ever be transparent with someone who didn't know anything about me: my ethnicity, my cultural background, my spirituality, and my life experiences. Being that I aspired to be ordained a priest, I deemed my spiritual-direction sessions as an entrée to making a "good confession." I wasn't willing to invest the energy to teach my spiritual director my African American culture and spirituality in the one hour allotted for our sessions. Being the only African American seminarian in my seminary formation, I was fortunate to have well-meaning "holy men" who were willing to invest the energy and engage me with appropriate probing questions such as, "As an African American man, how do you view God?" "How is our seminary liturgical worship different here than in your home parish, and how are you coping with that difference?" "What is God saying to you in this present moment?" My former spiritual directors were mostly white, middle-aged, or older religious-order priests or secular priests. This was the course of my spiritual-direction sessions for a large part of my life, until recently.

I am clear that spiritual direction is vital for my survival. With my fast-paced life of jumping on and off of airplanes, preaching revivals, conducting retreats, facilitating workshops, keeping speaking engagements, meeting deadlines for writing projects, occasional adjunct teaching, leading a Black Catholic theological organization, promoting a cause for Roman Catholic canonization, and serving on my religious community's leadership council, I reiterate: spiritual direction is vital for my survival. It grounds me and makes me stop and live in the present moment. It enables me to exhale and breathe in new life and to restore refreshment to my worn-out body and spirit. It brings balance to my often uncentered lifestyle. And because I know what I need, it is imperative that the one who accompanies me and leads me back to wholeness and holiness, to my best self—my spiritual self—is one who "gets me" and is strong enough to challenge me and gentle enough to comfort me when both I and life become too much.

My current spiritual director came as a rare epiphany. Remember, I was trained as a priest to have another priest guide me and ultimately help me to reconciliation, to penance, with the hope of absolution for my sins. However, someone whom I least expected entered my life: an African American nun more than eighty-years old. I had known of her for years, but it wasn't until a mutual friend who was staying with the nun invited me to her home, where she wanted to prepare a delicious Creole meal for us. During the course of the meal I listened to every word that she spoke; I was enthralled with her gestures and mannerisms. I knew instinctively that there was something exceptional about this vowed religious woman. She has been a nun for more than sixty years. She had been a teacher and principal in Catholic schools, a missionary in Nigeria, a superior general of her religious order, and a vicar of religious for an archdiocese. When I called her and asked if she would be my spiritual director, she said, "I don't think that I have anything to offer you." I did not let her bail out on me so easily. I implored her to at least meet with me and see if there was a connection (already knowing that there was).

The meeting that was scheduled for one hour lasted two hours. Externally we only shared race, religion, and being vowed religious; however, internally there was so much we had in common. This elderly black nun "gets me." She understands me and continues to give me sound and salient counsel and guidance. In my search for a spiritual director, I learned that a person has different spiritual needs for the different phases of their spiritual journey. It was evident, with the hectic pace of my life, that I needed not only stability but also a "seasoned stable person," one who had lived a full and active life of ministry and who could share with me the wisdom and insights of her lived experiences. Personally and culturally, I deeply respect the wisdom of my elders. I believe they have so much to impart about the joys and challenges of life. I also needed a woman— I needed a feminine and feminist perspective. Women think, feel, experience, cope, act, react, relate, and pray differently than men. "Different" was what I needed. I never imagined the difference that "different" would make in my spiritual journey. She listens intently. She questions unobtrusively. She challenges lovingly. She guides, nurtures, counsels, and prays profoundly. Because I give so much of my time to my ministry, I didn't realize how dry I was spiritually. My monthly spiritual-direction sessions are highly anticipated moments to be accompanied by the spiritual oasis of living water where I am replenished, refreshed, reinvigorated, revived, renewed, restored, and made ready to resume my life and ministry from a different perspective. Yes, a loving elderly black nun changed my life. Who knew?

Conclusion

The ministry of spiritual direction has undergone dramatic changes since the Second Vatican Council of the Roman Catholic Church in the early 1960s. The current manifestations of spiritual direction have expanded through ecumenical and interreligious outreach. Spiritual direction is constant and never stagnates; it has evolved and developed throughout the centuries to meet the spiritual needs of an ever changing world. Renowned theologian and mystic Thomas Merton surmised the nature and ministry of spiritual direction best: "God makes us ask ourselves questions most often when he intends to solve them."

Notes

1. Janet K. Ruffing, *Spiritual Direction: Beyond the Beginnings* (New York: Paulist Press, 2000), 1.

2. David G. Benner and Gary W. Moon, eds., *Spiritual Direction and the Care of Souls: A Guide to Christian Approaches and Practices* (Downers Grove, IL: IVP Academic, 2004), 11.

3. Ibid., 13.

4. Howard Thurman, *Deep Is the Hunger: Meditations for Apostles of Sensitiveness* (Richmond, IN: Friends United, 1951), 147.

5. José Manuel Martin, ed., *Principles and Practice of Spiritual Direction in the Catholic Church: A Collection of Readings* (Lexington, KY: CreateSpace, 2017), 9.

6. Ibid., 9.

7. The term "dark night of the soul" in Roman Catholic spirituality describes a spiritual crisis in one's journey toward union with God, like that described by St. John of the Cross (1542–91), a Spanish Carmelite mystic who was influential in the Counter-Reformation. His spiritual writings and poetry merited him a position as one of the thirty-six "Doctors of the Church" in Roman Catholicism.

8. Nouwen, quoted in Mary Frances Coady, "Nouwen Finds Rest at Daybreak," *Catholic New Times*, November 23, 1986, 3.

9. Henri Nouwen (published by his legacy trust), *Spiritual Direction: Wisdom for the Long Walk of Faith* (New York: Harper One, 2006), xii.

10. Ibid., xiv.

11. Ibid., xiv–xv.

12. Ibid., xvi.

13. Ibid., xvii.

2

Who Do You Say I Am?
Reflections on the Presence of the Spirit

Ruth Takiko West

TRAINING PRINCIPLE | SPIRIT

"Who do you say that I am?" is a central question of Jesus in the Gospel of Mark, as he helps the disciples clarify their relationship to and with him. It is also a crucial question for Jesus in his own identity clarification. We note the progression of questions: who do people say that I am, who do you say that I am, and, in Matthew's Gospel, who do people say the Son of man is? Each of these questions goes to the heart of every Christian's, or dare I say every person's, longing for a connection to the Divine, to their deepest self, and to the world they live in. Understanding that this is the central question of everyone seeking spiritual direction is foundational to the entire ministry of spiritual direction, soul care, and accompaniment on life's journey to wholeness and thus to holiness.

As a contemporary song goes, "There is a longing in our hearts, O Lord, for you to reveal yourself to us. There is a longing in our hearts for love we only find in you, our God."[1] The author of this chapter explains the process as "the cyclical interrelationship between yearning for the presence of Spirit and learning what and who we are in the presence of Spirit," which links us again with Sankofa, reconnecting with the stories of God, creation, and Jesus as a path to discovery of personal identity and our identity in relationship with the imago Dei (the image of God) that we are.

Spiritual directors for this kind of accompaniment must be skilled facilitators sensitive to cultural realities, expressions of hospitality, styles of communication, and interpretation that expand far beyond the Western European palette of experiences. The importance of the capacity to listen deeply and to hold the stories as sacred without refashioning them or commingling them with the director's stories, biases, and reactions is crucial. Undergirding this capacity is a capacity to do one's own personal work of introspection and identity awareness, growth, and integration that fosters the ability to draw good boundaries. As accompaniment happens, the gifts and blessings for directors and directees are mutual. The chapter ends with personal stories of how this process shakes out in reality.

Despite the normative notions of contemplation,
it is not limited to silence, not limited to
certain spaces or certain postures. It is
possible to be contemplative in other ways.

Introduction

For millennia, humankind has questioned and contemplated its origins. As much as there has been some kind of recognition of God the Creator, there has also been a yearning for connection to that being or life source. In belief systems across many cultures, this omnipresent, omniscient Presence shares space with us and through us in the earthly realm via an invisible yet tangible Spirit—a Spirit committed to dwell with us, guide us, and share our humanly existence. All that pertains to this Presence (Spirit) and our own essence (spirit) is what makes up the "spiritual" in spiritual direction.

There is an inherently cyclical interrelationship between yearning for the presence of Spirit and learning what and who we are in the presence of Spirit. In the Christian tradition, Jesus asks his disciples, "Who do you say that I am?" He is emphasizing that despite what the crowd might be saying about him, it is imperative that they know who he is. It is equally important that we know who Jesus, God, or the Spirit is for us. Our personal beliefs lead us to yearn to know more about our unique relationship to the Divine.

This awareness becomes the foundation upon which our spirituality is built.

Our questions about who God is lead us to simultaneously ponder our own significance to Spirit. Because Jesus taught by modeling, we follow his example and ask God, "Who do you say that I am?" Because we are the *imago Dei* (image of God), I believe God would say that we are God's Beloved, fearfully and wonderfully made. It is important to consider what we might know about ourselves and how we interact or respond in the ways we do, or what we perceive or believe about our own faith, theology, and identity. As we endeavor to live fully into this notion of belovedness, we must be introspective and self-aware, carefully uncovering and discovering our most authentic selves while staying connected to Spirit, utilizing the resources of prayer and other spiritual practices. This is the basis of how we live out our spirituality.

As we look in the mirror and at each other and Creation, once more we ask ourselves, "Who do you say that I am?" How might we represent the Holy in the world? How do we interact with each other and Creation? Our communal theologies, along with what we have already discovered about ourselves, are the responses that inform our ways of knowing how we might notice the presence of Spirit in our lives. How we see each other will impact our ability to notice the Spirit in the other. Doctrines are created, practices and rituals are learned and performed, identities are shaped, and behaviors become outward signs of belonging and acceptance. We must be mindful to revere the Holy in our neighbors—to share our stories about God's goodness and grace, companionship and love in the hopes of becoming the community that God has intended.

What Is Spirit? "Who Do You Say I Am?"

Pneumatology is the study of spirit. This study includes doctrines concerning the Holy Spirit and the doctrine or theory of spiritual beings.[2] It can also be the belief in intermediary spirits between humans and God. Each faith tradition or orientation has its own nomenclature for the Holy: Holy Spirit, Higher Power, Creative Force, Mystery, Essence, to name a few. My Christian understanding of Spirit comes from what I know about God through my own experience and from our sacred texts. It is essential for every individual to know God for themselves and to respect that others may have different and unfamiliar names for God even within the same tradition. In order to be a good listener and spiritual-journey partner, it is imperative that we not decide what these names are for someone else. (A concordance can be found for various sacred texts online.)[3]

Central to most Christian faith traditions is the understanding of God's triune nature: God the Creator (Father/Mother), Christ (Liberator, Teacher), and Holy Spirit (Sustainer, Reconciler, Mediator). These three act in perichoresis, intertwining or interrelating simultaneously with each other across time. It would be difficult to consider the Spirit's work in the world, through the Christian lens, without this knowledge.

Spirit is the transcendent God communing with us. Jürgen Moltmann explains, "[T]he Holy Spirit is the unrestricted presence of God in which our life wakes up, becomes wholly and entirely living, and is endowed with the energies of life."[4] Within Christian sacred texts we find that (among many other descriptions):

- Spirit is the Creator hovering over the waters of a formless earth (Gen. 1:2)
- Spirit is ever present (Ps. 139:7)
- Spirit gives life (Job 33:4; John 6:63)
- Spirit is a comforter, an advocate, and teacher (John 14:26)
- Spirit is intercessor, praying on our behalf (Rom. 8:26)
- Spirit is transcendent, poured out upon us to make the truth known (John 16:13)
- Spirit is the giver of gifts (1 Cor. 12:7–11); most important among them are faith, hope, and love (1 Cor. 13:13)

Although we can find examples through our spiritual or religious experiences, upbringing, or catechism, God is a mystery—not in the sense that there is a puzzle to be solved, but in the sense that we can never fully know all there is to know about God because we are so puny in comparison.[5] Our assumptions and images will always be inadequate; there will always be this "other" part that cannot be explained, examined, or encountered. "The fullness of God cannot be limited by any human concept or prediction," writes Henri Nouwen. "God is greater than our mind and heart and perfectly free to be revealed where and when God wants."[6]

Because we do not have the capacity to take in all that God is nor to understand God fully, we use metaphor and imagery to help us perceive and relate to the presence of Spirit. Moltmann asks us to consider the feminine nature of God, too, that the Spirit guides with a motherly hand and comforts as a mother comforts.[7] In that part of God's reality that is Mystery, gender should not matter; the image of God that we embody has more to do with our character and soul and spirit than with our physical selves. Daniel Migliore writes, "[T]he name 'Spirit' should primarily serve to remind us that God is beyond gender and that we must avoid the danger of making idols of any images and metaphors of God."[8] I choose to imagine God as energy, like a burst of light, so that God's image isn't trapped within any predetermined ideal. This image can then nurture my spirit at all times, especially within a society that is still patriarchal and where systemic racism is the norm. "To know God as Spirit," adds Migliore, "is to experience God as liberating rather than a coercive power."[9] Included in the ways we might experience or recognize Spirit is through symbols. The cross is one example, as are the rituals of sacraments, liturgical art, and simple everyday representations that are reminders that God is present with us: a simple bowl of water set on a table (baptism), butterflies (transformation), and live plants (Creation).

In the early Christian church, spiritual practices, including spiritual direction, were facilitated or mandated by church leadership. Only certain individuals (ordained men) were allowed to act officially as spiritual directors. Consequently, there is a long history of spiritual direction within the Catholic tradition. "The goal of the practice of spiritual direction was an individual's mystical union with God," writes Duane Bidwell in *Short-Term Spiritual Guidance*.[10] And it probably was directive, as it usually involved confession and moral or ethical guidance. Protestants were unfamiliar with this practice. It had no formal place or expectation in their church structure. However, it has become popular among Protestants who want to explore or question how Spirit journeys with us and thus want to participate in spiritual direction to find the answers.

Unless facilitators (spiritual directors, guides, journey partners, retreat planners) are sensitive to the lived realities of nondominant-culture people, the hospitality that is offered may be more stifling than respiting, more harm than blessing. An intentionally focused introspection is needed to find the source of this lapse in hospitality. It is a necessary ongoing practice that should explicate the heart's contribution to its complicity with oppression. Humanity continues to provide examples of how it wants to emulate the perceived power of God through its own control and manipulation. Unfortunately, the Eurocentric church has a history of erasing the personhood of some of God's people thought to be subservient to them. In many societies with a Eurocentric ecclesiological foundation, the extension of a privileged ideology leaks out into the public sphere and takes over. The result is the continuation of oppressive systems in which the holy text is used as the permission that is needed to keep those systems thriving. As centuries passed, the embeddedness of these assumptions of dominant-culture entitlement ran so deep as to appear completely normative and unquestionable. Those who do not fit into the dominant-culture paradigm must therefore experience Spirit differently than those in power. After all, the Holy Spirit is liberative and reconciling, not passive and acquiescent. Therefore, the ways that marginalized groups answer the question of who God is needs to be contemplated in a more authentic way than the "average" contemporary expression of spirituality might expect.[11]

Dominant cultures' collective historical legacy of power over all has precluded its need to identify the actions of Spirit who accompanies the struggle and strife of those who are least respected and most oppressed. This inherited inequity necessarily compromises one's humanity. Structures and systems in this paradigm are designed to retain control by reinforcing their own economic and social comfort zones at the expense of the dignity of the disempowered. These comfort zones diminish spiritual eyesight in such a way as to call into question the diversity of spiritual experiences that exist outside of those zones.

Because of this experience of control, which has godlike implications, the dominant-culture acknowledgment that God is in every space and that every person is the *imago Dei* has been relegated to the dust-covered tomes of dogma. As a result, many spiritual practitioners look outside of themselves for God, unaware of the movement of the Spirit in and through their immediate circumstance and social location. Henri Nouwen may not have been thinking about the effects of privilege as an impediment in this way when he wrote, "Self-rejection is the greatest enemy of the spiritual life because it contradicts the sacred voice that declares we are loved. Being the Beloved expresses the core truth of our existence."[12]

The definition of *contemplation* is: thoughtful observation; full or deep consideration; reflection; purpose or intention.[13] Despite the normative notions of contemplation, it is not limited to silence, not limited to certain spaces or certain postures. It is possible to be contemplative in other ways. One example of a form of contemplation that is rarely offered in imaginative ways occurs in the limited choices of "acceptable" music, such as the possibility of using music other than Taizé or classical as a centering exercise. I often found it difficult to settle into a sacred space where the music was not only unfamiliar but felt separating. My experiences of black gospel music and spirituals seemed a better place for me to examine or savor the lovingkindness of God. James Cone writes, "The spirituals were a ritualization of God in song. They are not documents for philosophy; they are material for worship and praise to the One who had continued to be present with black humanity despite European insanity."[14] Within these songs were the stories of spiritual strength and hopefulness despite the physical reality of subjugation. Contemplation is defined as purpose, intention, or deep consideration, and is found not only in the singing but in the hearing. The presence of God is evidenced by the movement of the Spirit that causes one to jump to their feet, hands thrown up in the air when the soloist hits that one note and sustains it as if he/she needed to make sure the sound would reach heaven. It is within that moment that there is communal solidarity around the awareness of God's grace. Cone writes, "The certain fact is always that God is present with them and trouble will not have the last word."[15]

Who Am I? Self-Identity

> The presence of Spirit invites us to introspection
> by helping us take note of our identities.

Who am I? What is my context or social location? Much of where
and how we have lived shapes who we are along the journey. The
better we know who we are, the more astute we can be when we
listen to the stories of those we accompany, those with similar
pathways, so that we don't unintentionally intermingle our history,
reactions, or embedded biases with theirs. Their story must always
be theirs alone.

I grew up as the oldest of two children in a multiracial, multi-
ethnic, multicultural, interfaith, one-income household in which
one of my parents is an immigrant. (There are more layers to my
identity.) We kids were nurtured to find our own path of faith. My
mother comes from the Shinto tradition, which is an indigenous
spiritual tradition of Japan based in nature. My father converted to
Islam when I was a child. He was raised in a Christian household. I
have memories of sitting at a home shrine beside my mother, going
to temple with my father, and to Baptist Sunday school with the
neighbor kids next door. I am an ordained Presbyterian Church
(USA) Minister of the Word and Sacrament. There is no doubt that
my faith, my theology, and the ways I have experienced God have
been shaped by my childhood experiences, which encompass only
one aspect of who I am.

If we believe that God has been with us from the womb to the
present, we must also look at other aspects of our identities so that
we might notice specific places in our timeline where our connect-
edness to God has girded our spirituality. These revelations may
help or enhance our empathic sensibilities, our compassionate responses, and our sense of hospitality. Our own spiritual practices
and/or spiritual director can be instrumental in helping us through
this. Some truths are difficult to bear. Some truths are hidden behind or beneath layers of denial or ignorance. In any case, the reality of our truths in the presence of Spirit, in the foundation of our
belovedness, is liberating.

My favorite prayer of encouragement was made popular by contemporary mystic Howard Thurman. I have used it as a centering piece many times in retreat settings or as an opening devotional. It is, for me, the quintessential account of life's purposeful living and our relationship with God in it. Here is an excerpt:

> Give me the courage to live!
> Really live—not merely exist.
> Live dangerously.
> Scorning risk!
> Live honestly.
> Daring the truth—
> Particularly the truth of myself!
> Live resiliently—
> Ever changing, ever growing, ever adapting.
> Enduring the pain of change . . .[16]

Throughout this prayer I can hear the pangs of longing—the yearning to live the only life I have in the best ways I can. Ultimately, it is about a deep reverence for the creation that I am, the honoring of God's gift of breath, of struggle, of really experiencing or savoring the days. The one line that grabbed me, "Daring the truth— / Particularly the truth of myself!" continues to guide my introspection. It allows me to be vulnerable and in need of courage, to be brave enough to stand in the face of the real. Courage helps us to unravel that part of us that yearns for connection to Spirit.

This kind of spiritual work moves me beyond simply asking myself why I made a certain decision or which path I should choose. It prompts me to lean into the grace of God who will not let me fall. That is the only way I can face a truth so frightful. Many of us cannot bear the truth of who we are as evidenced, for example, by our rampant consumerism, substance abuses, and failed relationships. This level of authenticity acknowledges the fear that wells up inside us that we try to hide and asks God to journey with us—to reveal to us slowly and repeatedly our real nature. In this way, Spirit encourages us to keep living.

Spiritual direction lets us embody this prayer with a companion (director). It can be used as a contemplative exercise or it can exist in our memories as a backdrop, something to be mindful of as we continue to explore our relationship with God. We can meditate on the ways we experience freedom. We might wonder what resiliency looks like and where God is in the midst of it.

What we find as a result of our introspection might benefit from further examination of other types of spiritual practices. Popular practices include Examen, *Lectio Divina* (consider also *Audio Divina* and *Visio Divina*), journaling (including dream journaling), Sabbath keeping, labyrinth walking, centering prayer[17] (or other various types of prayers), and guided imagery. Some of these are done individually or in small groups. All are done in the presence of God. Be mindful that regardless of the origins of these various practices, it is your authentic self within the practice that will lead to transformation. In practices facilitated by a director, *always* take care of yourself, resisting the assumptions of sameness that don't apply to you.

In one small-group guided-imagery exercise, our white facilitator told us to relax with our feet firmly on the floor. "Imagine your feet are shackled to the earth." Uh, no. I'm not doing that. I spent the time trying to calm my spirit and praying for freedom. Hopefully this example makes it clear how important context is to our spiritual growth.

Hospitality in Community

> The presence of Spirit invites us to recollect
> God's hospitality and to mirror that to others.

Who does community say that I am? The results of our deep spiritual work allow us to question our own openness; question our embedded assumptions about privilege, oppressive realities, cultural and/or contextual differences; and to face the unknown. The answers should help us to engage those we minister to in such a way that they feel at home, that they feel safe to be vulnerable enough to examine the layers of their own being, knowing there is no judgment or ridicule, no admonishment or shame.

One thing often missing in spiritual-direction training in a "dominant-culture" setting (Western, namely American) is the understanding of, or at least a depth of introspection, that incorporates how impactful oppression and oppressive systems are in creating the framework that shapes individuals and consequently either buffers or impedes our own comfort zones. Because this happens, without regard, seemingly neutral but normative statements or exercises can result in experiences of exclusion or perceptions of thoughtlessness. Well-meaning people can also be the most oblivious to this.

One white director trainee, in hearing his directee lament about what she perceived as a racist response from an encounter with another woman, skipped over the comment and instead asked how she was doing in the present moment. He explained later that he was too uncomfortable to address anything to do with racism because he actually did not know what to say. He was afraid that his own ignorance of the impact of his white privilege would make him appear racist. His failure to accompany his directee in the midst of her lament proved to be disconnecting. This created a sense that the space they occupied together was not a safe space for her to explore her spirituality.

We become able to provide hospitality that invites those to whom the "world" has treated harshly to let down their guard because we have experienced the freedom to do so ourselves. We should be able to stand back and ask what the welcome of the space looks or feels like. How do we as the accompanier (spiritual director) offer the love, care, acceptance, grace, and tenderness that might nurture a weary heart, a spirit exhausted from the weight of the burden society has placed upon them? In what ways can we be attentive to the Spirit to help another overcome the challenge to belovedness when their belovedness is an inherent contradiction of a society that doesn't hold an equitable definition of personhood?

Creation

> The presence of Spirit invites us to
> imagine creative ways to instigate new
> relationships with the natural world.

Who does nature say that I am? Meeting God in nature seems more effortless than all other meetings for the introvert in me. I marvel at the ways I see God's intention in both creatures and plant life. I notice God's sense of symmetry, especially in the creatures and how that carries over to our own human makeup. I am awed by how non-random our bodily compositions are. How is it possible that anyone could believe in accidental similarities after seeing a couple of dozen anatomical and biological examples? There is symmetry from the microscopic genetic composition to the organization of the internal placement of organs to the likeness in certain types of innate behaviors and the corresponding hormonal systems that make them possible. Randomness has an affinity toward chaos and not structure and symmetry. I am in awe at God's mystery as it shows up here as well. I see it in the way birds fly together turning simultaneously with razor-sharp precision. I see it underwater with schools of fish. The two groups have similar movements and are yet distinctly different creatures. There is also the force of maternal instinct that seems to cross species but not necessarily gender. I have learned to appreciate the ways that animals praise God by being precisely the animals God made them to be: dogs howling at sirens, guinea pigs grabbing food and hiding in a safe place to eat it. Sometimes our lack of patience and self-absorption prevent us from witnessing the subtle nuances of nature. I think of the intricacies of spider webs, the beauty of a peacock's plumage, the ways squirrels store food in their cheeks, and how ants follow each other in a straight line. They all are living into the purpose that God made specifically for them and for God's enjoyment. And because there are times when we miss the point because of our self-centeredness, we are blind to the ways we are destroying God's creation.

As much as our personal space is considered "nature," I sense that God is present and manifested in the things that we keep and display, the ways we arrange, the sounds that we prefer, and the safety and comfort that we perceive and receive in our environment. Our minds wander to meet God in the familiar ways that are nostalgic, hopeful, whimsical, and thoughtful.

Consider the ways that nature might help us get closer to God and the ways that we might care for Creation better as a contemplative practice. As available natural spaces are becoming scarcer, it may be difficult to find a way to wander in nature.

Integration

My spiritual-direction practice is mainly short-term direction in small groups. This would be the kind of spiritual direction that happens in retreat settings or workshops. It can be a one-time meeting or a series of meetings over a short period. These narratives include examples of Spirit moving in practice.

"The Power of Three Voices"[18] was a practice created for a discernment group of Chinese, Japanese, and Korean Christians in the planning stages for their future ministry. I was asked to provide contemplative spiritual exercises for a series of meetings discerning next steps in ministry. These meetings had been contentious at best.

In preparation for this practice, I prayerfully considered what might be helpful—what words could be heard in a silenced contemplative space without accusation or judgment. The truth was that the antagonists were actually on opposite ends of the same focus, the same intention. Their ultimate concern was overshadowed by their embedded theologies, which were at odds. Some of them couldn't listen to the others' voices. Some of them couldn't consider that our ways may not be God's ways even if that was their strongest desire. I chose Acts 10—mostly verses 9–15. I was intentional about my choices and took to heart the possibilities that there might be some discomfort because of them. After choosing the text, I went back to prayer hoping to have any unrecognized personal agenda diminished.

I arrived at the meeting about ten minutes early. I had decided that the text would best be presented in three different translations—NRSV, NIV, NLT—which I printed out on a single page. I prayed again while sitting in the car. It came to me that none of the voices reading the text aloud should be mine. Then I heard a Divine direction: "There would be three other voices reading each of the three translations simultaneously."

I had never experienced such divine direction before and was apprehensive about it considering for a moment that I might be seen as a fool. That notion was quickly squashed by my previous experiences of Spirit that were occasions for me to trust in who I knew God to be; I nodded and nervously went in.

The meeting started on time. I looked around the table at the fourteen or so faces staring back at me. No smiles. Three volunteers presented themselves and the reading began. There was no way for me to have anticipated how it would work out. It was the most amazing thing. These three voices all saying the same thing in slightly different ways, agreeing at times, and at times not. They spoke in a cadence which I likened to a spiritual heartbeat. And it all came from our sacred text. As the reading ended, I heard someone exhale and whisper, "That was awesome!"

It truly was awesome. Not only were we hearing Spirit encouraging us to consider that the habitual dogmatic ways we had done things while practicing our faith might be the thing that had us "stuck," unable to notice what else Spirit might be doing; we had also experienced in real time that God's word was still God's word even when different interpretations were spoken.

God often uses simple exercises to create profound experiences. I was prompted to consider in a new way how our embedded theologies—our own interpretations, learnings, and actions—might be what stifles our spiritual growth. I am challenged to go back and read again what I thought I knew for sure, to read it in a different way, a different place, at a different volume, and then to be still and listen.

"The Button" was a practice created for ecumenical, international, and interracial clergy participants. Days before I was to meet with my small group, I began praying for our particular experience. I had already prayerfully considered the scripture I would be using, and had already created the atmosphere of hospitality. As I prayed, an image of my button jar came to mind. I dismissed it because I couldn't see its relevance. My button jar holds a collection of buttons I've gathered over the years. It contained the extras that came with certain purchases, as well as buttons I bought specifically for sewing projects. In some ways, I was proud of my treasured collection because it was so varied. I put that image to the side and continued to pray.

The next day, I decided to use prayer partners in a *Lectio Divina*-style contemplation for my group. The button image came to my mind again. This time, I spoke to God aloud. "I don't know about this button thing. I'm not even sure where they are right now." I had used prayer partners in group sessions before. For example, if we were considering a sacred text about Creation, I would pass around shells or other little items from the sea, which became part of the contemplation "speaking" to us by being in hand, giving us visual companionship and therefore journeying alongside us as we considered the text. But buttons? Well, at least I had plenty to choose from.

Two days before the meeting, the button notion became stronger, which meant that Spirit was being insistent. I did not understand why it was important, but my experience with Spirit communicating with me in this way told me I had to comply. I started to panic because I couldn't find the jar. I began to question if it was my anxiety talking to me and not Spirit—until I found them. Buttons it would be.

On the day of my group encounter I thought two things. First, I was okay to be wrong and have the experience be a failure (though that was never my intention). Second, Spirit always knows more than I do. I said a quick prayer and acquiesced with wonder anticipating Spirit showing up and my being in awe again.

The table that was the centerpiece of our gathering was simply decorated with reminders of how God has been present to God's people: tall, clear vases filled with various levels of water (baptism, cleansing); a living vine (ivy); a cloth that had cultural significance; and three candles (Trinity).

After everyone settled in around the table, I introduced the day's contemplative process and offered an opening prayer. Each person was invited to take one to two buttons from a pouch. Included in the instructions for buttons as prayer partners was this narrative: Buttons can be memory holders. They can be representative of some place or time or person. They can be symbolic. Or they can just be buttons. Hold them and examine them and notice how they are alike and how they are different.

We prayed, meditated, and contemplated with the buttons as a text was read three different times. There was silence between each reading. At the end of the last silence, participants were invited to share something about their experience.

Let God grant us grace and bless us;

> let God make [God's] face shine on us,   *Selah*
> so that your way becomes known on earth,
> so that your salvation becomes known among
>   all the nations.
>
> Let the people thank you, God!
> Let all the people thank you! (Ps. 67:1–3 CEB)

There was a long pause before anyone shared their story. The following stories are paraphrased.

Story one. One of the buttons I got is an anchor button. It reminded me of the times I spent in my grandmother's sewing room. I spent a lot of time with her while my parents were at work. She'd be working on sewing projects and singing hymns. Sometimes she would stop, and we would sing together and play the piano. My grandmother taught me that an anchor button is the little button that is situated behind a bigger button. It anchors the bigger button in place so that it doesn't slip. While I was holding this anchor button and thinking of the fun times I had in that sewing room, I realized that my grandmother is the anchor to my faith.

Story two. I have been going through some challenging times lately. I didn't even know if I could be here this week. I'm glad to have this time to just be. I started to think back to my childhood where I grew up in the countryside. My family had horses. When I had tough times, I would go out and spend time with my favorite horse. The button I got has the name of my horse on it. What are the odds of that? I got a sense of security and memories of God's grace.

Story three. When you first mentioned buttons, I thought, "Buttons? How is that going to work?" Then I got this small button. I thought about the time I left home at a very young age to enter the priesthood. We were very poor and didn't have much. My mom gave me some buttons and a needle and thread and told me I needed to learn how to fix any buttons that might be loose. Over the years, I never learned how to put a button back on my clothes. But each time I met a new person who was joining the priesthood, I gave him a button, needle, and thread. I realize today that sharing these buttons was an expression of love and care. I am thankful for that.

Story four. I got this big button. (He shows us the button.) I thought this is the size button I need to have on my favorite shorts. My wife complains about those shorts because they're old and falling apart, but they are my favorites. They've needed a new button for a long time, and my wife keeps bugging me about it. I know it might sound awful, but I've been thinking if she wants them fixed so badly, she can sew the button on. Then I thought about all the things she has done for me over the years. I thought about how she cares for me, and that I don't thank her enough. I am blessed to have her.

I am not the only one who was in awe of how Spirit works—goosebumps and all. This was an amazing small-group encounter. We all were blessed by it and the ways that God accompanies us in and through each other and the retelling of our stories. *Selah.*

Conclusion

It is curious how often we wonder about where Spirit is in the midst of our struggle or lament, yet in times of jubilation we either "know" that Spirit is present and say nothing or we acknowledge Spirit's presence and quickly move on. Our dedication and commitment to assuring ongoing encounters with Spirit benefit from the actualization of our most fervent efforts to make thoughtful spiritual practices routine. We must develop meaningful practices that are organically created out of genuine personal experiences of Spirit rather than those that ask for voluntary assimilation into a paradigm that assumes the pathways to wholeness and the end results for spiritual maturity and satisfaction are the same. We must also always be mindful that the journey of spiritual direction is designed to be a mutual blessing for both director and directee. It is an honor and a holy privilege to be invited into the circle of conversation with God and the one who shares the story, asks the questions, and yearns to notice the Spirit moving in their lives.

Notes

1. The song is "There Is a Longing," with text by Anne Quigley and tune by Anne Quigley © 1994. Published by Oregon Catholic Press.

2. "Pneumatology," Dictionary.com, accessed September 24, 2018, https://www.dictionary.com/browse/pneumatology.

3. There is also a book by John Mabry, *Noticing the Divine: An Introduction to Interfaith Spiritual Guidance* (New York: Morehouse, 2006), which is about interfaith spiritual direction and may be a good resource to have on hand.

4. Jürgen Moltmann, *The Source of Life* (Minneapolis: Fortress Press, 1997), 10–11.

5. *Puny* is not meant to be a pejorative term. Instead I use it here to signify the contrast between us and the vastness of God.

6. Henri Nouwen, *Spiritual Direction* (New York: Harper Collins, 2006), 77–80.

7. Moltmann, *Source of Life*, 356.

8. Daniel Migliore, *Faith Seeking Understanding: An Introduction to Christian Theology* (Grand Rapids: Eerdmans, 2004), 230.

9. Ibid., 225.

10. Duane Bidwell, *Short-Term Spiritual Guidance* (Minneapolis: Fortress Press, 2004), e-book location 136.

11. Margaret Guenther addresses this disconnect in the ways facilitation of spiritual practices with women is not contextually sensitive in her book *Holy Listening: The Art of Spiritual Direction* (New York: Cowley, 1992). More specific to the African American women's experience, in *Soul Talk: The New Spirituality of African American Women* (Rochester, VT: Inner Traditions, 2001), Akasha Gloria Hull challenges the status quo by pointing out that "spirituality among African American women eventually veers into and takes into account racial oppression and other socio-political conditions" (81). This would change the landscape of a "typical" spiritual practice offered by the dominant culture.

12. Nouwen, *Spiritual Direction*, 31.

13. Dictionary.com, accessed September 26, 2018.

14. James H. Cone, *The Spirituals and the Blues* (Maryknoll, NY: Orbis Books, 1992), 65.

15. Ibid.

16. Margaret Stanton, "A Prayer," in Thurman's essay "What Shall I Do With My Life?" in *A Strange Freedom: The Best of Howard Thurman on Religious Experience and Public Life*, edited by Walter Earl Fluker and Catherine Tumber (Boston: Beacon Press, 1998), 33–34.

17. Gustave Reininger, ed., *The Diversity of Centering Prayer* (New York: Continuum, 1999), 52–54, writes of an experience of this practice as not just Eurocentric but that has roots in the desert Mothers and Fathers of African tradition as well.

18. Excerpt from "The Power of Three Voices," Placing My Stone on Awesomeness, August 10, 2017, http://ruthtwest.wixsite.com.

Part II: Art of Spiritual Direction

Why do we use the word "art" to speak of spiritual direction? If we take a moment to recognize the significance of art within our human contexts, the answer seems obvious. However, for most of us the answer is not so obvious. Just what is the function of art in our lives? If we define art as "creative human activity concerned with the production of imaginative designs, sounds, or ideas," or "human skill (aptitude, or knack) as opposed to nature," then perhaps we can grasp more readily what art has to do with spiritual direction. Art helps us to connect to the whole of our lives, the spiritual-imaginative realm, our inner lives, and the physical-concrete, even scientific realm . . . the physical world in which we live. It influences the development and evolution of consciousness of a person and the whole of humanity; it makes us think about life at a deeper level, challenges us to consider eternal questions, and to mine the meaning of symbols that point to deeper realities and that help us express ourselves. Art is where creative ideas are born. Art connects us with and to other people's realities, interests, ideals, and concerns. In this sense, we can say it is a vehicle fostering and undergirding Ubuntu, connecting persons to one another in the human endeavor.

The art of spiritual direction then involves the creative action of the director to create internal and external spaces for the directee to encounter the self, the creative processes of the Holy Spirit, and the realities of our times. The preface to the book Holy Listening: The Art of Spiritual Direction *states, "The art of spiritual direction lies in our uncovering the obvious in our lives and in realizing that everyday events are the means by which God tries to reach us." The concreteness of this art form takes place as we create "sacred space," "deep listening to self, God, and life's contexts," "a place of hospitality, welcoming, and knowing the guest," and "a framework for discernment, for understanding the Divine and the Divine's role in one's life and in one's call."*

*Each of these features of this art will be guided by the prin-
ciples of the craft of spiritual direction; however, they will find different
manifestations depending on the expressions of the artisan, the Spirit
at work within the particular director, and the level of reception to the
activity of the Spirit the directee can receive at any given time. Thus,
the title "Art"—God painting, singing, writing poetry, or dancing
within our particular skills, experiences, and creativity.*

❁

3

Creating Authentic Sacred Space

Gibbon Bogatsu

TRAINING PRINCIPLE | SACRED SPACE
Creating authentic sacred space is crucial to the spiritual-direction experience if we are to prepare the way for encountering the self, the other, and the Divine. Perhaps one would ask: What does that mean? What makes a space sacred? How do I create it? How do I know it is authentic? In anticipation of these questions, the chapter begins by defining the terms and then turns to the task of creating sacred space. Drawing inspiration from scripture, we outline two basic rules to follow: intentionality and purpose, both having to do with interior disposition for connecting with the Divine. Then, we explore histori-cal practices that facilitate creating an exterior authentic sacred space of encounter. These practices include silence and solitude, gazing and listening, virtual contemplation, music and singing, art and icons, as well as rituals and traditions. Each of these practices for shaping the authentic sacred space is illustrated to provide clarity and provide op-tions for practice within the spiritual-direction setting.

As a young child, I was always fond of throwing pebbles into ponds so I could watch with excitement the ripples extend from the cen-ter outward. I would imagine how much bigger I could make the ripples with the throw of my next pebble, and I would do it over and over with awe. This imagery speaks volumes to me about the force and power that can emanate from the center of being. It conjures up for me what it means to create an authentic sacred space.

To fully comprehend the title of our chapter we need to define the words *authentic, sacred*, and *space*. To be *authentic* is to be all that you can be in truth without adding or subtracting anything. In other words, it is to be real and true to yourself. To create something that is authentic is to create something that is meaningful and embodies truth that resonates with one's spirit. *Sacred* is a reference to the Divine, the Holy, and the Ground of one's being. *Space* speaks of a place or a state. On the one hand it refers to the environment such as nature, buildings, and altars; on the other hand, it refers to a person's state of the mind or the person's state of being. Thus, authentic sacred space requires divine presence in one's physical environment and inner state as a habitat for the embodiment of spiritual truth. Two rules need to be in place to create an authentic sacred space: the Rule of Intention and the Rule of Purpose. We create authentic sacred space by being intentional with a pure desire for God and by assigning meaning and purpose to our encounters, contexts, or sacred spaces—such was the experience of Jacob in Peniel when he wrestled with God.

> And Jacob was left alone. And a man wrestled with him until the breaking of the day. When the man saw that he did not prevail against Jacob, he touched his hip socket, and Jacob's hip was put out of joint as he wrestled with him. Then he said, "Let me go, for the day has broken." But Jacob said, "I will not let you go unless you bless me." And he said to him, "What is your name?" And he said, "Jacob." Then he said, "Your name shall no longer be called Jacob, but Israel, for you have striven with God and with men, and have prevailed." Then Jacob asked him, "Please tell me your name." But he said, "Why is it that you ask my name?" And there he blessed him. So Jacob called the name of the place Peniel, saying, "For I have seen God face to face, and yet my life has been delivered." (Gen. 32:24–30 ESV)

Jacob was determined to be blessed by God, and that is why he prevailed. He knew the intention of what he wanted, and he understood his purpose for seeking the blessing. We may not be able to make sufficient spiritual progress in the art of creating authentic sacred spaces if we are not intentional about what we want and why we want it before God. If we understand and apply these two rules, then we can have a sacred space wherever we are and whenever we desire. We create sacred space by being intentional and by discerning purpose in context. That means knowing what we want and knowing where we are and why we want what we want from the Divine. I can testify from my own experience that whenever I am intentional in seeking the Holy, the Divine flow becomes intensely palpable. Wherever I am at that moment becomes holy ground—an authentic sacred space.

The Rules of Intention and Purpose in a seeker's life are foundational to our Divine encounters. For us to deepen our understanding of sacred space, we need to draw our inspiration from a few Bible passages. Please bear in mind that I speak as an African who is a believer in the Christ and who has had a personal encounter with Jesus the Messiah. In other words, I speak from a personally realized Christian faith perspective.

Rivers of Living Water

> On the last day of the feast, the great day, Jesus stood up and cried out, "If anyone thirsts, let him come to me and drink. Whoever believes in me, as the Scripture has said, 'Out of his heart will flow rivers of living water.'" Now this he said about the Spirit, whom those who believed in him were to receive, for as yet the Spirit had not been given, because Jesus was not yet glorified. (John 7:37–39 ESV)

This passage is a powerful revelation for all parched souls and seekers of spiritual direction to fathom: faith in the Christ is critical for creating interior center points of authenticity, impact, and influence. Faith is a starting point, similar to a pebble hitting still water and triggering a ripple effect. Because the Holy Spirit is constantly within us and with us (John 14:17), we are emboldened to enter sacred space wherever we find ourselves, so that the ripples of living water can emanate from within us to bless all our human interactions. This is our true nature in Christ: by our faith we have access to the Divine, and we carry the celestial atmosphere with us.

Treasure in Jars of Clay

> But we have this treasure in jars of clay, to show that the surpassing power belongs to God and not to us. (2 Cor. 4:7 ESV)

Seekers look for direction, answers, solutions, and to know the will of God for their lives. Often, the treasure of what they are seeking is buried within them. We need to be conscious of what we carry, apply our two rules to create authentic sacred spaces to uncover joy, love, and peace that can flow out to all our human interactions and encounters. We must dare to seek intentionally and purposefully.

Rule one: sincerely desire intimacy with the Holy and be intentional about our wants and desires. Despite the distractions we may encounter, God responds to the primary intentions of our hearts. It is paramount that a seeker enters attentively and intentionally into any context that may serve as a sacred space.

Rule two: assign a purpose to why we are seeking and assign a purpose to the space in which we find ourselves. This can be in an office, a study, a kitchen, a bedroom, a lounge, a sports field, outdoors in nature, or while commuting. Sacred space can occur spontaneously.

Often, our intention can define the purpose and the significance of the space. You may have heard stories of people who encountered God in the most undesirable circumstances, such as in the prison cell, or while hospitalized. We are continually surrounded by the presence of God which we cannot escape. The psalmist reminds us that we cannot hide from God (Ps. 139:7). The Bible also tells us, "In him we live and move and have our being" (Acts 17:28 ESV).

Jesus's Mountain Prayer

> In these days he went out to the mountain to pray, and all night he continued in prayer to God. (Luke 6:12 ESV)

Nature offers us a variety of elements that we can gravitate toward as authentic sacred spaces because of the beckoning atmosphere of the Divine. For Jesus, it was often the mountain and the night sky that symbolized a blanket of stillness over the hustle and bustle of human daytime activity.

Of all the elements of nature, I am personally drawn to water—be it rivers, streams, lakes, waterfalls, or oceans. I also love mountains and forests, and I find it very easy to be consumed by the sacred where I know that I am eternally loved and valued, and I am usually filled with an overwhelming sense of joy and peace.

Elijah's Mountain Prayer

> And after the earthquake a fire, but the LORD was not in the fire and after the fire, the sound of a low whisper. And when Elijah heard it, he wrapped his face in his cloak and went out and stood at the entrance of the cave. And behold, there came a voice to him and said, "What are you doing here, Elijah?" (1 Kings 19:12–13 ESV)

Sometimes when we are seeking the face of God in our sacred spaces, we may be inclined to want to find the Divine in some dazzling spectacle or grandiose epiphany. The scripture above teaches us that the creation of authentic sacred space should be accompanied by a spirit of attentiveness to all of life's mysteries, to see the Divine in the faces of the marginalized and the downtrodden, and to hear the contemplative, still inner voice that spurs us on to perform acts of social justice.

Authentic sacred spaces are not just for us to feel at peace, but are for us to hear the instructions of God for our lives and for us to walk in obedience so that we are able to fulfill God's plans and purposes for our lives. We are not accidents. In full expectation of our arrival, God has given each one of us an assignment, and that is why it is important for us to create authentic sacred spaces that enable us to remain true to our nature, culture, ethnicity, status, and origin. Sacred spaces help to validate the sense that God loves us eternally and that we were created for a definite purpose.

Integration

Practical Ways Which Can Help Us
Create Authentic Spiritual Spaces

Apart from my suggested two Rules of Intention and Purpose for creating authentic sacred space, which is primarily an interior disposition for connecting with the Divine, there are historical practices that we can initiate to create an exterior authentic sacred space in order to facilitate our holy encounters with the Divine Presence. These practices include silence and solitude, gazing and listening, virtual contemplation, music and singing, art and icons, as well as rituals and traditions.

Silence and Solitude

There is no doubt that our modern environments are saturated with manufactured sounds that emanate from our means of transportation, machinery, television, radio, computers, and phones. We suffer from noise pollution more than at any time in history. The advertising world is constantly screaming at us for attention. The healing natural sounds of the twittering birds, the rustling leaves, the gentle breeze, the barking dogs, and the sounds of our own breath are lost in the tumultuous noise that plagues us day by day.

Creating authentic sacred space by seeking silence and solitude is crucial to our livelihoods and imperative for our sanity and restoration. There is great wisdom in the psalmist's reminder to "be still, and know that I am God" (Ps. 46:10 ESV) We are called to cease struggling and to rest in the caring bosom of our Creator in order to experience the restorative salvation of our God.

Being still can make some people uncomfortable, because they are conditioned to a life of activity and busyness. We are so programmed to doing rather than to being that entering into solitude and silence can be challenging. It is also possible for some people to confuse aloneness and loneliness. No one goes on a date with an entourage. They go alone for an encounter, with a person of significance, to a quiet intimate space where they can be attentive to one another.

Stepping Into Silence

1. Select a space. Choose a room or corner in your house and remove any clutter that can cause distraction. Create a prayerful atmosphere by using cushions and candlelight. Go into the garden or to some facet of nature such as a stream, a beach, a forest, or a mountain.
2. Seek solitude or aloneness intentionally in the space you have selected.
3. Position yourself comfortably, close your eyes, and become aware of your sensations—your breath and the God within—while you relax and breathe slowly and deeply.
4. Ask the Holy Spirit to help you and to reveal the mysteries of God.
5. Choose a meaningful mantra or phrase such as "Jesus is Lord" as a centering prayer.
6. Abandon yourself to the grace of the present moment and be attentive to God's voice.
7. Rest in what God is saying or meditate on God's Word found in the Bible.
8. When distractions come, return to your mantra and deep breathing to center yourself.
9. When you are filled, offer a prayer of gratitude to God and quietly exit your space.

Gazing and Listening

Two wonderful passages from the Bible reveal that God speaks to us through creation. The first is:

> The heavens declare the glory of God,
>   and the sky above proclaims his handiwork.
> Day to day pours out speech,
>   and night to night reveals knowledge.
> There is no speech, nor are there words,
>   whose voice is not heard.
> Their voice goes out through all the earth,
>   and their words to the end of the world.
> In them he has set a tent for the sun . . . (Ps. 19:1–4
>   ESV)

The second is:

> For what can be known about God is plain to them, because God has shown it to them. For his invisible attributes, namely, his eternal power and divine nature, have been clearly perceived, ever since the creation of the world, in the things that have been made. So they are without excuse. (Rom. 1:19–20 ESV)

Children are naturally full of joy because they have an unspoiled sense of wonder and they are completely immersed in the world. Through the discipline of deliberate contemplative meditation, we can bring ourselves to a childlike sense of wonderment so that we are able to hear God by looking and listening. Try the practice of quietly looking at any given facet of creation, and we will be amazed at how quickly our souls are flooded with a sense of love, joy, and peace. We will get the same results if we attentively listen to the natural sounds of creation.

When we are engaged in this contemplative act, we don't have to do anything else except to look and listen attentively. The last century's inventions of photography, film, and recordings have provided us with an effective virtual reality whereby we don't need to travel far to enjoy the natural wonders of the earth.

Virtual Contemplation

Today it is possible to enter authentic sacred space in a virtual mode and still get the benefits of the real thing because of how our brains function and because of the power of the human imagination. The internet has copious, astounding images and films of scenic visuals, as well as amazing recordings of sounds of creation. YouTube is replete with free relaxation and meditation videos of all types.

I have used stunning Google images of nature for my daily meditation and contemplative practice. I have arranged an array of PowerPoint slides of mountains, flowers, seas, rivers, and waterfalls that lead me to relaxation and peace. I have also used recordings to listen to soothing ocean waves, rainfall, singing birds, and animal sounds. With high-definition technology, what we see and hear virtually is realistic and compelling.

By our creative abilities, humans resemble God the Creator, and we can use our creativity to infuse in us the same sense of wonderment we feel when we are in the awesome wonder of God's creation. We need to utilize other people's creations, such as music, art, icons, customs, and rituals to enhance our sacred spaces. Most of our creativity is harmonious because we bear the likeness of the Creator. We need to be discerning of creation symbols, however, because not all creations aim to glorify God.

Music and Singing

The following passage shows how Paul was conscious of the value of continually inhabiting sacred space.

> And do not get drunk with wine, for that is debauchery, but be filled with the Spirit, addressing one another in psalms and hymns and spiritual songs, singing and making melody to the Lord with your heart, giving thanks always and for everything to God the Father in the name of our Lord Jesus Christ, submitting to one another out of reverence for Christ. (Eph. 5:18–21 ESV)

The practice that Paul instilled among the Christians of Ephesus is akin to what Brother Lawrence advocated in his famous booklet, *The Practice of the Presence of God*. What they both advocate is the habitual cultivation of a spiritual discipline that enables spontaneous and continuous authentic sacred spaces through what is traditionally referred to as ejaculatory prayers, or prayers of the heart. Spontaneous psalms, hymns, and spiritual songs stem from the rhythm of the heart that pines for God who is the ultimate ground of our being. Melodies of the heart create authentic sacred spaces and bring us into intimacy with God Almighty.

Along with singing melodies in order to bring heaven to earth, we can also invest in good inspiring praise and worship music in order to create authentic sacred spaces. We may not even have to purchase any music per se, because we can find websites that provide sacred space music and prayers for free. Two such websites I like to visit are Pray as You Go (https://pray-as-you-go.org), produced in several languages by the Jesuits in Britain, and the Secret Place (www.secretplaceministries.org), which produces worship songs of the heart. The site is hosted by Ray and Pam Watson, who pastor a church in Auckland, New Zealand.

Songs and music are essential for altering our atmosphere. They can change our mood and emotions for the better. It is important for us to choose music that lifts our spirits so we can use it to enter our sacred space. Many African Independent churches play drums to create and enter into a rhythmic atmosphere of prayer and worship. For some it may be classical music, contemporary classic, Gregorian chants, chimes, or gongs.

We are created with different tastes and preferences, which is why self-knowledge is the key to creating sacred space. To be authentic, we must be true to our inner beings because that is who God loves. One particular singer and song writer who I like is an Irish woman named Enya. Her music creates within me the deepest longings for faraway places. It is music that my spirit can easily soak in, allowing me to be who I truly am with my longings before God.

Singing and music play the important role of connecting us to God and, therefore, is the correct metaphor for entering sacred space—as the Bible prompts us to "make a joyful noise to the LORD, all the earth! Serve the LORD with gladness! Come into his presence with singing!" (Ps. 100:1–2 ESV).

Art and Icons

One of the most controversial and misunderstood practices among Christians is the use of sacred art and icons in our worship of God. Some people see the value of using imagery to depict divine truths, and some people see it as idolatrous and forbidden.

When it comes to religious art, icons, and sacred or blessed objects, we need to be attentive to the revelation poured out to us by the Holy Spirit through these objects instead of dogmatically discounting their use. The Bible carries the message of God through paper, letters, and ink. In the same way art, icons, and stained-glass windows carry their message. Historically, religious art was used to teach the mysteries of God to illiterate people. God spoke to the Hebrews through images and art.

> And the LORD said to Moses, "Make a fiery serpent and set it on a pole, and everyone who is bitten, when he sees it, shall live." So Moses made a bronze serpent and set it on a pole. And if a serpent bit anyone, he would look at the bronze serpent and live. (Num. 21:8–9 ESV)

Jesus went further by saying, "And as Moses lifted up the serpent in the wilderness, so must the Son of Man be lifted up, that whoever believes in him may have eternal life" (John 3:14–15 ESV). The crucifix has served as one of the most powerful pieces of religious art for centuries. Two great saints of the thirteenth century, Francis and Clare, are known for their contemplating the crucifix as the mirror of the ineffable love of Christ. In fact, the figure of the crucified Messiah made the love of God so tangible to them that they wept when they thought of the suffering Jesus. Francis was graced with the stigmata in the last two years of his life as a result of the love he had for Christ through his contemplation of the crucifix.

When we venerate icons or religious art, we are connecting with the reality behind the symbols and not with the substance that is wood and paint. Religious art, icons, and other sacred objects are points of contact for access to the sacred. They help us to create authentic sacred spaces for meditation. Religious symbols have the power to evoke a sense of the holy because they tell faith stories.

Much of the art was created as a spiritual discipline, through prayer and fasting, that allowed for openness to revelation.

It is important to have religious symbols blessed by an ordained servant of God. One can also bless them with holy water. Select the religious symbols that are most meaningful to you and arrange them in a place designated to signify sacred space for your private prayer and worship. You may adorn the space with cushions, draping, flowers, candlelight, or use a tabletop as an altar for sacred space.

Rituals and Traditions

There is fine distinction between the meaning of traditional *practices* and *rituals,* and, therefore, I intend to use the terms interchangeably. I have heard people accuse others of being ritualistic, religious, or too traditional. We are all ritualistic and traditional by nature of being humans. Even animals and other living species perform certain rituals for specific purposes, such as mating. Rituals and traditions are guidelines for living, and they are part of how we communicate and assert ourselves.

Rituals and traditions are a series of regularly practiced actions or behaviors, such as what one does when they first get up in the morning. There are day-to-day rituals, and there are religious rituals and traditions, which are ceremonies and actions performed according to the prescribed order of a particular faith system.

Day-to-day rituals are things like shaking hands, embracing, kissing, or waving goodbye. They are engagements with other people as forms of communication, or patterns we follow for ourselves, such as our daily cup of coffee in the morning to get us going. Rituals and traditions serve the purpose of anchoring us. When we don't follow them, we often feel out of sync. Rituals and traditions are reassuring. They provide certainty and stability.

Because rituals and traditions are part of who we are, they are vital for creating authentic sacred space because they help us to set a consistent and well-founded stage for our Divine encounters. They may be things like making the sign of the cross, genuflecting, closing our eyes when we pray, silence, singing, reading the Bible, and assuming a variety of prayer postures. Rituals and traditions are only a means to an end. If we hold on to them dogmatically, we inhibit the action of the Holy Spirit in our lives. Rituals and traditions are meant to liberate us for authentic worship and not bind us or oppress us in any way. Jesus cautioned against the following of rituals and traditions without the spirit of love when he said, ". . . thus making void the word of God by your tradition that you have handed down. And many such things you do" (Mark 7:13 ESV). He also spoke to the tradition of the Sabbath: "And he said to them, 'The Sabbath was made for man, not man for the Sabbath. So the Son of Man is lord even of the Sabbath'" (Mark 2:27–28 ESV).

While rituals and traditions can help to guide us in the creation of our sacred spaces, the spirit of love infused by the Holy Spirit must take precedence in our sacred spaces for them to be truly genuine in our encounters with the Divine and in our interactions with all of humanity. Let love lead, and let us answer the call to social justice by means of creating and forging ahead with our authentic sacred spaces.

4

Contemplative Listening

Ineda Pearl Adesanya

TRAINING PRINCIPLE | LISTENING
Listening is a central element in spiritual direction, the required foundational skill. Alice Fryling, in Seeking God Together: An Introduction to Group Spiritual Direction, *gives us a few good guidelines for the task and discipline of listening within the spiritual-direction context.*

> [T]here are three things that define the posture of good listeners: a contemplative attitude, an open spirit and a humble perspective. When we listen contemplatively, with openness and with humility, the words that follow our listening will more likely be loving ones.[1]

For those who are not familiar with this skill called variably contemplative listening *or* deep listening, *the author begins this chapter with a prayer of African American mystic Howard Thurman for the grace and skill to be desired by every spiritual guide, "a listening ear that can see." This gift of an ear that can both hear well and see well is invaluable to the spiritual guide. For this is a listening ear that has a disciplined mind and heart that can see the meaning of the ordinary, the commonplace—a listening ear that can see personal faults and likable qualities in others and see God in all things.*

Following this introductory prayer for grace, Rev. Adesanya begins an investigation of contemplative listening, grounding this foundational skill of spiritual direction in the contemplative life and prayer tradition. Out of this grounding, she broadens her definition of contemplation to include "an embodied experience of the presence and action of Spirit." After giving examples of what this might mean in the day to day, we are led through a basic skills-development process to help us internalize what we have learned in this chapter and acquire the basic skill of contemplative listening, or to deepen skills we already have. In the final pages, Rev. Adesanya outlines a "Contemplative Listening and Responding Process" for continued skill development and growth in the art of contemplative listening.

Give Me the Listening Ear

Give me the listening ear
The eye that is willing to see.
Give me the listening ear. I seek this day the ear
that will not shrink from the word that corrects
and admonishes; the word that holds up before me
the image of myself that causes me to pause and
reconsider; the word that challenges me to deeper
consecration and higher resolve; the word that
lays bare needs that make my own days uneasy,
that seizes upon every good decent impulse of my
nature, channeling it into paths of healing in the
lives of others.

Give me the listening ear. I seek this day the
disciplined mind, the disciplined heart, the disciplined life that makes my ear the focus of attention
through which I may become mindful of expressions of life foreign to my own. I seek the stimula-
tion that lifts me out of old ruts and established
habits, which keep me conscious of myself, my
needs, my personal interests.

> Give me this day the eye that is willing to see the
> meaning of the ordinary, the commonplace; the
> eye that is willing to see my own faults for what
> they are, the eye that is willing to see the likable
> qualities in those I may not like, the mistake in
> what I thought was correct, the strength in what
> I had labeled as weakness. Give me the eye that is
> willing to see that thou hast not left thyself with-
> out a witness in every living thing. Thus to walk
> with reverence and sensitiveness through all the
> days of my life. Give me the listening ear, the eye
> that is willing to see.
> Give me the listening ear
> The eye that is willing to see.[2]

Thurman seeks in his prayer a listening ear that can see. Our sight accesses not only the object of our focus, but also the foreground and the background of the object. We see the periphery surround-ing the object, and we see the movement—the changes in the object. Contemplative listening requires an ear that is willing to see. This is the basis from which I will approach this chapter on listening.

Before we tackle contemplative listening, let us consider con-templation. We can't be expected to listen contemplatively if we do not have an understanding and agreement on what is meant by contemplation for our context as spiritual directors. The term *con-templation* is used variously in the twenty-first century. Though it has acquired multiple meanings and connotations, the word had a specific meaning for the first sixteen centuries of the Common Era.

Saint Gregory the Great summed up this meaning at the end of the sixth century as the knowledge of God that is impregnated with love. For Gregory, contemplation was both the fruit of reflecting on the Word of God in scripture and a precious gift of God. He referred to contemplation as "resting in God." In this "resting," the mind and heart are not so much seeking God as beginning to experience what they have been seeking. This state is not the suspension of all activity, but the reduction of many acts and reflections to a single act or thought in order to sustain one's consent to God's presence and action.[3]

Jean Stairs offers one of my favorite explanations of contemplation:

> Contemplation is both a lifestyle and a way of praying—a way to listen carefully, incline our ears, and come to deeper awareness of God. Contemplative living contributes to spiritual wholeness by restoring balance, perspective, and mental, physical, and spiritual health. Contemplative living and praying embody a concern for the whole person and for the development of souls that experience a stronger integration of the sacred and secular, body and soul, heart and mind, and the inner and outer worlds.[4]

An act of contemplation is one that requires an essential "letting go" of one's innate desires and tendencies to react, immediately respond, and fix. Spiritually, contemplation and contemplative living may benefit individuals personally from the focus and centering that allows for fuller and possibly more effective connection with Spirit and with God's desires for our lives. I have broadened my definition of *contemplation* as that which allows one an embodied experience of the presence and action of Spirit.

In my practice of spiritual direction, I have appreciated the opportunity not only to cultivate the charism of contemplative listening with others, but also the experience to attend more deeply to God's presence in my own arenas of life. I regularly experience how contemplation can influence listening, and likewise how listening contemplatively can influence and impact our day-to-day lives. In my work with small groups, I encourage women and men to begin a process of spiritual awareness, spiritual healing, and spiritual empowerment through the simple but complex act of listening. For so many of us, what we need first and foremost is to be truly heard—to be truly seen. With regard to listening with "others," remember that culture is not limited to ethnicity or race. Consider differences in age, social location, and geographical lineage. The most difficult cultural/religious dichotomy may possibly be liberal versus conservative. When we feel disconnected and have not done the work of letting go, we can begin to rely upon stereotypes and other implicitly biased thoughts. Contemplative listening requires the listener never to assume anything. Assumptions always serve as ways to construct the world around us versus organically seeing and receiving.

Contemplative listening, also called "deep listening," is not only good for use by spiritual directors. Mary Rose O'Reilley describes a form of contemplative listening used among friends. In a relationship of spiritual companionship, she and her friend Peter meet weekly for two hours, each speaking for one hour while the other listens. In describing this relationship of deep listening with her friend, O'Reilley describes an accompaniment that gives each participant the freedom to chart a spiritual path outside the norm. This freedom helped them to see what the norms were, what they were good for, and where they may have actually impeded spiritual progress. In response, she noticed within herself that if someone pays attention to the part of her that struggles to know God, her search intensifies. She ends her article with a quote by Douglas Steere: "To listen another's soul into a condition of disclosure and discovery may be almost the greatest service that any human being ever performs for another."[5]

This process of letting go in contemplation is vital in becoming an effective spiritual director. There may not be much worse than seeking comfort, companionship, and spiritual guidance from a stressed-out spiritual director. Spiritual directors, too, benefit from spiritual direction. My spiritual director listens contemplatively to me, and this has been a very freeing experience. It has given me a safe, comfortable space to express my spiritual joys and challenges without concern for judgment. It has helped me to better recognize Spirit moving in my own life. Through the art of spiritual direction, I have been provided with the tools to develop personal contemplative practices. This formation provides for responses to life's stressors by pausing and considering more deeply with an eye toward Spirit. Whereas in the past I would react to challenging situations with a quick "fix-it" approach, I now contemplate the individual or situation before responding to it. This is possible in even the noisiest part of the day. When God becomes displaced in our lives, not only do our spirits suffer but the well-being of our mental, emotional, and physical selves also suffers.

I propose that spiritual directors can avoid such pitfalls and hazards of the vocation by drawing into God. What do I mean by *draw into God*? Howard Thurman says we must center down. He explains that even in our worship and praise, we must locate the stillness of centering down as the first step toward restoration and renewal. We have discussed the value of stillness in and of itself; however, this particular asset of spiritual formation goes beyond restoration and renewal. One of my colleagues in the Spiritual Directors of Color Network, Lerita Coleman Brown, does an exemplary job of presenting the teachings and practices of Thurman on contemplation, inner authority, and spiritual direction. In regard to those experiencing life's most difficult challenges, Brown summarizes, "Both Jesus and Thurman believed that no matter how repressive the external circumstances, God created an inner sanctuary in each of us. It is only by our (inner) authority that we allow it to be disturbed."[6] One way to "draw in," "center down," or attend to one's "inner sanctuary" is to seek regular, personal spiritual care with a spiritual director. It is through this private contemplative work that I have learned to embrace the "letting go" that is essential for true contemplative listening.

I am fully invested in the Hindu proverb that claims, "To learn, read; to understand, write; to master, teach." One of the subjects I have come to teach regularly is contemplative listening. My students and I together experience what happens when we truly and deeply listen, not only to each other, but also to ourselves and most importantly to Spirit. We discover that listening helps us to grow and mature; keep us accountable; is essential to good discernment; shows that we honor and respect others; and can provide healing. Reflect upon your own listening experiences. When you are in prayer, conversation, meditation, and reflection, how well are you listening? Do you pause in your prayer time to see if God is trying to put a message on your heart? Do you wait in conversation to allow others to complete their thoughts before inserting your own? How about taking time alone just to listen to your own soul? Stairs writes:

> Listening happens best when we pause and take
> time to hear more deeply and reflect upon the

depths we hear. Our souls simply cannot thrive in a fast-paced life without claiming some time to take things in, uncover what lies deeply within, and mull things over. If we are gulping things down without taking time to chew on them well, then we don't know what we've just eaten, let alone what effect it will have on us.[7]

There are some basic skills, sensibilities, and sensitivities that underscore contemplative listening and helpful spiritual direction. These are taught in most spiritual-direction training programs, though the names may vary: bracketing, noticing, probing, waiting, summarizing, savoring, awareness, affections, paraphrasing. Details on how these skills are used in practice are included in the "Resources" section toward the end of the book.

Integration

In the week following your read of this chapter, offer an ear to another, having no plan to fix their problems or to even offer your advice. See if you can just listen to another, fully engaged in what they are saying to you, but resisting the temptation to share your own story. Next, see if there is one who will listen to you! Do the same in prayer and in prayerful meditation.

For further integration, I have included the contemplative listening and responding process that I use and teach. It is an adaptation of the process I learned as a student spiritual director.

Contemplative Listening and Responding Process

This process of contemplative listening and responding involves a presenter and a group of listeners.[8] Both the presenter and the listeners have specific tasks to which they attend during the process.

1. Form a small group of three to five persons to participate in a contemplative listening session. Select the presenter at least one day in advance. Establish a covenant together.

2. Tasks of the Presenter
   a. Prior Reflection and Writing
      i. Attend to some aspect of your own experience, an experience that caught your attention even briefly. You might use your senses to put yourself back into a particular situation in order to amplify it.
      ii. At least one day in advance of your listening group, write a paragraph that describes the experience concretely in as much detail as you recall.
   b. Presentation of your Experience to the Group
      i. Read your experience slowly to the group.
      ii. Listen contemplatively to the responses from the group.
      iii. Reply to the responses, moving further into your story to the extent that you desire.
      iv. Listen again to the group's next response to your shared experience continuing the dialogue for as long as you wish.
         • Feel free at any time to tell group members to slow down the pace of the process.
         • Feel free at any time to let the group know that the process has gone as far as you desire or that the process seems finished to you.
   c. Reflection on the Process
      After you have finished your story and have had a few moments to reflect upon the process, reflect back to the group anything you would like to say about how you experienced their comments.

3. Tasks of the Listener
   a. Listening contemplatively to the speaker who is sharing an experience:
      i. Attend to whatever you notice about the speaker and the experience.
      ii. Attend to your own inner life, noting your thoughts, feelings, sensations, and desires as they arise.

- Learn what they have to say to you. Does your inner experience relate to the speaker? Will your experience assist the presenter in this given moment?
- Call yourself back to the present if your attention is drawn away from the presenter.

b. Pause and reflect: Is there something you noticed that might magnify or enhance the presenter's experience?

c. Respond to the presenter, helping to enlarge his or her experience in a way other than asking a question.

Noticing: This is what I notice . . .
              This is what I hear . . .
              I am struck by . . .

Experiencing: As you speak about . . . , I feel . . .
               When I hear you say . . . , I get an image of . . .

d. Listen as the speaker responds to what is said and listen, also, to yourself and to the responses of the others in the group.

  i. Remain aware of the speaker and how he or she may be deepening the story in his or her responses to what is shared.

  ii. Remain aware of your own inner experience as it relates to the speaker.

  iii. Enlarge your attention to include an awareness of the whole group.
    - the group's responses to the speaker and how they interact with one another
    - what moves in you as you hear the responses of the group

e. Keep moving with the speaker, responding to what the speaker is communicating in the present in order to follow the speaker as his or her story develops.

f. Reflection on the Process
   After the speaker has finished the story and time has been spent allowing the speaker to remain with what has occurred, the group discusses the process.

Reflect back to the group anything you would like to say about the process, not the presenter's experience.

   i. What you noticed about yourself or the process while attending to the presenter.

  ii. What you noticed about yourself as you attended to your own inner experience.

 iii. What you noticed about yourself or the group as you attended to the movement of the group.

Notes

1. Alice Fryling, *Seeking God Together: An Introduction to Group Spiritual Direction* (Downers Grove, IL: InterVarsity Press, 2009), 40.

2. Howard Thurman, "Give Me the Listening Ear," in *Meditations of the Heart* (Boston: Beacon Press, 1953), 208.

3. https://www.contemplativeoutreach.org/christian-contemplative-tradition, accessed January 21, 2019.

4. Jean Stairs, *Listening for the Soul: Pastoral Care and Spiritual Direction* (Minneapolis: Fortress Press, 2000), 38, 39.

5. Mary Rose O'Reilley, "Deep Listening: An Experimental Friendship," *Friends Journal*, November 1, 1994, 25.

6. Lerita Coleman Brown, "An Ordinary Mystic: Contemplation, Inner Authority, and Spiritual Direction in the Life and Work of Howard Thurman," *Presence* 18, no. 1 (March 2012): 17.

7. Stairs, *Listening for the Soul*, 21

8. Adapted from the contemplative-listening model created by Elizabeth Liebert for the Diploma in the Art of Spiritual Direction program at San Francisco Theological Seminary. Used by permission.

5

Knowing the Guest
Crossing Over and Coming Back

Daeseop Daniel Yi

TRAINING PRINCIPLE | HOSPITALITY

Hospitality is an art that embodies both giving and receiving. Many gravitate toward the giving and pay less attention to the importance of receiving. Daeseop Daniel Yi dives in to the interplay of the two in his theme of "crossing over and coming back." This chapter calls our attention as well to the importance of "welcoming and knowing the guest," taking into consideration the cultural context and worldview of the directee, including language, culture, meaning making, relationship to and about authority within the director-directee relationship, as well as how to attend to these issues in both the physical and the virtual space. By using the term "guest," the author deemphasizes the often misplaced power differential that typically accompanies the use and notion of "other." The director is called to recognize that each person brings a unique journey formed in the worldview of their culture and current life context. "Sensitivity to the differences of worldviews one meets in the spiritual-direction relationship is thus a prerequisite for fruitful, grace-filled sharing and discernment in the one Spirit of God."[1] Yi gives us a peek into experiences of how this type of hospitality works in a concrete setting.

The Korean Ethnic Self in Spiritual Direction

I have lived in America for fourteen years and have worked as a spiritual director, pastor, and faculty in Korean American churches and at San Francisco Theological Seminary. While giving spiritual direction to first-generation Koreans living both in the United States and in Korea, I have noticed that Korean directees have a different understanding of themselves as compared to Americans. Here are two Korean directees' stories. If you were their director, imagine how you would approach or respond to them.

The first directee is a Korean man who is in his late forties in Korea. "In general, my life is fine, but I feel something is missing in my life. I have been working as an assistant minister of strategy design and budget in my current church for seventeen years. I should keep doing this work because my church needs me. I am going to stay here since I am working for the kingdom of God." What is your understanding of his core issue? How would you explore this issue more deeply?

The second example is a Korean directee who is the wife of an assistant pastor and who graduated from an M.Div. program in Korea. "There is going be an opening for a position in youth ministry in our church. Right now, I have been playing the piano and helping my husband with the children's ministry. If the session can't find a minister and asks me to do the children's ministry as a minister while my husband does the youth ministry, I would like to do that." What do you notice about her identity and what she is saying? What questions would you ask to explore with her?

What I have noticed, first, is that Koreans have a different cultural understanding about the authority of the spiritual director. They tend to have strong expectations that the spiritual director will tell them what to do and will confirm what they are supposed to do. In the same way, in their community they expect authority figures to notice their desires and tell them what they are supposed to do. They are very cautious about sharing their true desires. Instead, if the spiritual director points out that "you have this kind of desire or need" and says that "this path is right for you," they will be glad. This creates a temptation for the spiritual director to act as an advisor or authority figure instead of as a companion to the directee in consideration of the directee's desires and needs.

At the same time, the Korean understanding of the self is consciously or unconsciously shaped by their relationships with significant others. According to Hee An Choi, the Korean self emphasizes the community and prioritizes obtaining a good quality of life for the community over that of the individual.[2] Even though individual Koreans have their own needs or desires, they tend to sacrifice them and put a priority on the community's needs. However, what if the spiritual director has a Western concept of the self as belonging to an individual and thinks that individuals need to possess a good quality of life as individuals? What if the director, out of his or her own understanding of the self, questions the directee's hesitation to express their desires and needs to the authorities in their life? This kind of thought or question might interfere with the ability of the director to be present with the directee, without prejudice or judgment, and hinder their ability to listen to the stories of the directee. Thus, being aware of one's own and the other's cultural senses of the self is essential for a director to know authentically a directee.

The Spiritual Director Creates a Guest House

In spiritual direction, whether cross-cultural or not, the director passes over to the directee and comes back from the directee. John Dunne uses this method in interreligious dialogue, and I think that this can naturally happen in the spiritual-direction context. He says, "Passing over is a shifting of standpoint, a going over to the standpoint of another culture, another way of life, another religion. It is followed by an equal and opposite process we might call 'coming back,' coming back with new insight to one's own culture, one's own way of life, one's own religion."[3] This requires the director to be attentive and fully present to the directee without any judgment or prejudgment, and without imposition of the director's values and beliefs. Being authentically present demands a real openness from the very center of one's being, which is in God.[4] As I pass over to a directee's journey and experience, they become the center of my world for a brief time. As I am truly present to the directee's stories and experiences, all my experiences and my whole being are available for the directee. This is possible because the Holy Spirit is between us. In this process, at the same time, I can have new, deeper insights about myself after I come back to myself.

Rumi's poem "The Guest House" describes this process of "passing over and coming back."[5]

> This being human is a guest house.
> Every morning a new arrival.
>
> A joy, a depression, a meanness,
> some momentary awareness comes
> as an unexpected visitor.
>
> Welcome and entertain them all!
> Even if they are a crowd of sorrows,
> who violently sweep your house
> empty of its furniture,
> still, treat each guest honorably.
> He may be clearing you out
> for some new delight.
>
> The dark thought, the shame, the malice,
> meet them at the door laughing,
> and invite them in.
>
> Be grateful for whoever comes
> because each has been sent
> as a guide from beyond.[6]

Changing "this being human" in the poem to "this being a spiritual director" gives us new insight about the process of "passing over and coming back." One of the most important qualities of the director is the ability to create a safe, open, free, friendly space that allows the guests to be comfortable as themselves and to be transformed as they explore their stories, their experiences, and even their hidden woundedness. A part of creating this space is welcoming and being grateful for whatever they bring, their being and their experiences, without resisting or judging. If I as the director am fully present with them, later they may give me a new insight that I didn't pay attention to previously, leading me to want to rearrange or clean my furniture or decide to treat something new with the highest regard. In this sense, every directee can be a guide who lets me know and understand myself more deeply. As Leslie A. Hay says, as a director, I welcome directees (strangers or guests) and provide hospitality in the form of "shelter" (space) and "food" (nurturance) so that they can explore God's presence in their lives.[7] Furthermore, in this process, I would say that my identity as a director is not that of the host; instead, the Holy Spirit is the true host who welcomes the directee and provides real hospitality. The directee and I become mutual beneficiaries as the guests in the guest house of the Spirit. In this triad relationship, the director helps the directee to be aware of the Holy Spirit, to experience the Spirit's presence, and to respond to any invitation, guidance, or call that arises from this encounter.[8] One of the critical elements of spiritual direction is an encounter with the Spirit of God so that the directee can find their own identity, path, and vocation on their journey.

Lessons from Korean Directees

When I met with each of the two directees described above in spiritual-direction sessions, I tried to be fully present with them without offering any advice. As I listened to their stories, I asked open questions such as, "If you imagine that you can put aside the community's needs for a moment and focus on your own real desires, what would you like to do with your gifts? If God were to give you everything you want and need so you could do whatever you want to do, what comes up in your mind now?" These questions helped them to go deeper and find their own desires planted by God instead of thinking of their community's needs first.

The first directee answered, "I want to do mercy ministry with people who are in need. So, I want to create a baseball team with homeless people and let them experience recovery with God. I want to spend more time with people so we can share our stories with each other and know God more intimately." The second directee responded, "I would like to take over the children's ministry and tell the church we need to start the process of getting green cards for myself and my husband." When I asked each of them to stay in the moment, their faces shone with happiness because they had touched their own deeper desires. I was guiding them to notice their true selves in God and to listen to their own voice first. I was also allowing them to notice, at the ego level, the voice within them that was being shaped by their culture.

Next, I asked them to find a harmonious and more creative way to hold both their own desires and their communities' needs. They became more courageous about being aware of their desires and sharing them with others. Gradually, they have found a way for their desires and their communities' needs to coexist. As a result, the first directee eventually established a baseball team in his city and had a joyful time with them while he negotiated with his church, so that the time he spent on administrative work gradually shifted into more of what he wanted to do. The second directee started expressing her own desires in her church, and the session listened to her desires and decided to let her work in the children's ministry. Out of this experience, she moved out of a mild depression that she experienced when she thought no one recognized her own calling was subsequently not helping her to meet her own needs in her church.

What I noticed from working with these two directees is that in Confucian culture the priority is not on individual liberty or equality but on communal harmony. However, this harmony is not real harmony since it is achieved by people sacrificing their own individual freedom in a culture of patriarchal hierarchy. With this awareness, what I was doing with the directees was letting them go deeper into their own true selves in God, beyond their cultural concept of their identity. Then, I let them come back to reality and create a new way of living as their true selves. This reminds me of Thomas Merton's understanding of spiritual direction, which is concerned with the whole person not merely as an individual human being but also seeks to recover the person's perfect likeness to God in Christ by the Spirit of Christ.[9] My role, then, as a director is not only to help directees be aware of how their sense of self is limited by their cultural identity but also to help them uncover their true identity and destiny as they come to know the Christ who dwells at their center. As they sense their identity and encounter the Christ at their center and start living their life in the fabric of their own ministry and culture, they become more free to engage with others, not only in their ministry but also in the liberation of all people.[10] They can create a new way of living their lives within their culture. Sometimes they can change their culture to find a new way because they are grounded in the Christ at their center.

In this process of helping directees to find their true identities and callings, I become more deeply aware of myself as a director. As I pass over the boundary of myself and come into their world, listening to their struggles and stories naturally sheds light on my own experiences—how I have lived my life putting a priority on my community and have silenced my inner voice; how I have been afraid to say my truths out of fear of being rejected by my community; and, at the same time, how I have been courageous in expressing my real desires and have actually lived my life successfully. As I come back from the space I shared with the directee, I can reflect on my past and current experiences and listen to God's invitations. In this sense, after finishing a session, reflecting on my inner self is a crucial way to know myself better. Also, bringing some issues revealed in the session to my supervisor is one of the best ways of getting to know myself and growing in God. It is in this process of passing over and coming back that the director and directee get to know each other and have a true, intimate relationship with each other because the Holy Spirit reveals in the Light that they belong to each other and God.

In short, when directing Korean directees, helping them to become aware not only of their cultural concept of the self but also of their true selves in Christ and to listen to their desires about vocation is essential. As a result, they are able to find a way to live their vocation. In the process, I am able to know myself in a different way and sharpen my identity in God through self-reflection and supervision. To help directees in this way, what kinds of qualities do I need to cultivate as a director?

Qualities of the Spiritual Director That Create Hospitality

As a director, one of the essential qualities of a guest house is providing the real hospitality of listening. Listening is indeed one of the central modes of hospitality since it is a real presence that allows directees to be themselves and to find their vocation. Therefore, listening is an important art for the director to cultivate because it offers the full and real presence of people to each other.[11] Nouwen writes, "Listening is paying full attention to others and welcoming them into our very beings. The beauty of listening is that, those who are listened to start feeling accepted, start taking their words more seriously and discovering their own true selves."[12] The Chinese philosopher Chuang Tzu has a similar insight about listening: "The listening that is only in the ears is one thing. The listening of the understanding is another. However, the listening of the spirit is not limited to any one faculty, to the ear, or to the mind. Hence it demands the emptiness of all the faculties. And when the faculties are empty, then the whole being listens."[13] Both Nouwen and Chuang Tzu realize that we listen with our full being, and in this way, we let others find their beings. This is real listening in a space in which the director freely welcomes and accepts the directee without having any need to change the directee. Why is listening at the level of being-to-being essential? If I listen to my guests' stories on a superficial level because of my prejudice or judgment, there will be no real transformation or healing that allows them to find their true selves. However, if I really listen to guests from my own being, they can understand their past and current stories from the perspective of their true self and God, and it will provide them a new direction in which to go. This listening leads to a real transformation or healing that occurrs in the process of telling stories.

Nouwen also notes that listening can be healing and transformative because "it makes strangers familiar with the terrain they are traveling through and helps them to discover the way they want to go."[14] Healing, he says, means first of all allowing strangers to become sensitive and obedient to their own stories. Therefore, "Healers are hosts who patiently and carefully listen to the story of the suffering strangers. Patients are guests who rediscover their selves by telling their story to the one who offers them a place to stay. In the telling of their stories, strangers befriend not only their host but also their own past."[15] The process of finding themselves occurs through the telling of their stories. True listening is a way for guests to refresh themselves and be healed because, in this real listening space, guests can uncover new treasures hidden in their misunderstood or unrevealed stories. My most important role as a director, therefore, is to develop a sufficiently empty inner space where guests can reflect on their pain and suffering without fear.[16] In a natural way, transformation and healing occur in this space through true listening. How can I truly listen to the directee with my real presence of being?

Emptying myself is the crucial thing I must do as a director since I cannot truly listen to the guest without being empty. This reminds me of the poem "The Woodcarver" by Chuang Tzu, in which he describes how a master carver empties himself before making a bell stand.

> When I began to think about the work you
> commanded
> I guarded my spirit, did not expend it
> On trifles, that were not to the point.
> I fasted in order to set
> My heart at rest.
> After three days fasting,
> I had forgotten gain and success.
> After five days
> I had forgotten praise or criticism.
> After seven days
> I had forgotten my body
> With all its limbs.
>
> By this time all thoughts of your Highness
> And of the court had faded away.
> All that might distract me from the work
> Had vanished.
> I was collected in the single thought
> Of the bell stand.
>
> Then I went to the forest
> To see the trees in their own natural state.
> When the right tree appeared before my eyes,
> The bell stand also appeared in it, clearly, beyond
> doubt.

All I had to do was to put forth my hand
And begin.[17]

The woodcarver was aware of others' projections on him about his identity, work, and skills. Instead of being caught up in other people's projections about his self, he engaged in "guarding," "fasting," and "forgetting" and arrived at a deeper level of the inner place. Because of this, he could name his fears and temptations and obstacles. As he went to a deeper sense of self, he could see the bell stand appearing in the tree. He saw that the guest (the tree) had its own nature, limits, potentials, and real vocation within itself, without prejudices.

As a director, I pass over to the directee by emptying myself. Nouwen says, "The paradox of hospitality is that it wants to create emptiness, not a fearful emptiness, but a friendly emptiness where strangers can enter and discover themselves as created free; free to sing their own songs, speak their own languages, dance their own dances; free also to leave and follow their own vocations."[18] In this emptying of myself to create hospitality, what kinds of "fasting" and "forgetting" do I have to practice in order to pass over into the directee's real sense of self without my projecting anything onto the directee or myself? In this sense, having an ongoing practice of contemplation or silent prayer is essential for the director because, in this free space, the guest can find the root and purpose of their life on their life journey. How do I know that I am creating a space in which guests can become themselves and find their vocation?

This question brings me to the poem "Fire" by Judy Brown, which addresses how to find a balance between response and silence in a spiritual-direction session by describing how a fire burns:

What makes a fire burn
is space between the logs,
a breathing space.
Too much of a good thing,
too many logs
packed in too tight
can douse the flames
almost as surely

as a pail of water would.

So building fires
requires attention
to the spaces in between,
as much as to the wood.

When we are able to build
open spaces
in the same way
we have learned
to pile on the logs,
then we can come to see how
it is fuel, and absence of the fuel
together, that make fire possible.

We only need to lay a log
lightly from time to time.

A fire
grows
simply because the space is there,
with openings
in which the flame
that knows just how it wants to burn
can find its way.[19]

Integration

How might a director create space for the flame to burn in a spiritual-direction session? As I listen to the guest, using various contemplative listening skills such as clarification, summarizing, paraphrasing, noticing, mirroring, affirming, or asking open questions, I know that too many responses will douse the flames. One of the ways to build open spaces is simply to wait in silence and let the guest savor the experience of God when they are moved or touched by the Holy Spirit. Silence is a gift and a way of knowing the guest, myself, and God. Instead of trying to fill the space with responses, taking time to reflect on what is happening right now is a way of creating a space in which the Holy Spirit naturally works and leads the guest along the best way. At the same time, too few responses will make the guest wander without any sense of direction. With awareness or sensitivity to the movements of the Holy Spirit, following the movements and sometimes leading the guest by responding to their inner movements like we are dancing together, gives the guest the space to find their own way. Practicing silence cultivates my discerning heart and sense of awareness. Sometimes, even though it seems that nothing is happening in the session, I try to trust that the seeds planted in the session will keep growing in the days ahead instead of trying to build a fire with my own efforts in the moment.[20] This is also a way of creating a space for me as the director to be open to any outcome.

After coming back to myself, being aware of myself and reflecting on the session prayerfully is very critical. I ask myself what I have noticed or learned about myself. Some of the questions I might use after a session are as follows:

- What insights arose about me as a person or as a director?
- What are the significant areas of unfreedom that surfaced during the session?
- What did I notice about myself and the directee and God's presence in the session?
- What realizations are clearer about the directee's experience of God, life, prayer, identity, and resistance?
- What graces do I need to ask God for in order to help the directee grow closer to him or herself and to God and to find their own path?
- What did I learn about the directee's cultural background and perspectives, and how did I hold them for the directee to explore them freely?
- In what specific ways can I maintain an open, free space?
- To what in the directee's worldview, image of God, self, and community am I not open?

- Am I aware of my own cultural identity, assumptions, social privilege, power, and gender as a male with a directee who is different from me?
- How do my own cultural experiences enhance or block my being present?
- What am I afraid of and what do I enjoy in the challenge of "passing over and coming back"?[21]

Usually, I write my responses to these questions in my journal right after a spiritual-direction session. It is my privilege to witness directees' profound journeys and mirror their experiences to my own. Also, participating in my peer-supervision group and in individual supervision enhances my self-awareness as a director. The more I am aware of myself, the more the gifts of passing over and coming back enrich me in new, refreshing ways. I am aware of not only my ego level of identity, which is created by my mind and by society's expectations, but also of my true self, which is my radical union with God. As I keep connecting with God as the branch is connected to the vine (John 15:5), I can sense that I am accepted as I am, and I am able to see God's presence in the directees more clearly. Furthermore, I can bring my contemplative loving gaze to the directees and people around me to connect with them in God's love because I am aware of my absolute identity, which is in God. If I do not spend time with God in contemplation, I feel small, limited, and partial in my narrow interests and caught in my own perspective. It is crucial to have this time of reflection because it allows me to be in the intimate silence and not lose my real connection with God, my directees, myself, and the world. In this way, in order to provide hospitality during a spiritual-direction session, having a balanced approach of being aware of my two identities, one that is culturally shaped and the other that has its foundational being in God, is healthier than staying in only one of these identities.

In conclusion, as Merton says, the purpose of spiritual direction is finding the truth of a person's life. The truth is discovered when the purpose for a person's life is discerned in the love of God unfolding in his or her life journey.[22] The critical role of the director, therefore, is to provide hospitality for the guests so they can become their true self and find the inmost truth of their vocation—the act of grace in their soul. The director offers the guest hospitality by creating a free, open, friendly, and safe space in which the real director, the Holy Spirit, is able to lead and teach the directee everything he or she needs. In this sacred place, under the Holy Spirit, the directee and I can experience an intimate bond with humble and open hearts. In doing so, as I become aware of myself and my companion or friend, we get to know each other and are enriched through knowing our own identities and our vocations during our journeys together. It is then that we have truly experienced "passing over and coming back."

Notes

1. Susan Rakoczy, ed., *Common Journey, Different Paths: Spiritual Direction in Cross-Cultural Perspective* (Maryknoll, NY: Orbis Books, 1992), 17.
2. Hee An Choi, *A Postcolonial Self: Korean Immigrant Theology and Church* (Albany: State University of New York, 2015), 31.
3. John S. Dunne, *The Way of All the Earth: Experiments in Truth and Religion* (New York: Macmillan, 1973), ix.
4. Susan Rakoczy, "Unity, Diversity, and Uniqueness: Foundations of Cross-Cultural Spiritual Direction," in idem, *Common Journey, Different Paths*, 19.
5. James Neafsey originally saw this poem as an evocative description of a contemplative approach to supervision, but I expand this as a process of "passing over and coming back" in spiritual direction. James Neafsey, "Seeing Beyond: A Contemplative Approach to the Supervision Relationship," in *Supervision of Spiritual Directors: Engaging in Holy Mystery*, edited by Mary Rose Bumpus and Rebecca Bradburn Langer (Harrisburg, PA: Morehouse, 2005), 29.
6. Jalāl al-Dīn Rūmī and Coleman Barks, *The Essential Rumi* (San Francisco: Harper, 1995), 109.
7. Leslie A. Hay, *Hospitality: The Heart of Spiritual Direction* (Harrisburg, PA: Morehouse, 2006), 29.
8. Elizabeth Liebert, "Supervision as Widening the Horizons," in Bumpus and Langer, *Supervision of Spiritual Directors*, 37.
9. Thomas Merton, *Spiritual Direction and Meditation* (Collegeville, MN: Liturgical Press, 1960), 7.
10. Conrad C. Hoover, "Going Deep to the Truth: Thomas Merton and Spiritual Direction in a Cross-Cultural Context," in Rakoczy, *Common Journey, Different Paths*, 73.
11. Henri J. M. Nouwen, *Reaching Out: The Three Movements of the Spiritual Life* (Garden City, NY: Image, 1986), 89.
12. Henri J. M. Nouwen, "Listening as Spiritual Hospitality," Henri Nouwen Society, https://henrinouwen.org/meditation/listening-spiritual-hospitality/, accessed November 25, 2018.

13. Marshall B. Rosenberg, *Nonviolent Communication: A Language of Compassion* (Del Mar, CA: Puddledancer Press, 1999), 77.

14. Nouwen, *Reaching Out*, 89.

15. Ibid.

16. Ibid., 90.

17. Chuang Tzu, "The Woodcarver," quoted in Parker J. Palmer, *A Hidden Wholeness: The Journey toward an Undivided Life—Welcoming the Soul and Weaving Community in a Wounded World* (San Francisco: Jossey-Bass, 2008), 95–96.

18. Nouwen, *Reaching Out*, 69.

19. Judy Brown, *The Sea Accepts All Rivers and Other Poems* (Bloomington, IN: Trafford, 2016), 34.

20. This insight comes from the Circle of Trust touchstones developed by Parker Palmer and the Center for Courage and Renewal.

21. Maureen Conroy, *Looking Into the Well: Supervision of Spiritual Directors* (Chicago: Loyola University Press, 1995), 129–31. I have adapted some of Conroy's questions and use them to reflect on myself. At the same time, I have also adapted some of the questions in Rakoczy, "Unity, Diversity, and Uniqueness," 19–20.

22. Hoover, "Going Deep to the Truth," 69.

6

The Gift of Discernment

Betty Wright-Riggins
with Ineda Pearl Adesanya

TRAINING PRINCIPLE | DISCERNMENT
Howard Thurman once again allows us to segue into the arena of the next topic, discernment: In the quiet, Thurman observes, one discovers the will of God. For Thurman, a mystic, discernment was not just a spiritual activity one takes on from time to time to make a decision; discernment was a way of life. "God," he writes, "is a part of the very content of one's own life." Betty Wright-Riggins and Ineda Pearl Adesanya explore the many definitions of discernment and offer contemporary and historical reflections in order to set us up for discovering "the art of discernment."

In the end, we return with the authors to Howard Thurman's insight that "discernment is a way of life." The chapter ends by looking at sample guidelines for discerning decisions and identifying various methods for discernment. Some of the methods of discernment are included in the resources toward the end of the book.

In the quiet time I may seek to discover the will of God for my own life. This quest must be pursued with great diligence and consecutiveness. It is well to use a part of each period in seeking to find the answer or, more important, clues to the answer, to this deeply felt need. A man wants to know that his life's purposes and plans are floored by a structure that is more than he is, that is comprehensive, significant and good. When there is the assurance that such a structure has been found, then the sense of being adrift, of living a meaningless life, disappears. The simple assumption is, that God is in each one of us, a part of our very life structure, and we are in Him. We need not concern ourselves over much with the many speculative questions that may range through our minds as a result of such assumption. For the assumption is in itself something more; it is an insistent fact, a category which is the rock upon which we stand. It is its own evidence. Very important indeed is it to be aware of the direction which begins to take shape within us as we seek to know the Will with all our hearts. Often, the will of God becomes apparent in the central concern of our spirits, which leads us to act or function in accordance with its urgency. Or it may become clear to us only after we have exhausted all our plans and schemes for doing certain things or achieving certain results with our lives. Sometimes a man goes along very sure of his direction and then, under the scrutiny of a deadly serious searching in the experience of prayer, finds that all along he has been mistaken. Often, only one step at the time becomes clear, while for some other, in a flash of insight, the total meaning of their lives is made clear. God is a part of the very content of one's own life. Sometimes, His will is seen in simple earnestness and intense desire. Sometimes the quieting of one's spirit in prayer exposes the area of sensitiveness to God's spirit which is submerged by much traffic. Sometimes, there is the marshaling of one's ideas, plans and purposes in accordance with the sense of direction which looms larger and larger as the must for one's life. Always there is the checking and rechecking, testing and retesting, of one's life in the light of what seems more and more the right course, the right way for one's life. At length one's entire life—no particular aspect of it but one's entire life—becomes pervaded with a quality which is divine quality, an accent which is divine accent.[1]

What Is Discernment?

Thurman says that "God [the Divine] is a part of the very content of one's own life." He likewise affirms that "always there is the checking and rechecking, testing and retesting, of one's life in light of what seems more and more the right course, the right way for one's life." This process that he describes is one of discernment.

Discernment is about more than making good decisions. It requires an understanding of the Divine and the Divine's role in one's life and in one's "call." Thus, it requires an awareness of what the Divine is doing in the whole of your life. When asked of a class of spiritual-direction students, these are some of the expressions they gave to describe the many manifestations that represent their whole lives—inner life; dream life; emotional, social, church or religious life; school, family, creative, and imaginative life.

Because we are logically oriented beings, it helps to systematize things, so we need a structure or "map" for all of these manifestations of our lives. Referring to this map as "arenas" of the Divine's activity, John Mabry, in *Noticing the Divine: An Introduction to Interfaith Spiritual Direction,* historicizes these arenas back to the renaissance physician and alchemist Paracelsus.

> Disease, Paracelsus felt, was caused by disharmonies in what he called the five *entia,* or entities. These *entia* are spheres of human endeavor that, until Paracelsus, were not thought of as being related. First there is the *ens astrorum,* or the historical field, containing the history and culture of a specific geographical place. Attention to place, and to a people's culture is of utmost importance for one's health. The second *entia* is the *ens veneni,*

the healthiness of one's food. Long before organic gardeners began warning us that toxic substances used in growing our food could be dangerous to our health, Paracelsus was beating a similar drum. The third *entia* is the *ens naturale*, or the innate predisposition towards health or illness we are granted by our parents. In other words, Paracelsus took genetics into account in his schema. The fourth *entia* is the *ens spirituale*, or the field of social endeavor, as Paracelsus was convinced that the healthiness of our human interactions had a great effect on our health as well. Today, we might call this psychological health. The final *entia* is the *ens Dei*, or that all-encompassing field that is the Divine, for as Paracelsus tells us, our relationship to the Divine is just as important to our well-being as any other aspect.[2]

Paracelsus was looking for balance, harmony, and health in each of these arenas, because disharmony in any would cause disease or "dis-ease" in the whole—the whole of one's life.

Discernment Defined

The etymological root of the word *discernment* is the Latin *discernere*, which comes from the Indo-European meaning "seer." The *Online Etymology Dictionary* defines it as keenness of intellectual perception, insight, acuteness of judgment; and as an act of perceiving by the intellect. *Discerning* is an adjective that is often affiliated with the Old French *discerner*, meaning to distinguish between, or to separate by sifting. This affiliation aligns well with the etymological root as someone with discerning tastes or a discerning eye, someone good at distinguishing the good from the bad and sifting out the gems from the junk. Etymologically, *discernment* requires the ability to "see" by way of cutting, separating, and sifting.

Spiritual discernment has been defined and described in numerous ways. Here are a number of definitions and several descriptions, given by both seers and seekers, that may or may not ring true for you:

- "That habit of faith by which we are properly disposed to hear God's Word and properly disposed to respond to the Word in the practical circumstances of our lives."[3]
- Discernment gets to the heart of the matter: it is the heart of the Spirit engaging our hearts and spirits.
- "A hermeneutical capacity by which we interpret the religious meaning of various influences that bear upon human awareness and activity."[4]
- Discernment strips away the counterfeit and reveals the essence of what is or could be.
- "Not a specific process, but an attitude, a hunger, a search to have the course of one's life correspond to God's gracious purpose and plan."[5]
- Discernment builds up the kingdom of God and lifts kingdom dwellers.
- Any process of approaching decisions that assists a seeker to find God's call in that decision.

Discernment is:

- Knowing the right answer.
- The ability to distinguish between good and evil spirits.
- Knowing and resting in the character and will of the Spirit of God.
- A gift, not a skill.
- A companion to wisdom yet cannot be accessed by increased education, high intellect, or years of Christian service.
- Granted at the Spirit's good measure.
- Characterized by love centered in Christ, directed by prayer and scripture.
- Rooted in an egalitarian spirit and just relationships.
- Obscure.

Clearly discernment has been perceived and approached in many different ways. This chapter does not seek to give the right way or ideal method, but rather to provide helpful insight and places to enter what is often a daunting concept and an obscure venture.

A Contemporary Christian Reflection

The word *discernment* has been used more often recently in a non-spiritual context.

I have heard it used as a descriptor, such as "I thought she was more discerning than that." There was even a commercial on television talking about making the right choice that indicated the "discerning choice" was that of the insurance company being promoted. Why is there so much interest in the use of this word? What does it mean, really? Why is *discernment* not included in the Ephesians 4 passage that enumerates the gifts given to the church, or in Galatians 5 that list the gifts of the Spirit? If discernment is a gift from God, why do we have to pray for it?

The Bible records in 1 Kings 3:8–9 the account of Solomon, who had just inherited the throne upon the death of his father, King David. He prayed and asked God for an understanding mind to govern the people: the ability to discern good from evil.

God responds and says, "Because you have asked this, and have not asked for yourself long life or riches, or for the life of your enemies, but have asked for yourself understanding to discern what is right, I now do according to your word. Indeed I give you a wise and discerning mind" (vv. 11–12a). It is noteworthy that Solomon asked for discernment to govern; God granted much more. God joined wisdom together with discernment, the ability to know, hear, and recognize the voice and will of God and wisdom to follow through on what was revealed. God continues in the passage to promise Solomon that these gifts of wisdom and discernment will be his for as long as he lives, if he continues to follow God's commandments and keep God's statutes. God also promises long life and declares no one will be as wise as Solomon; none will be his equal. This does not appear to be a gift given for a particular circumstance or a gift given to be used only when a decision is necessary, but it is a life choice and a lifelong engagement to live close to the will and heart of God. This begs a question for me, which is why do we consider discernment mostly when there are problems to be solved or decisions to be made?

I was talking with a colleague recently who was in a planning stage with his church leadership. He was seeking resources, to include a discernment process. He said he wanted to make sure the Spirit of God was included in their plans. Is not that the point? Are God's will and desires are always integral to our plans, or is it the other way around? We are to be integrally included in the plans God desires for us and our churches. Maybe this is the reason we must pray for discernment. It is our choice as to how much of God we want in the interior.

Often discernment is experienced as a process, an extended time of prayerful seeking. However, there are times of instant knowing. Call experiences are considered spontaneous knowing. The recipient knows without a doubt that the desire of God for them is being expressed. The "call" is defined as being summoned by God to a spiritual vocation. It can be a dramatic and unexpected occurrence. It can occur in dreams, while engaged in particular situations, or in nonengaging activities. The experience is one of certainty and can be accompanied by auditory, visual, or kinesthetic mediums. The call is always confirmed and upon revisitation is as real as it was initially. In the African American Baptist church, context call experiences were common. Each call was considered unique. The congregation always embraced the calling and provided opportunities for the recipient to engage the new vocation as well as to tell the experience again and again as a testimony of God's grace and power. Call experiences are life-changing events. They have included accounts of being transported to the foot of the cross and hearing a heavenly vocal commissioning. They have included seeing the face of Christ in a sunset and hearing the voice to go be my witness.

Scripture is filled with instant knowings:

- Hagar seeing the angel in the desert, revealing water.
- Mary's visitation by Gabriel, announcing she had found favor and detailing the events of her new life.
- Isaiah being caught up in the temple on the Lord's day.
- Ezekiel seeing the wheel in the middle of a wheel.
- Jesus's confirmation after baptism.
- Peter's dream and being instructed to eat what he considered unclean.

All represent instant knowings indicating God's absolute will for those divinely addressed.

A Discernment Manifestation

> Days pass and the years vanish, and we walk sight-less among miracles. God, fill our eyes with seeing and our minds with knowing; let there be moments when Your Presence, like lightning, illumines the darkness in which we walk. Help us to see, wher-ever we gaze, that the bush burns unconsumed. And we, clay touched by God, will reach out for ho-liness, and exclaim in wonder: How filled with awe is this place, and we did not know it. Blessed is the Eternal One, the Holy God![6]

There is no particular path the gift of discernment takes when op-erating in the lives of God's people. Following are a few samplings of discernment in action.

Years ago, an elder woman was seeking ordination. She was na-tionally known for her gifts in Christian education. She ministered principally among senior pastors desiring advanced seminary de-grees. She was a motivator, a patient tutor, and even taught many the art of writing that enabled many to publish books. She was a national treasure, yet no pastor would ordain her. This was a time in the African American church culture when women were not wel-comed in the pulpits of many churches. Based on an interpretation of the scripture, pastors believed women were not allowed to pas-tor. For fear she might pastor someday, no pastor would convene an ordination service.

There was a pastor of great respect who was also nationally known as one who walked closely with God. He was affection-ally called "holy one." Upon hearing the elder woman's dilemma, he agreed to convene the service. This was great news around the country. He was praised for his obedience to the Spirit's leading de-spite outward discouragement from other pastors.

Two weeks before the service the "holy one" called the candidate, saying the Spirit has directed him not to convene the service. The candidate, along with women of color around the country, was devastated and confused. This ordination signaled a major breakthrough in the role of women in ministry in the African American church. If this woman would not be ordained, then no woman would be ordained. The holy one's answer to the questions of why was simple: "Spirit said, 'No.'"

Not apparent to many, in another part of the country, another pastor who advocated for women of color in the ministry was praying and asking God for ways he might be of service in helping women become ordained. He was a seminary professor and welcomed all women called to the ministry to come study with him and minister in his church. Women from all over the country did so. This pastor contacted the candidate and invited her to have her service at his church. His church would pay her expenses. His openness to the Spirit had a wider impact. Hundreds of men and women attended the service, and it served as a major source of encouragement to women ministers in training and to those who longed to be ordained but felt they were too old or would not live to see this change.

The movement of the Spirit of God is often dynamic. Still, the movement can be received as if the gift of discernment is obscure. The outcome of what is being prayed for may not be evident immediately. Sometimes it takes time. In retrospect, this was a two-part event. The first was the possibility of what appeared impossible when the first pastor said yes. This opened the door for the second pastor to walk through and yielded a grander impact. There is a saying in the African American church community: "God may not come when you want, but God is always right on time."

A Spirited Tradition Meets Ignition Discernment

Timothy Gallagher makes it clear in his book *Discernment of the Spirits: An Ignatian Guide for Everyday Living* that knowing the will of Spirit in our lives is possible by being alert to the movements of consolation and desolation in our hearts.[7] Using the Ignatian model, Gallagher stresses that being fully conscious to the movements that draw us close to God's will or away from it is central to the discernment process. In other words, if the thoughts and feelings in the interior indicate joy, then moving forward toward that joy is an adherence to God's will. Conversely, if the thoughts and feelings conjure actions that move away from God, it is not of God.

Gallagher's assertions find residence in the African American spiritual context. Phrases like: "This just doesn't feel right," "My Spirit is troubled," and "I can find no peace." These are all expressions of adherence that would prevent movement away from the will of God. Following the movements of the heart can often be expressed on the exterior through embodied practices, audible prayers, and in the charismatic shout. "Working it out" is often the explanation. Such exterior expression is an indication that the person is proactively seeking spiritual clarification and direction, discerning within the safety of spiritual community. Afterward, people often share that they have received an answer. Gallagher does emphasize that the full measure of the Spirit leading is made complete in the fourteen rules inherent in the Spiritual Exercises. This type of sharing applies closely to rule one, during the first week of the exercises, which offers a set of considerations to ponder about why God has put us on this earth. The purpose is to overcome the self, ordering one's life on the basis of a decision made in freedom from any ill-ordered attachment.

Historical Christian Reflections:
The Arc of Discernment

Henry Nouwen, in the series *A Spirituality of Living*, defines *discipline*. "Discipline means to prevent everything in our life from being filled up. It means having space in our interior being that is not otherwise occupied."[9] He continues, "Discipline means to create space in which something can happen that we have not planned or counted on."[10]

When one prays for the spirit of discernment, there must be space within one's heart to receive it. Prayer, silence, and solitude are some of the vehicles used to create unencumbered interior space. Therein lies a mystery.

Ruth Haley Barton, in her book *Sacred Rhythms*, gives us insights as to how to be positioned for the Spirit, leaning in, obtaining discernment. First, we pray for it. We pray the prayer of indifference. We search deeply within, asking if we want what God desires for us or if we are confirmed in knowing that what we want is what God wants for us. Praying to be indifferent to the outcome and desiring only what God declares is the intent. To be open and honest with oneself requires a fundamental belief that God's will for our lives is best regardless of the circumstances. Praying for indifference takes us deeper into our interior and deeper into the heart of God. Praying this way frees us from attachments, from our eyes, and from our sense of entitlement. It is living a prayerful, radically open stance before God. It is desiring the will of God above all else.

Second, Haley Barton suggests we pray for wisdom: wisdom to choose not just between the good and not good but choosing between the good and the best. Scripture confirms our asking for wisdom: "If any of you is lacking in wisdom, ask God, who gives to all generously and ungrudgingly, and it will be given you" (James 1:5). Wisdom is vital in executing God's will. It is understanding the how of the discerning journey.[11]

In addition to praying for indifference and wisdom, incorporating the spiritual practice of Examen is key. Examen focuses our senses on God's movements each day. Gallagher says:

> The presence of examen begins when the fundamental desire of our hearts is to see and find the divine will in the disposition of our lives; when we long for a means to embrace this will in the concrete circumstances of our everyday living. The root of the practice of examining will always be desire. A desire that is an awareness of the immense love of the God who is ever close to us. It is a desire that is enkindled within us when we wish to respond daily moment by moment to God's love . . .[12]

Practicing the discipline of Examen in praying for discernment opens our heart to see the presence of God in the daily activities of our lives. It sensitizes our hearing to the voice of God echoed in routine conversations. It calls us to pay attention to the emotional and physical movements of our spiritual interior. Practicing

Examen at the culmination of each day pushes us—initially in the interior, but over time shapes our inner ears and heart eyes to recognize the presence of the God who loves us and desires a close relationship with us.

Silence and solitude are a bedrock for spiritual discernment. Scripture records numerous occasions of Jesus slipping away for times of silence and solitude to quiet his spirit. He would often leave his disciples or remove himself from the crowd to spend time praying, listening, and reflecting. In Luke 6, Jesus prayed before choosing his disciples. Luke 22 describes the Garden of Gethsemane experience of struggle in confirming his ultimate mission. Silence, listening, and solitude are paramount in discerning God's desire for our lives. Struggle is intricate to a discernment lifestyle. Determining our desires from God's will is the journey. It requires trusting more in the Spirit of God than trusting in ourselves. Discernment is a lifestyle. It is a complex, deeply interior discipline. It requires personal reflection and spiritual practice.

Integration

> God, we have no idea where we are going. We do not see the road ahead of us. We cannot know for certain where it will end. Nor do we really know ourselves, and the fact that we think we are following your will does not mean that we are actually doing so. But we believe that the desire to please you does in fact please you. And we hope that we will never do anything apart from that desire. And we know that if we do this you will lead us by the right road, though we may know nothing about it. Therefore, we will trust you always though we may seem to be lost and in the shadow of death. We will not fear, for you are ever with us, and you will never leave us to face our perils alone.[13]

Five Key Components of Discernment

1. Desire (must want to do it/inner disposition)
2. Indifference (to Divine will)
3. Attentiveness (willingness to hear)
4. Love (if no love, just say no!)
5. Discrimination (Mystery, Divine guidance)

Sample Guidelines for Discerning Decisions

Although discernment is a spiritual lifestyle there are guidelines when specific decisions are warranted. The following steps are comparable to individual and group decisions. They are based on Haley Barton and Ignatian Spirituality concepts:

> Create interior space through silence and solitude.
> Pray for indifference.
> Pray for wisdom.
> Practice daily the discipline of Examen.
> Be informed. Gather all necessary data pertinent
>   to the subject at hand.
> Contact experts in the subject field.
> Engage in a pros and cons dialogue on the subject.
> Ask the following questions of oneself:

- Are you leaning toward going forward consistent with what your experience of God has been?
- Does this decision going forward fit with the overall calling and direction of your life?
- What is the response when Jesus asks you, "What do you want me to do for you?"
- What scriptures are being brought to your mind?
- Will this decision going forward develop your spiritual life?
- Where is the love of God in this decision personally and for the community?
- Will going forward draw you closer to God or pull you away?

- Does the choice bring joy and peace?

When you have reached a decision, pray again and wait a few days for settling and confirmation.

If this process does not yield a clear decision, revisit the process.

Please note that these suggested steps to discerning a decision are not to be initiated linearly. Praying and engaging in silence and solitude througout the process may dictate repeating a step or staying in a particular place for a period of time. These suggestions are effective in groups or as an individual endeavor. What is sure is that this process must begin with silence and solitude in order to make space in the interior for the Spirit's leading.

Haley Barton reminds us that discernment is risky and there are no guarantees. We can never be absolutely sure we are in God's will. But we can rest in the promise that God will never leave or forsake us and that our intention to please God and be in God's will is honored by God.

Spiritual Direction and Discernment

The task of the spiritual director in sitting with African Americans seeking clarity about the gift of discernment is to listen intently to what the client is asking.

- Is there a need for clarity concerning discerning evil spirits?
- Is there a desire to live a discerning lifestyle?
- Is there a decision that must be?
- What has been the directee's experience with discerning the Spirit of God?
- Does the directee trust that God desires the best for their life?

The spiritual director does not ask these questions or others that come to mind directly. But the spiritual director listens to clues that reveal the client's past and current experience with the Spirit of God. Listening will reveal the areas of openness.

Haley Barton reminds us that most religious leaders are experiencing discernment at the second spiritual level (using Ignatius's second set of rules for discernment). At this level, the movement toward that which gives joy and peace can be a distraction from God's true desire, which will yield the best choice for them. It is the difference between a "good choice" and the "best choice."

She cautions leaders when leaders begin to feel there is no need for the ministry of a spiritual director in their lives, as this is just the time the need for a spiritual director is most paramount.

Thomas Merton states, "The spiritual director's function is to verify and encourage what is truly spiritual in the soul. They must teach others to discern between good and evil tendencies, to distinguish the inspirations of the spirit of evil from those of the Holy Spirit."[14] He continues, "A spiritual director is, then, one who helps another to recognize and follow the inspirations of grace in his life, in order to arrive at the end to which God is leading them."[15] The ministry of the spiritual director is to be a conduit of listening and praying with and for the directee. It is not to tell or script the discernment process or layer the discerning lifestyle with rules and prescriptions. Modeling and suggesting spiritual practices and discernment methods, the spiritual director journeys alongside at the pace of the traveler. The spiritual director must be knowledgeable about discernment processes for decision making and the practices useful in developing a daily discerning way of living close to the heart of God.

Sample List of Discernment Methods

1. Bio-spiritual focusing (somatic method)
2. Discernment groups
3. Divination (tarot)
4. Experience circle (wholeness method)
5. Ignatian discernment
6. Quaker clearness committee
7. Reliable and unreliable signs—Jonathan Edwards
8. Social-discernment cycle
9. Zarathustra (cognitive-intuitive method)

Notes

1. Howard Thurman, "In Quiet One Discovers the Will of God," in *Meditations of the Heart* (Boston: Beacon Press, 1981), 20–21.

2. John R. Mabry, *Noticing the Divine: An Introduction to Interfaith Spiritual Direction* (New York: Morehouse, 2006), 44–45.

3. Luke Johnson, *Scripture and Discernment* (Nashville: Abingdon Press, 1996), 110.

4. Michael Buckley, "Discernment of Spirits," in *The New Dictionary of Catholic Spirituality*, edited by Michael Downey (Collegeville, MN: Liturgical Press, 1993).

5. Elizabeth Liebert, lecture on defining discernment in the class "Art of Discernment" (SP 2499), San Francisco Theological Seminary, January 2012.

6. "A Prayer by Chaim Stern," in *Mishkan T'Filah: A Reform Siddur-Shabbat*, edited by Elyse D. Frishman (New York: Central Conference of American Rabbis, 2007), 53 [171].

7. Timothy Gallagher, *The Discernment of Spirits: An Ignatian Guide for Everyday Living* (New York: Crossroad, 2005), 52.

8. John Mogabgab, *A Spirituality of Living: Henri Nouwen* (Nashville: Upper Room Books, 2011), 16.

9. Ibid.

10. See Ruth Haley Barton, *Sacred Rhythms: Arranging Our Lives for Spiritual Transformation* (Downers Grove, IL: InterVarsity Press, 2006), 67.

11. Timothy Gallagher, *The Examen Prayer: Ignatian Wisdom for Our Lives Today* (New York: Crossroad, 2006), 52.

12. Adaptation of "A Prayer of Thomas Merton," in *Thoughts in Solitude* (New York: Farrar, Straus & Giroux, 1958), 83.

13. Thomas Merton, *Spiritual Direction and Meditation* (Collegeville, MN: Order of St. Benedict, 1960), 16–17.

14. Ibid.

Part III: Contemporary Matters

In Part III, we turn our attention to contemporary issues and "powerful shaping forces" that touch and influence the lives of directees as well as spiritual directors themselves. Issues that impact the civil society and life generally have real consequences and devastating effects on everybody. It stands to reason that whatever effect the directee personally experiences will in fact affect the spiritual life of that person. The spiritual director will be impacted as well. For people of color, the weight of carrying the fallout from these issues could cause a block within the spiritual-direction context. Social issues such as the economy, race and racism, gender oppression, human sexuality, the criminal-justice system and mass incarceration, poverty, and violence leave none untouched. When these are coupled with personal woundedness and loss, particular attentiveness to empathetic, contemplative listening is required. The task is made even more complicated by the simultaneous woundedness of the director.

The chapters in this section explore relationship tools and strategies as ways to interrupt the deafening and paralyzing effect of the contemporary social scene that suppresses the ability to hear the divine connection. Storytelling and visual arts help us to access the imaginative world and places where we can encounter God. A guided navigation to "the inward journey" to freedom opens up for us the search for the genuine within, leading to liberation to live as an authentic self. Because of the pervasiveness of trauma, both social and personal, within the lives of people of color, the final chapter of this section looks at a womanist relational ethic that can help us foster collective- and individual-care strategies for the healing of both directors and directees.

7

Discovering the Creative-Imaginative in the Spiritual Direction of Color Experience
Storytelling, Creativity, Imagination, and Dreams

Naisa Wong

TRAINING PRINCIPLE | CREATIVITY
This chapter explores the relationship among "imagination, dreams, storytelling, and creativity and how this relationship intersects with the art of spiritual direction and soul care." Naisa Wong takes us on a journey with her into the process and "powerful shaping force" of the creative arts that leads to discovering the "shape of her spirit" and en-countering the Divine. Uncovering in her own story a genuine experi-ence and connection with the Divine, we enter the author's experience through these two quotes:

> Often when I lose my way, I rely on stories to get
> me through the deafening silence.
> > Renita J. Weems, *Listening for God*

> Imagination is more important than knowledge.
> > Confucius

These illustrations are provocative and instructive. Wong challenges the reader to come along with her to explore how, as practi-tioners, to make the creative-imaginative realm accessible and inclu-sive for all people within the art of spiritual direction itself. Our guide offers us a primer of methods and tools for "complex conversation about how creativity, imagination, dreams, and storytelling can both shepherd and be shepherded into one's encounter with God when practiced with informed sensitivity, intentional awareness, and compassionate intuition and grace."

❁

"No one told me I had to follow Oprah!" I exclaimed to myself as I tried to catch my breath behind the stage wings. Of course, in light of those present, and considering the active desolation that permeated the air of the ballroom that morning of June 19, 2015, Oprah seemed to be the more appropriate figure to open the morning's session, given what had recently transpired. The audience's response to the pop-culture icon's video message of encouragement had just begun to dissipate. I stood backstage, trying to collect my frayed nerves and focused on my breath. "Remember why you're here," I thought to myself. The text to the inspirational reading I had encountered in the early hours of my morning's meditation came to me. Rising at 5:30 A.M., I had been crying out to God for a word, any word, to offer to these great servant-leaders of justice. "Remain in me and I will remain with you," I repeated as I quieted my thoughts. I had been tasked to open the first general assembly session of Sojourner's Leadership Summit, an invitational event for three hundred of the world's formidable leaders on the frontlines of social justice, activism, peacemaking, and spiritual leadership. The topic for the panel discussion following my opening was on trauma and moral injury—an arena I had just begun studying in my graduate-certification program in trauma and spiritual care. Truly, no one could have anticipated just how Divinely orchestrated and filled with grace the convergence of this subject matter and opening would be for the community that had gathered that morning.

As I looked out at the audience, I saw the delegation of South African leaders still fighting to restore communities that had endured decades of apartheid. There were individuals who were working in transitional programs for women and children coming out of sex trafficking. There were many more community leaders from around the United States who were attempting to bring a more inclusive and reconciliatory narrative to their respective communities, many of which were serving the most marginalized sectors of the world. And then, there was the cohort of young leaders from the front lines of the Ferguson uprising in the wake of the murder of Michael Brown. These leaders, predominantly young women of color, had endured a racial and political war zone and had just begun to enter some kind of transition into regulated daily life, even as the work and mission carried on into what was now a global stage. Because life often moves at a perplexing rate at best, and at an offensive and disregarding rate at worst, we had all been rocked by a new traumatic event within the past twenty-four hours. News of the mass shooting at Emanuel African Methodist Episcopal Church in Charleston, South Carolina, had broken forth. Leaders from the surrounding community, some with very personal connections to those who had been killed and injured, were present at the summit. As we came together as a community, the devastation of the event began to take its toll—morally, spiritually, and physically. All of us on some level were grappling in real time with the intrusion of indescribable pain, trauma, triage, and disorientation.

Often when you are called upon as a care practitioner in this work of spiritual care in contemplative justice, you are caught off guard. There truly is no way of being fully prepared for the moment. It can feel as if your breath is being stolen from your body as you face the circumstances presented to you and as you attempt to move through the pain and the suffering. I remember feeling that metaphysical strangulation especially as I attempted to prepare for this plenary moment. I thought about how much specific care was needed within the community. At one point, in the early-morning hours, I was holding great desolation. As I attempted to lean into my own spiritual exercises to get through the night, I was led to lament. Out of that lament, in that mysteriously synergistic way, the Spirit expanded to hold a greater capacity within a suffering moment and met me and offered me strange grace and peace. That morning, as I held the hope of John 15, which had been born in the night, I began to respond in a series of body movements using the tradition of Qi Gong. I had first learned Qi Gong as a young child from my great-aunt. I moved into the Spirit's invitation to "remain," and a kind of prayer movement evolved as I continued to hold the image of the vine and the reminder to breathe. Somehow, out of that meditative and sacred space, I found the shape of how I might meet the needs of the summit leaders and the ever present darkness around us. I took the stage and introduced myself,

> Good morning, my name is Naisa. Naisa is Asian spelled backwards—I was born to Chinese American hippies in the late 1970s and raised in Berkeley, California. I have grappled most of my life with what it has meant to be a backwards Asian. I have come to the conclusion that it speaks to a kind of liminal identity which entails both honoring my cultural heritage as a second/third generation Chinese American, but it also serves as a birthright and commission to live into a new empowerment as an Asian American female. In some ways, I see my life's story as learning to exist in the in-between spaces. For many of us Asian Americans, this is the stamp of our experience of marginal dwelling. More importantly, I can't introduce myself without telling a story, and ultimately, this is who I am. I am a storyteller and a practitioner of storytelling as well as a spiritual director and care practitioner. I believe it is in our stories where we are able to find connection and restoration and even a genuine experience of the Divine.

What proceeded after that introduction was a version of what I had discovered early that morning in body prayer with God. I invited the audience to lean into the picture of John 15 and Jesus's invitation to abide, to choose to remain despite present experiences of hardship, pain, and suffering. We began in one of my centering breath exercises and, then, I invited them into a blend of Qi Gong and somatic movement that focused on renewal, diffusing stress, and regulating the central nervous system. I explained things slowly, as I went. I gave people the option to not stand, to sit, or to be as they needed in order to be comfortable. At the end, I asked us to breathe together and to notice that universal sigh by placing hands (with consent) on each other's shoulders so that they could feel the universal rise and fall. Remain, as the vine, abide with courage and with hope. Perhaps, in community, there would be a collective resilience that would emerge. As ever, the Spirit showed up in a way I could not imagine that morning and afternoon. What I did not know, and would discover after my opening, was that the leadership staff had planned a communal response around John 15. They had brought a large symbolic vine in which people could leave messages of lament. It was truly a morning of Spirit meeting the spirit and the need of the people in an intricately woven tapestry of creative experience.

When I trace my way back to the formative years of my life, I see that the two great companions of my heart have always been God and creativity. I remember starting to play simple melodies by ear on a small, plastic air organ at the age of three and a half or four. I would spend extended periods of time making up songs and performing them for an audience of stuffed animals or the foliage in my mother's garden. When I was eight, still unable to master Mozart or Chopin like the other Asian kids I was growing up with, I composed my first piece of music—a piano solo called "Spring Rain." As a child who lived with an extreme sense of otherness on multiple levels including chronic health issues, the creative arts became a safe haven for me—a home base. It was through music, dance, poetry, and other artistic mediums that I discovered the shape of my spirit. Contrary to what I was learning from the world around me, I saw that my spirit was strong. She had a voice, and she would be resilient.

It was on a playground in Berkeley, California, when I was about five years of age that I first encountered the presence of God. I distinctly remember walking the perimeter of the playground, running my hands along a chain-link fence as the others played. That day, I remember feeling especially set apart, alone, and in need of something I could not yet explain. Whatever compelled me to start singing words of praise, I can't recall. I can remember a sensation of deep longing and feeling compelled to respond to it. Through my imperfect, childlike, and honest rehearsal of Sunday school worship, I began to lament and praise. Teachers would later attest to the fact that I was actually singing quite loudly. Somehow, out of the depths, I sang my way out of my loneliness and into the loving arms of God. I distinctly remember feeling that shift—that divine awareness cementing in me. I encountered joy that day. To this day, that singular moment spherically connected the two most fundamental pieces of myself: the power of the Divine's response and the power of the creative spirit as a gateway to Divine experience.

The Intersection and Multiplicity of the Creative-Imaginative Arena

What makes the journey of writing this chapter so daunting is the sheer magnitude of what could be said individually about imagination, dreams, storytelling, and creativity and how they intersect with the art of spiritual direction and soul care. Each arena bears the potential of a unique thumbprint of experience with the Divine. To contextualize the language of this chapter title a bit more specifically: I attempt to address the creative-imaginative arena of human spirituality, which includes the sub-arenas or subcategories of storytelling, artistic expression, and dream interpretation, which in themselves are arenas of experience. Additionally, I view these three subcategories as the language or expression of the creative-imaginative. The beauty and grace of the creative-imaginative is its multiple nature. It is both a component of one's personal spiritual identity as well as a realm or arena that offers a multiplicity of discovery and practice which can deepen and expand one's spiritual experience. I believe that the human spirit's most authentic expression is by nature creative and imaginative. As the Divine is inherently a creative source—so are we made to be creative in God's being. As God is multiple in God-self, we too desire to be our most authentic selves in a multiplicity of expression and, most often, this employs the language and access points of the creative-imaginative arena. These experiences expand our capacity toward wonder, and it is in wonder that we experience divine presence and companionship.

I have also encountered the opposite opinion. The alternative is being met with intense scrutiny or fear around how to incorporate creative practices within spiritual care or seeing creativity, imagination, storytelling, and dreaming as an unacceptable way in which to "hear or experience God." This is especially true within more traditional systems of theology as well as spirituality methods and practices. When this belief system is conjoined with the person-of-color experience, entering into the creative-imaginative may feel inaccessible and overwhelming. Perhaps, for some, it may even be triggering. To that end, although the potential for authentic experience within the artistic and creative-imaginative realm is vast and fluid, one must take into careful account a client's or group's cultural, religious, traditional, and personal-identity markers. This should be of paramount consideration when choosing creative and imaginative tools in the practice of spiritual direction and other forms of therapeutic care. Being able to assess and anticipate the potential resistance or triggers one may have when engaging with the creative-imaginative is often disregarded when incorporating the arts into a care experience.

I have often found there to be an assumption that all art, all avenues of imagination or creative spaces, are inherently safe. This is not true. As a professional artist with more than twenty years of experience in multiple fields, this inquiry has been at the heart of my creative teaching and practice. How do we make the creative-imaginative realm accessible and inclusive to all people? What is required for this to become a reality? Though it may be obvious to the reader and to the audience of this book, it bears repeating: just as it is true of the art of spiritual direction itself, there is a systematic component to the ways in which the creative-imaginative arena is endorsed, taught, and experienced. For the most part, these models are Western European in their approach, in their language, as well as in practice and pedagogy. When I came into my calling and subsequent training as a spiritual director following nearly sixteen years of professional work as a director, producer, writer, and musician/composer, I was disappointed to see the same systematic assumptions being subsumed, even in seminary. The most fundamental inquiry of this chapter is how to promote a person of color's story—their history, their cultural and traditional background, and their spiritual language as the primary focus of how creative-imaginative and artistic spaces are constructed and introduced into practice, rather than as an afterthought.

As a practitioner called to both fields of the creative-imaginative as well as soul care, I believe I can offer a distinct perspective around how the creative-imaginative arena meets people, how people meet the creative-imaginative arena, and how these two things can co-alesce to meet the Divine in a place of safe exploration. What tools, what setups, what environments need to change or be adjusted to accommodate the PoC experience? How do you make these adjustments without being too prescriptive or inauthentic? Perhaps a certain amount of prescription is necessary. On a macro level, what makes spiritual practices creative? By sharing my stories of experience, my hope is to offer a primer on a much deeper and more complex conversation about how creativity, imagination, dreams, and storytelling can both shepherd and be shepherded into one's encounter with God when practiced with informed sensitivity, intentional awareness, and compassionate intuition and grace.

Navigating the Art of Story and Storytelling

In many ways, stories are a unique component to the DNA of our experience. Stories are both the structure by which we remember an event as well as the language or script that we use to substantiate the event's meaning. Before we have the ability to gain understanding or to derive meaning from a life event, we rehearse these experiences in sharing what happened—sometimes to ourselves, sometimes to someone else. Storytelling occurs when we are able to move from recounting the memories of what took place to an authentic connection to the event. Moving beyond the rehearsal of the details into a present engagement with those memories moves us into a deeper realm of experience. Coupled with witness, this allows us to make meaning out of what transpired. Storytelling is the most elemental component of the creative-imaginative arena of identity and experience. By leaning inward to extend outward in sharing our stories, we become open to the possibility of reconciliation and healing.

For some, the oral practice of telling one's story is uncomfortable and daunting. Sometimes it is unsafe. I have found this to be particularly true for individuals who have grown up with traditions that have caused them to detach or dissociate from their feelings and emotions. Too often, this is true of the experiences of people of color (PoC) and can be associated with heavy shaming and trauma.

It is important to remember that the oral tradition of storytelling is not the only way in which to engage it. Discovering what allows your client to experience explorative freedom and devising creative ways in which to engage with their stories will be the trust and spaciousness that is needed to be witnessed in the process. For a spiritual director, learning to identify and catalog the client's story is the most important artful practice. From first contact, the client is often offering pieces of their story that can eventually build toward a storytelling moment. I have often found that a client is encouraged to proceed when I reflect back or summarize their events for them, as it indicates how carefully and sensitively I am listening. Learning what to hold onto or discerning what details to bracket until you sense the client and/or the Divine are moving toward an opening for further authentic storytelling is skillful.

I have also discovered that sharing pieces of my own story, specifically in the intake process of first meeting with a client or within the introduction to my group experience, is actually vital to building trust. Building trust at the foundation of a caregiving relationship is especially vital when I am working alongside people of color, particularly those who do not identify as Asian American. This may not be comfortable for some directors, but I have found it to be an essential component to my work with clients of color. I have discovered that coming into my own story often mirrors the only connective experience a client may have had with the elders of their own communities. Stories level the playing field and allow for an exchange of vulnerability and transparency. Beyond regulating an experience, stories offer permission that directees may need in order to look inward. As many cultures thrive in the collective experience, entering into storytelling by way of exchanging stories honors a sense of familiar ritual and sacredness.

Another unique component of PoC-centered spiritual direction is that I rarely stop a client from engaging with their story, and often this means our sessions will be filled with dialogue. This form was not modeled for me in my own training in traditional spiritual direction, where silence and slowing down is key to the posture of contemplation. I argue that for some persons of color, the freedom and ability to dialogue or to be provided with a space to unhinge their voice, is itself a form of slowing down. Silencing and compartmentalizing one's emotions, feelings, and experience so often accompany the PoC experience, specifically for women of color, who comprise the majority of my one-on-one practice. More often than not, clients are led to wonder when they are given a gracious and wide, nurturing space in which to be seen and heard. As is universally true, this feeling of being known allows for a deeper experience and often leads one to an authentic encounter with the Divine. Maintaining an inviting tone is quintessential to this slowing down. Too often, spiritual directors adopt a directive and pedantic tone that can be easily misinterpreted.

To invite the tradition of spiritual direction into these spaces, I am intentional about beginning and ending our time with stillness or a creative way to approach quieting down. In addition, finding places to pause in the midst of the storytelling in order to savor the movement of the Spirit is another way of engaging the more traditional model of spiritual direction. Often, within these savoring spaces I invite the creative-imaginative and artistic expression into the space to capture moments or to go even deeper. Silence and quiet and methodical slowness are not requirements for spiritual direction. In some cases, such as the PoC experience, this can lead to furthering desolation and a feeling of being misunderstood or silenced. Finding ways to adapt these postures leads to a more creative and authentic experience.

Interacting with the Creative-Imaginative

Within my practice, I have found that storytelling is a process of unfolding, and beginning the process is often the hardest part. Safety, trust, hospitable space, time, and a fluid structure to guide the directee are needed to hedge the experience of entering into storytelling. I believe that creativity is vital to that fluid structure and quintessential to promoting accessibility and inclusivity. Working with the added layer of trauma care also necessitates the creative-imaginative space, as it often serves as either the language of experience that cannot be expressed in words or it allows for a client to translate and interact with their experience and response with an additional filter or safety harness. For me, as an artist and spiritual director, artful creativity is the framework for my practice. It is also often necessary—imperative even—to seek outside the parameters of what is traditional, methodical, and practiced in order to meet someone in difficulty and strife.

In addition, creating or providing spaces that are culturally specific in their offerings may open up a unique portal into wonder. Although much of my work has led me into diverse spaces, I have also been called into specific work with Asian American evangelicals who are attempting to grow the language and the practice of their spirituality and perhaps imagine God and especially Jesus and Spirit within an Asian context. This work has been incredibly transforming, even for myself. In a workshop I co-created alongside a dear colleague and friend, Claudia May, PhD, we explore the dynamics of how culture, heritage, and tradition impact our images of God and also our ability to encounter the grace, love, and mercy of Jesus. Opening with a circle process, I start the group by facilitating a conversation around what it means to be Asian American today and how that differs from what it has meant historically. We listen deeply in the story circle as I help to navigate the conversation to truly dig deep for what dissonance and what desolation we may be experiencing culturally. It may be possible to accentuate existing narratives of shame, erasure, ridicule, and apathy. We move through historic wounding. As we move through a process of adaptive Examen, we invite the group to move toward exploring how they sense Jesus may be inviting them specifically to the table of grace. Being invited to the table is essential to the reconciliation experience for Asian Americans. We then disperse the group into creative experience stations (generally four to five) for a good hour of soaking. They are given the prompt to choose whichever experience draws them. Some may stay in one station for the entire hour. Some may choose to attempt to fit in time with each station or two out of the four or five offerings. It would be up to them.

As I had created some of these experience stations at more diverse gatherings, I wanted to see if I could adapt some of them to be more Asian-specific. The stations included (*a*) an open artistic space with tools to create something original; (*b*) a worship-centric music station focusing on Asian American song leaders and writers; (*c*) a contemplative music station with original music I had composed with an accompanying guide that allowed you to step into the lament experience; (*d*) a station of sacred images and icons; and (*e*) a food/sensory experience.

To adapt the stations, I invited those who participated to consider bringing what had come up for them into each experience station. More specifically, within the free-art station, I provided a prompt to consider (*a*) creating an image or expression that spoke to the beauty of the Asian American experience or (*b*) creating an image or expression that offered a sense of peace, consolation, or the fruits of the Spirit when holding the experience of what it has meant to be loved by God. Within the worship experience, I chose original worship music composed and performed by Asians/Asian Americans, or I chose well-known worship music led by those of diverse Asian backgrounds. Some of the music was sung in different languages—Korean, Tagalog, Mandarin. I asked those experiencing this station to observe what it felt like to witness being led into such intimate spaces by someone that looked like them. Further prompts were offered to go deeper with what was coming up for them. In the original music station, my hope was to provide a space of guided lament which, outside of funerals, was not always welcomed within the Asian diasporic experience. Interestingly enough, I have also found that within a white/European American context, when I have offered this station, many have confronted feelings of resistance toward such vulnerable expression. This makes it difficult to sit transparently with desolation. Within an Asian American social context this could be interpreted as "performing goodness." Within most Asian cultures, not complaining is a form of respect to those that have sacrificed so much for our freedoms. To enter into a space of longing and desire and lament before God is for many often a struggle. The music seems to illicit an invitation toward a deeper opening. In the fourth station, I included images of a non-European Jesus. I offered sacred art created by Asian artists like He Qi and Sadao Watanabe. I would also lay out cultural pieces like rabbit-hair calligraphy brushes, fans, origami paper, katsugi pottery, and bells—items that may spark a storytelling moment and an unpacking of one's emotional and spiritual response.

The fifth and final station was perhaps most important as it included foods from many Asian cultures. Individuals were asked to simply partake and to serve one another. They were asked to delight and to allow nostalgia to guide their imaginings. As the meal is perhaps one of the most universally sacred spaces in PoC experience, this station has grown into the primary experiential component in our workshops. Often, we simply engage the whole group in this as a closing exercise. The meal begins by the "breaking" of an orange or piece of fruit typical to the Asian experience. Slices are passed among those gathered. Then, each person takes a turn to serve someone tea. In some cases, when addressing the themes of inherent patriarchy and misogyny of our cultural experience, the men serve the women intentionally. I ask the experience group to consider the practice as they would communion. This exercise has always been most profound. Within the circle, an engagement of conversation and storytelling flows organically, and we are able to access the essential question of how God might be inviting us in specific ways to deeper grace and love—for ourselves and for our parents and children.

Providing Hospitable Entryways That Invite the Creative Spirit

For spiritual directors who feel intimidated by creativity or feel that creativity is less intuitive, remember that, on an elemental level, creativity may be any adjustment that allows a client and the director to deepen into spiritual freedom, which often generates more connectivity to their stories. Creativity should always be hospitable and invitational. There should always be several offerings, and the directee should be encouraged to opt into the exercise. Creativity employs a certain amount of humility, because some tools or methods of engagement may not work, and that is okay. Learning more of your client's story will help to navigate the types of offerings in order to provide an authentic experience.

In my practice, I make paper, pens, pencils, art supplies, collaging tools, yarn, a table and basket of icons, artistic images, an assortment of music, and symbolic items available to my clients so that they can have various "creative entryways" with which to respond. Often, before each new client enters my space, I change the elements on the sacred altar in my office as a symbol of invitation to that particular client's individual spiritual signature. On a creative level for me as practitioner, it reminds me that I am entering a new space with each client. The creative-imaginative items in my office often act like a safe portal, especially when the directee is allowed to choose their interaction. Promoting agency is a crucial component to building trust and ensuring safety. Standing by on the ready are also several readings, blessings, poetry, movement, postures, or other interactive or contemplative exercises that I may also employ if the client or group is in need of even more prescriptive ways to engage with their stories.

Long before I entered spiritual care, I developed a creative entryway that helped artists center and to come into sacred space. It would be many years later that I realized I was leading people in a form of Examen. At the time that I developed this exercise, I was looking for a creative offering that would be universal to the human experience, as I was often working within a social-justice context with a culturally divergent group of people (age, race, gender, economic status, religious beliefs, etc.). Over the last ten years of using this exercise, I have found it to be accessible in almost every gathering.

When commencing work with one-on-one clients, I often invite them to step into this exercise and share what has led them to seek out spiritual care. I invite them to sit with it for several days leading into our intake. This form of Examen tends to be a good prompt to begin the process of entering into contemplation. When I am asked to work within groups with diverse backgrounds—often interfaith or even secular environments—I use this simple creative entryway as a way to access spiritual engagement so that they can become open to the possibility of authentic storytelling. The process asks three questions: (a) where is your longing, today? (b) what might your fear(s) be? (c) how might you be invited to hope today or in this season of your life? (On many occasions, I use the language of Examen to nuance this experience.) If the client or the group is able, we stay in these questions for a good twenty minutes (the length of three or four pieces of music). If the client/group appears to be intensely engaged, I extend the time for this exercise. I often use music from a specific playlist I've created to also hedge the space. As a musician and composer, I am extremely intentional about what music I choose. And, I even ask the directee what type of music they respond to the most. Something about the melody, the orchestration, or the musical experience should be inherently inviting and should illicit a sensation of being accompanied. At the end of the last piece of music, I invite the directee to "come to a gentle close, even if it is not perfect or complete." And, I ask them how they feel about sharing their experience. Sharing can also include everything from the asking of the questions, to how they are feeling in the moment, to their response to the music I played. Some kind of opening to a deeper conversation presents itself in this exercise, and this is where the art of spiritual direction can take flight.

Imagination and Dreamscaping as a Bridge

Fundamentally, I believe that imagination sets the stage for wonder, and the ability to enter the realm of wonder is what ultimately leads us to the table of grace. Often regarded as a transpersonal experience, imagination often exists in the paradigmatic liminality of either mental escapism or as a highly animistic experience. Within more conservative theological and doctrinal denominations, imagination is often looked at with great skepticism and even caution. As such, some clients harbor a great deal of hang-ups and resistance around imaginative invitations and language. When introducing intentional use of imagination within my practice, I begin simply, slowly, and often in a classical space of contemplation. We often start with the imaginative language of the Bible. We stay in images and parables and metaphors found in the Psalms, the wisdom literature of the Old Testament, as well as the teachings of Jesus. To interact with them, we gradually begin to incorporate *Lectio Divina,* as well as imaginative prayer, into the experience. What is also undeniable is the incredible imagination that can be found within the sacred texts of so many religions. Whether through parables, metaphors, or full-on imagery, the language of imagination is particular to spiritual experience and is often the necessary agent to illicit a human being's connective response toward empathy, conviction, humility and even fear.

In the beginning of my training in spiritual-direction practicum, my first clients were all Korean pastors studying on religious visas.

What was so intriguing about that experience was how much I could not depend on language as a way to thread the session. Most of my clients spoke very little English. In the beginning, I often understood only about 70 percent of what they were attempting to communicate within a fifty-minute session. I can recall feeling as if I was disappointing my clients with my inability to use the finer skills of spiritual direction, which often depend on language or silence, which often felt oppressive for my Asian clients. Additionally, as I was meeting most of them at the library, I couldn't even rely on the image of the burning candle as a way to link us together to the Spirit of God. I remember having to bracket a lot of feelings of inadequacy, constraint, and frustration in the initial sessions. At the time, I was imposing a rather classical interpretation and expectation of spiritual direction onto my clients. Part of this was also the limitation I was perceiving from the conservatism that I was confronting in most of my client's stories. Yet, they had each expressed in some common way a desire to truly "feel" the presence of God and to deconstruct the system of religiosity that governs the church in Korea. So many of them came from long lineages of pastors, and trying to decipher their own experiences of authenticity with God was a true longing.

As I thought of my clients within the constraints of their cultural system, I imagined them as being trapped. I can remember thinking and praying into how I might experience freedom and in turn promote more freedom for these clients. I thought about the community I had grown up in as a child and teenager, a bilingual and multigenerational Chinese American church that modeled a lot of similar dynamics of family, a recapturing of the village, and the implications of spiritual piety. I thought about growing up surrounded by "Chinglish" (Chinese + English) and decided to lean into more open communication. In essence, I imagined what it would be like to hold the space of spiritual direction for my grandmother or my grandfather. There would have to be a lot of banter, a lot of gesticulations, and back-and-forth language building where I was helping to piece together what they were trying to say and offering back more construction than is typically advised in standard spiritual direction. The minute I tried it and refused to get locked up in a predetermined way of spiritually directing, the session opened up completely. The experience also made me think of what it was like to musically riff with another musician or what it was like to do improv with another actor. There was a back-and-forth energy that was essential in creating and discovering the emergent narrative.

I had also started to bring different icons into the space that helped to ground us to the sacred. I would bring an Asian fabric and lay it in the middle of the table, with a wooden bowl at the center filled with water, and I would invite us to imagine Jesus as living water. Sometimes, I would place a flower in the water and include a second bowl that would remain dry, with rocks in it, to offer an image of the desert as counterpart to the spring. And, within our work together, I began to discover that leaning into scripture was a good entryway to imaginative prayer and even some visualization work. In one incredibly meaningful moment, a client with whom I continue to work was able to picture themselves on a baseball field with God. They tossed the ball back and forth until the end of the game. They would then sit together and, at some point, even recline against each other like a father and son. This movement of imagination was born out of a longing to redeem the directee's experience of Father-God, because their father was not present emotionally in their childhood. In another session, when trying to draw near to the love of God, the breakthrough for this client was the image of God as a nurturing and loving grandmother. We would spend time discovering how God as Korean grandmother could lavish love on her grandchild. Suddenly, we were experiencing a depth that could only be described as a gift of grace.

Prayer, too, became a unifying element within our sessions. I would often invite the directee to pray in their own language. I would hold space, listening for the rise and fall of their vocal patterns and the presence of tears and other emotional responses. I would close those times in English, praying blessing upon them. It was always a vibrant and charged experience of connection. There were times when I still struggled to understand what exactly my directees meant by a broken word or phrase. There were other times when we would get lost in translation and would have to let go of a moment so as not to get stuck in confusion and frustration. There was an ongoing complexity of emotional engagement for each of them, due to cultural restraints. Still, we knew we were being met by God in an astonishing way. Always, we attempted to draw nearer to grace, to love, and to mercy which were in themselves virtues that often ran in opposition to the narratives of shame, of over-responsibility, of perfectionism, and emotional detachment. My clients constantly reiterated how thankful they were for the compassionate and flexible accompaniment, and I felt exactly the same.

When I work with a client and their dreams, I often hedge the space by explaining that it is less about literal interpretation and more about unpacking whatever emotion has emerged from the dream itself. Employing the visualization and centering techniques I used as a theater director as well as the tools of drawing, writing, poetry, and painting, we often sit with only one part of the dream at a time and lean into new images that may emerge in our creative-imaginative space, as we attempt to connect authentically with the images and emotions of the experience and invite God to be present in it. If a client seems emotionally hypervigilant or is experiencing a negative arousal from the dream itself, first we work to enter into a more regulated space before attempting to unpack the event of the dream. In this work I use the language of story to construct the space as if we were reading through or deconstructing a script. This often helps to diffuse the disorientation of reality versus surreality within the work of dreamscape.

Conclusion

It would be years later before I recognized that embracing and reconciling who I was as an artist and storyteller was truly who God desired for me to be in my life, in my work, and in the world. As I continue to live into this vocational call—be it in a theater, on a studio backlot, a South Central Los Angeles neighborhood, or my spiritual-direction office—I have witnessed the power of how story and creativity can meet a person in the most intimate and vulnerable places within themselves. I firmly believe that the creative and imaginative arena is a fundamental access point to God, and it is a delight, a privilege, and a joy to be present when that intersection takes place. For people of color, this is a unique experience. The melodies are more complex, the colors have more tonal gradation and saturation, and the language(s) of creativity comes from a much deeper and often lamenting well. Navigating such intricate experience requires humility, patience, and leaving one's presuppositions (even with regard to the very structure of spiritual direction) at the door. Letting the directee's story and the Spirit guide you toward ripe openings is paramount.

As a practitioner who has the privilege of serving a diverse populace of clients in multiple arenas of care (one-on-one spiritual direction, integrative soul care with an emphasis in trauma care, group work, artistic coaching, reconciliatory circling processes and restorative justice processes in interfaith or non-faith-based organizations, story-circling), I find that my own identity as a creative woman of color allows me to distinctly and fluidly care for my clients. Ultimately, I have discovered that my primary posture is as both an artist and as a spiritual director. As I have sought and experienced a deeper synergy between these two vocational callings, I have come into a growing awareness of how the creative-imaginative arena and the art of spiritual direction (or soul care) complement and counterpoint one another to harmoniously provide internal freedom, authentic expression, and a genuine encounter with both the Divine and with one another. I have continually discovered that, despite our inherent differences, more often than not, story and creativity allow us to meet in a safe harbor of mutuality and trust.

8

Internal Liberation

Therese Taylor-Stinson
with Paula Owens Parker

TRAINING PRINCIPLE | FREEDOM
*Spiritual direction seeks primarily to enable the seeker to achieve a
deep relationship with or grounding in God and thus to live a life
of total freedom, individuality, and deep love . . . an awesome and
complex process which entails ridding oneself of past psychological
injuries and traumas, false ways of thinking and acting, and undue attachment to any person, possession, or spiritual practice. At the same
time it encourages and fosters a practice of deep prayer so that one can
discover one's deepest self, and thereby find the will of God in one's life.*[1]

*How does one negotiate this journey to "discover one's deepest
self" having experienced trauma, disenfranchisement, or marginalization? What approaches in spiritual direction are helpful for the seeker/
directee to enable them to hear deep within the sound of the genuine?
The authors point the way with Jesus as the incarnational model and
Howard Thurman's embodied spiritual guide as navigator of the "Inward Journey" and the "Inward Sea." Thurman, the African American
mystic, provides the explanations and guideposts for the search for the
genuine within, developing a habit of discerning what is authentic and
what is not. "Finding the genuine in yourself helps you to see the genuine in others," write Taylor-Stinson and Parker, "which leads to healthy
interdependence and freedom to be fully who you are created to be."*

*The authors reference Thurman's strategies to deal with the
forces opposed to internal freedom or that would attempt to prevent
us from living in the freedom we seek: fear, deception, and hate. "One's*

internal liberation is tied up with one's spirituality" as well as with one's self-love. The authors provide exercises to help the directee navigate the rough waters of the complex emotional and spiritual life.

❁

The Inward Sea

> There is in every person an inward sea,
> And in that sea there is an island
> And on that island there is an altar
> And standing guard before that altar is the "angel
>   with the flaming sword."
> "Nothing can get by that angel to be placed upon
>   that altar unless it has the mark of your inner
>   authority."
> "Nothing passes 'the angel with the flaming sword'
>   to be placed upon your altar unless it be a part
>   of 'the fluid area of your consent.'"
> This is your crucial link with the Eternal.[2]
>   Dr. Howard Thurman (1900–1981)

Are you free? Really free? Most people believe their freedom is external—no chains, enough money, knowledge. True freedom is internal, and Thurman submits that was Jesus's message for the Jews of his time, and the message to the disinherited of all time. Instead of embracing Jesus's wisdom, the Jewish authorities under Roman oppression, and Christians today, turn Jesus into a scapegoat. Our freedom, we generally believe, comes from the sacrifice of another rather than our claiming our own area of consent. We deny the truth deep within, and the relationship that follows, for the external lie, which is used to devalue and dominate.

Howard Thurman was a scholar, pastor, and practical mystic during the twentieth century. He was also a man of African descent born in Florida in the United States. He is known as one of three spiritual advisors to Dr. Martin Luther King Jr. during the U.S. civil rights movement, and, though he was shunned for not participating in forms of civil disobedience, he is responsible for undergirding the movement and its protests in contemplative practice. Thurman co-planted the first multiracial, interdenominational church in the United States, in San Francisco, in 1944. He was the first African American to meet with Mohandas "Mahatma" Gandhi in India in the 1930s, which sparked the flames of the interfaith movement in the United States.

In his book *Jesus and the Disinherited*,[3] first written in 1949 as a response to Gandhi's critique of Christianity, Thurman makes clear that Jesus, himself, was one of the disinherited. He was born out of wedlock, raised in Nazareth, where it was queried, "What good could come out of Nazareth?" Jesus's "father" Joseph was a poor carpenter, and there were siblings. Jesus was a Jew. The Jews in the Roman Empire were oppressed. Jesus fully identified with those on the margins, but he did not fully embrace that status. He self-differentiated from his peers. Did he do it by assimilating to the dominant culture like the Jewish religious leaders of his time—the Pharisees and Sadducees? No. Jesus sought his own path, liberated himself from internal oppression, and he called that place the kingdom of God. Jesus said "the kingdom of God is within in you," "in your midst," "near." This internal liberation gave Jesus the power to stand against his oppressor despite fear, to reach out to his peers, and to teach them of this internal state he referred to as God's reign on earth. Thurman wrote:

> It has long been a matter of serious moment that for decades [centuries] we have studied the various peoples of the world and those who live as our neighbors as objects of missionary endeavor and enterprise without being at all willing to treat them either as brothers [and sisters] or human beings. . . . [I]t is not an issue in which vicious human beings are involved. . . . [I]t is one of the subtle perils of a religion which calls attention—to the point of overemphasis, sometimes—to one's obligation to administer to human need. . . . The issue is not what it [religion] counsels them to do for others whose need may be greater, but what religion offers to meet their own needs.[4]

In other words, we use religion to bolster our own position under the guise that we are following the Golden Rule, doing our part, answering God's call, and standing up to the political system. In reality, rather than our religion freeing us, it sets us up to develop a "savior complex"—a situation where one acts to help "the other." This help in some contexts is self-serving, feeding our ego, giving us undeserved value over those we are trying to save. Internal freedom is not only freedom from the external oppressor but also from the need to satisfy societal expectations in order to be valued and approved. Jesus's message called for a radical change in one's inner attitude. He recognized that oppression is won over another from within—spiritual warfare. Jesus with great clarity and accuracy placed his focus on the inner life of a person—"the inward center," according to Thurman. This was the decisive ground for fortifying a people and determining their destiny.

Jesus and the Inward Journey

Thurman attempts to interpret Jesus as religious subject rather than religious object. He examines the religion of Jesus against the background of his own age and people, and inquires into the content of Jesus's teaching with reference to the disinherited and the underprivileged. Thurman submits that it is impossible for Jesus to be understood outside of the sense of community that Israel held with God. Thurman says that Jesus was revealed as the product of the constant working of the creative mind of God upon the life, thought, and character of a race of people—the Jews.[5] He states, "Here is one who was so conditioned and organized within himself that he became a perfect instrument for the embodiment of a set of ideals."[6]

Jesus was a poor Jew. The economic condition with which he was identified from birth places Jesus with the masses of people who are poor: the disinherited. In his poverty, he was more truly human. Jesus was also a member of the Jewish community, a minority group, in the midst of Rome, a larger, dominant, and controlling group. He grew to manhood in the surging currents of common life that made up the climate of Palestine. He was aware of the people with whom he lived and was affected by them, as we all are affected by our environments. What sets Jesus apart, however, is his ability to not internalize his oppression. Thurman states, "There is one overmastering problem that the socially and politically disinherited always face: Under what terms is survival possible?"[7] Jesus's message to the house of Israel focused on a radical change of the inner attitude of the oppressed.

In Mark's Gospel, Jesus delights in a Canaanite woman from the region of Tyre and Sidon, where people were apparently thought of as "dogs." After asking Jesus if he would come and heal her daughter, who was tormented by demons, Jesus insults her, saying that it was not fair to take the children's food (meaning the Jews) and give it to the dogs (the Gentiles). The Canaanite woman responds, "[B]ut even the dogs under the table eat the children's crumbs" (Mark 7:28 NIV). Jesus sees in the Canaanite woman her emotional freedom from the slurs used against her people. What's important to her is her daughter's healing, and that healing is granted because the Canaanite woman had faith to believe her daughter was worthy of healing even if someone on the outside compared them, as Gentiles, to dogs.

Thurman tells a story of a Korean woman asked to attend a convention of the Student Volunteer Movement to talk about her impression of American education. Very personable and somewhat diminutive, she came to the edge of the platform and said, "You have asked me to talk with you about my impression of American education. But there is only one thing that a Korean has any right to talk about, and that is freedom from Japan." Thurman submits, "This is the position of the disinherited in every age,"[8] and this is the question of the African American, and the people of the land across the globe: How do we overcome oppression and find freedom from the oppressor?

The Jewish minority had two choices: to resist or not to resist. Nonresistance could mean imitation of the oppressor and repudiation of one's own culture, customs, and faith traditions and/or to keep contact with the enemy to a minimum, resulting in cultural isolation, bitterness, hatred, and fear. Resistance could mean the physical, overt expression of an inner attitude or inward resistance that leads to emotional liberation. This is spirituality. And still the spirituality of the disinherited is denied in the dominant culture.

The Sound of the Genuine

In Howard Thurman's 1980 commencement address at Spelman College, he shared the following:

> There is something in every one of you that waits, listens for the sound of the genuine in yourself and if you cannot hear it, you will never find whatever it is for which you are searching and if you hear it and then do not follow it, it was better that you had never been born. . . .
>
> You are the only you that has ever lived; your idiom is the only idiom of its kind in all of existence and if you cannot hear the sound of the genuine in you, you will all of your life spend your days on the ends of strings that somebody else pulls. . . .
>
> There is in you something that waits and listens for the sound of the genuine in yourself and sometimes there is so much traffic going on in your minds, so many different kinds of signals, so many vast impulses floating through your organism that go back thousands of generations, long before you were even a thought in the mind of creation, and you are buffeted by these, and in the midst of all of this you have got to find out what your name is. Who are you? How does the sound of the genuine come through to you? . . .
>
> The sound of the genuine is flowing through you. Don't be deceived and thrown off by all the noises that are a part even of your dreams, your ambitions, so that you don't hear the sound of the genuine in you, because that is the only true guide that you will ever have, and if you don't have that you don't have a thing.
>
> You may be famous. You may be whatever the other ideals are which are a part of this generation, but you know you don't have the foggiest notion of who you are, where you are going, what you want.

Cultivate the discipline of listening to the sound of the genuine in yourself.

Now there is something in everybody that waits and listens for the sound of the genuine in other people. And it is so easy to say that anybody who looks like him or her, anybody who acts as this person acts, can't hear any sound of the genuine. I must wait and listen for the sound of the genuine in you. I must wait. For if I cannot hear it, then in my scheme of things, you are not even present. And everybody wants to feel that everybody else knows that she is there.

I have a blind friend who just became blind after she was a grown woman. I asked her: "What is the greatest disaster that your blindness has brought to you?" She said, "When I go places where there are people, I have a feeling that nobody knows that I'm here. I can't see any recognition, I can't see . . . and if nobody knows that I'm here, it's hard for me to know where I am."

There is something that waits and listens for the sound of the genuine in your mother, in your father, in the people you can't stand, and if you had the power you would wipe them out. But instinctively you know that if you wipe them out, you go with them. So you fight for your own life by finding some way to get along with them without killing them.

There is something in you that waits and listens for the sound of the genuine in other people. And if you can't hear it, then you are reduced by that much. If I were to ask you what is the thing that you desire most in life this afternoon, you would say a lot of things off the top of your head, most of which you wouldn't believe but you would think that you were saying the things that I thought you ought to think that you should say.

But I think that if you were stripped to whatever there is in you that is literal and irreducible, and you tried to answer that question, the answer may be something like this: I want to feel that I am thoroughly and completely understood so that now and then I can take my guard down and look out around me and not feel that I will be destroyed with my defenses down. I want to feel completely vulnerable, completely naked, completely exposed and absolutely secure.

This is what you look for in your children when you have them, this is what you look for in your husband if you get one. That I can run the risk of radical exposure and know that the eye that beholds my vulnerability will not step on me. That I can feel secure in my awareness of the active presence of my own idiom in me.

So as I live my life then, this is what I am trying to fulfill. It doesn't matter whether I become a doctor, lawyer, housewife. I'm secure because I hear the sound of the genuine in myself and having learned to listen to that, I can become quiet enough, still enough, to hear the sound of the genuine in you.

Now if I hear the sound of the genuine in me, and if you hear the sound of the genuine in you, it is possible for me to go down in me and come up in you. So that when I look at myself through your eyes having made that pilgrimage, I see in me what you see in me and the wall that separates and divides will disappear and we will become one because the sound of the genuine makes the same music.[9]

You might ask, how do I hear the genuine within? I think Thurman gives some hints in his speech. First, you must pause with the intention to listen for the genuine. There are contemplative practices, such as centering prayer, the Ignatian Examen, and spiritual direction that can provide the pause you need to give your intention toward the genuine. Determining what represents the genuine for you requires a habit of discernment, where you become adept at noticing what's real and what's not real for you. You have to believe and know that the genuine is within and, through practice, separate the noise that clutters from within and without from that authentic voice that bubbles up from your soul.

Thurman makes clear in "The Inward Sea" that each of us has the power of consent for what we allow to be placed on our altar—our soul. You must own that authority, and in that authority lies your internal liberation. You allow what is needed to give your authentic self life, and you reject those things that have you attached to strings that others pull. That is why a habit of discernment is needed, not just a practice for particular situations or problems to be solved.

You cultivate a habit of discernment through self-care, through giving yourself regular times to be still, go within, and listen for the genuine in yourself. All good practices should become habits, which means that they become so integrated into your way of being, so congruent with who you are, that they become your lifestyle, not just a practice you hold out of compulsion. Finding the genuine in yourself helps you to see the genuine in others, which leads to healthy interdependence and freedom to be fully who you were created to be.

Integration

Practice
You may adapt as needed for individuals.

1. Give participants time to gather their thoughts and to ponder their own emotional freedom. Ask them to journal a bit if it feels right.
2. If a diverse group, form a fish bowl with two groups: The disinherited of this age and those of the dominant culture. Have each group take a turn in the center of the fish bowl, and ask them to answer the following:
   - Name, where are you from, where do you live?

- In what ways are you internally free, and how does your internal freedom assist you in supporting those who are not free?
- How aware are you of your personal privilege, and how aware are you of how your use of that privilege may oppress others?
- In what ways are you oppressed, and how does your awareness of that oppression move you in understanding the oppression of others?
- What is the state of your internal journey? What is the next step for you on that journey? What today is the sound of the genuine in you?

The Hounds of Hell

Without memory, our existence would be barren and opaque, like a prison cell into which no light penetrates; like a tomb which rejects the living. . . . If anything can, it is memory that will save humanity. For me, hope without memory is like memory without hope.

Elie Wiesel, Nobel lecture, 1986

Children often catch the brunt of adult sin.

Rev. Charles L. Booker Jr.

Thurman holds up three emotions as consistent with oppression. These he calls "the hounds of hell": fear, deception, and hate. He ends with what he believes to be the solution to all, and that is love. Thurman submits that although these "hounds of hell" have legitimate reasons for appearing in the oppressed and may start with good outcomes, their continued practice leads to isolation, illness, and a devaluing of self and others. Let's take a look at each of these in light of our investigation into liberation.

Fear comes from isolation and helplessness in the face of varied dimensions of violence—one-sided violence, breeding contempt on the part of the disinherited. Thurman writes:

The disinherited experience the disintegrating effect of contempt in some such fashion as did Goliath. There are few things more devastating than to have it burned into you that you do not count and that no provisions are made for the literal protection of your person. The threat of violence is ever present, and there is no way to determine precisely when it may come crushing down upon you. . . . The underprivileged in any society are the victims of a perpetual war of nerves. The logic of the state of affairs is physical violence, but it need not fulfill itself in order to work its perfect havoc in the souls of the poor.[10]

Fear produces the following conditions:

Control, sometimes with assistance from the disinherited. Paternalism, saviorism, isolation from one's own group or the larger society—segregation. Thurman writes, "In the town in Florida in which I grew up as a boy, it was a common occurrence for white persons to attend our [black] church services and share in the worship. But it was quite impossible for any of us to do the same in the white churches of the community."[11] During enslavement, Africans were not allowed to congregate as a group, and that "shadow behavior" continued during segregation and even into the twenty-first century.

Inferiority, insecurity, devaluation. Racism is the economic, mental, and emotional devaluing of the lives of an oppressed group (anti-Semitism is a form of racism). Thus, Black Lives Matter is a necessary cry to bring attention to our knowledge of our continued devaluation. Devaluing of another group is a deep confession of one's own sense of inferiority and moral insecurity.

Health disparities. Thurman writes, "[F]ear actually causes chemical changes in the body, affecting the blood stream and the muscular reactions, preparing the body for flight or fight."[12] Increased or decreased amounts of natural chemicals in the body, such as adrenaline, dopamine, and serotonin, may cause mental and physical illnesses, rewiring the brain, and/or causing overfunctioning of the organs. Epigenetics has revealed a trauma gene in Jews and people of African descent. That gene could very well be present in other oppressed groups, such as First Nations people.

One-sided violence is being exposed to somebody or something that can inflict terrible harm with no escape. There is no element of contest; the power and tools of violence are on one side. There is no available and recognized protection from trauma and terror on the other side. Lynchings, police shootings, and mass incarceration are examples of one-sided violence. The results are deeply terrifying, and for African Americans chronic, because the danger never passes. Studies show that traumatized people keep secreting large amounts of stress hormones long after the actual danger has passed. The continued secretion of stress hormones is expressed as agitation and panic, and in the long term, wreaks havoc with their health. Rachel Yehuda, who studied post-traumatic stress disorder (PTSD) in war veterans and Holocaust survivors at Mount Sinai Hospital in New York, found that their stress hormone cortisol was low because it was depleted by sustained levels of stress. Cortisol puts an end to the stress response for fight/flight/freeze by sending an all-safe signal. But what if the fight/flight/freeze stress response signal is sustained for long periods of time . . . or never ends? She also found lower levels of cortisol in their children, which could lead to vulnerability to PTSD, hypertension, and obesity.[13]

Humiliation—a loss of a sense of self. Who am I? What am I? What is mine to do? I am thinking about the children who often grow up not knowing that there might be another way for them. There is a ceiling placed on their ability to see past their poverty, their humiliation, sometimes by their despairing elders. Generations of poverty lead to the belief that this is all there is to life, and there is no way out—it is enslavement. Devalued persons learn to put a hold on their expectations and, therefore, their ability to hope.

Regarding concentrated poverty, Thurman writes, it ill behooves the person who is not forced to live in a concentration of poverty, where poverty consists of more than a lack of money, to tell those who must how to transcend its limitations.[14]

Deception

Does the fact that a particular course of action jeopardizes a person's life relieve the person of the necessity for following that course of action? Are there circumstances under which the ethical question is irrelevant? Where does one draw the line? Is there a distinction between literal honesty and honesty in spirit and intent? Are there times when to tell the truth is false to the truth that is within you?

Three Alternatives to Deception

- Accepting the fact there is no sensible choice offered. "The penalty of deception is to become a deception."
- Juggling the various areas of compromise, on the assumption that the moral quality of compromise operates in an ascending-descending scale.
- Complete and devastating sincerity. Jesus's appeal was, "Let your yes be yes and your no be no."[15]

Deception is a survival tactic. How do you show the disinherited that deception can have negative results when what is at stake is simply not to be killed? It is not about keeping the body alive, it is how not to be killed. In order to release the hold and move toward internal liberation, three things have to occur. First, there must be spiritual surgery on the psyche of the oppressed. The barren rocky places in the soul must be revitalized and brought to life before they can be challenged. This can be offered through guided prayer and meditation. Second, people have to live in an environment in which they are not required to exert supreme effort in just keeping alive, where they are able to make choices for other purposes besides those for mere physical survival. Directees such as domestic-violence victims and refugees may need additional support to alleviate the stress of daily living. Group spiritual direction may be able to create space for reflection. Until survival is not the pressing issue, there is no psyche space for reexamination and self-awareness. Finally, internal liberation is cultivated by having the ability to see oneself in the other—to have a sincere relationship with the other. When you can truly see God in the other—no hypocrisy, when there is a sincere relationship between human beings—it marks the supreme moment of human dignity. In spiritual direction, as one focuses on developing a sincere relationship with God, the results are sincere relationships with others. As God provides compassion and loving kindness, it overflows to the other.[16]

Hate: Anatomy of Its Development

> Hating is something of which to be ashamed unless it provides for us a form of validation or prestige.[17]

- Hatred often begins in situations where there is no relationship, where there is contact without a sense of connection and without genuine kindness—a sense of humanity. It is easy to gravitate toward such fellow-ship when the encounter is on our own terms.
- Contacts outside of genuine relationship tend to develop without empathy for the other.
- A relationship without empathy tends to be performance-based and easily leads to conflict when one does not please the other.
- "Ill will" toward others becomes a way of life and a cyclical event and a toxic way of being that exudes hatred instead of love toward those encountered.[18]

Thurman writes:

> Hatred, in the mind and spirit of the disinherited, is born out of great bitterness, a bitterness that is made possible by sustained resentment which is bottled up until it distills an essence of vitality, giving to the individual in whom this is happening a radical and fundamental basis for self-

> realization. . . . [F]rom within the intensity of their
> necessity, they declare their right to exist, despite
> the judgment of the environment. Hatred makes
> this sort of profound contribution to the life of the
> disinherited, because it establishes a dimension of
> self-realization hammered out of the raw materials
> of injustice.[19]

Hate develops out of bitterness and sustained resentment to injustice felt, whether it is real or imagined. If the oppressed accept the judgment that they don't deserve anything other than that which is being visited on them, their self-esteem is compromised, their sense of worth and agency undermined, and their yielding becomes a countersignature to the judgment. If the oppressed reject the judgment, hatred may serve as a device for rebuilding their self-esteem, so that from within the intensity of their necessity they declare their right to exist despite the judgment of the environment.[20] Examples of this are the creation of liberation theology, womanist theology, and feminist theology, where the marginalized interpret the gospel out of their own experiences, where God hears the cries and identifies with the oppressed. Movements such as Black Lives Matter, #MeToo, and Gay Pride are born of this rejection to injustice. Anger can serve as a protection. It is not difficult to see how hatred, operating in this fashion, provides moral justification for the weak. The illusions of righteousness are easy to create. There is a thin line between bitterness, hatred, self-realization, defiance, and righteous indignation. The oppressed can give themselves over with utter enthusiasm to life-affirming attitudes toward their fellow sufferers, and this becomes compensation for their life-negating attitude toward the strong. For the weak, hate serves a creative purpose. However, hate has no boundaries, and behaviors such as hypervigilance, suspicion, negativity, resentment, and bitterness will eventually spill over into other relationships.

In order to set themselves free from the grip of hatred and injustice, there has to be forgiveness: forgiving God, self, and the other. Forgiveness is not something that can be introduced too soon. Underneath the hate is anger, and underneath the anger is hurt, and the hurt has to be healed. Healing happens when persons feel seen and heard, when one is fully present with the other. Healing happens through prayer and confession. Healing happens when the directee experiences the love of God and the love held by the spiritual director. Healing happens when the directee learns to love themselves.

Love

> Behold the miracle! Love has no awareness of merit or demerit; it has no scale by which its portion may be weighed or measured. It does not seek to balance giving and receiving. Love loves; this is its nature. This does not mean that it is blind, naïve, or pretentious, but rather that love holds its object securely in its grasp, calling all that it sees by its true name but surrounding all with a wisdom born both of its passion and its understanding. Here is no traffic in sentimentality, no catering either to weakness or to strength. Instead, there is robust vitality that quickens the roots of personality, creating an unfolding of the self that redefines, reshapes, and makes all things new.[21]

"The Clearing" in Toni's Morrison's "Beloved"

Author Toni Morrison's novel *Beloved* is based on the true story of an enslaved women, named Sethe, who kills her infant daughter (known as Beloved) because she feels her death is better than living through the traumas of enslavement. Sethe, who married a man named Halle, lives with Halle's mother, Baby Suggs, in House 124. Though Baby Suggs suffers the deep traumas of enslavement, she makes her home a hub of love for all that pass through—food cooking on the stove, a place to rest, family (those who understand their plight).

Baby Suggs is described as a "pagan preacher," as many of the women preachers were not trained and licensed by the slaveholders, who trained some of the enslaved males to preach a gospel of submission. Baby Suggs would hold service in "The Clearing," and although she suffered much from the loss of her sons and grand-daughter Beloved, whom Sethe murdered to set her free, Baby Suggs preaches to those gathered a theology of love of oneself and holds celebrations where they dance, sing, moan, and embrace in a liturgy of release and acceptance of self. Baby Suggs would encourage them to see the beauty of nature around them despite their circumstances and to see the beauty within themselves and each other as acts of subversion and liberty from the realities of their enslavement.[22] Baby Suggs grows weary and dies of a broken heart, but Sethe remains at 124 haunted by her own traumas in the person of a young woman named Beloved.

People of color, especially First Nations people and those of African descent, are still in need of this self-love—both individual and communal—that reminds them of their origins, that they are fearfully and wonderfully made in the image of that which some call God. This is our liberation. It must be internal before it can ever manifest externally. Spiritual directors sitting with people of color must encourage self-love in their directees, who often come burdened by life and caring more for others than themselves. PoC carry their traumas and burdens in their bodies. In the Christian tradition, Jesus advises us to love our neighbors as we love ourselves. We tend to put the emphasis on love of neighbor, but Jesus's directive assumes love of self first. Women, especially, often forget about self in order to care for others. The truth is that no one can truly love others if they do not possess self-love, body and soul. The Golden Rule, in all traditions, advises us to treat our neighbor as we desire to be treated. Without self-love and the desire to be loved, we cannot fulfill our direction to treat others in a loving way. Spiritual directors' ethics require them to practice self-love by being accountable, practicing self-care, and walking the walk with which we are called to accompany others. Directees should also be encouraged to be loving of themselves, body and soul. Spiritual directors can both model and mirror self-love in the way they accompany people of color, who almost always are carrying the weight of centuries of devaluation within a racist culture.

Love of Enemy

Three groups of enemies:[23]

- the personal enemy
- those who make it difficult to live without shame and humiliation
- the moral enemy—"Rome"

Thurman writes, "Love of the enemy means a fundamental attack must first be made on the enemy status."[24] The enemy status can only be attacked when we see the "other" as human like ourselves. However, to see the other's humanity first means we embrace our own humanity. It is impossible to change the enemy status of another until we embrace, without condition, love of self.

Practice

Break into four groups: Fear, Hate, Deception, and Love. Each group must choose a scribe and reporter to the larger body. Each group must answer the following questions as they relate to the group's assigned emotion.

- What emotions do you employ to navigate through your oppression?
- What are the benefits of those emotions for your current circumstances, and what are the long-term effects?
- What is your greatest fear?
- What deception(s) do you entertain?
- What evokes feelings of hate in you?
- The Golden Rule assumes love of self. What are your ways of being in the world that reflect love?
- What are your ways of being that indicate a lack of love for yourself and others?

Conclusion

One's internal liberation is tied up with one's spirituality. The enslaved Africans, some who may very well have come to the West as Christians, some as Muslim, and others devoted to indigenous belief systems, found their freedom in their spirituality. Through their spirituality, the enslaved Africans have passed on their ways and wisdom through generations of diasporas. They are in some ways responsible for our modern Christian theology, which imagined their emancipation. In African American spirituality, liberation and justice are key. Just like the Romans in Jesus's time, the current dominant culture has devalued the culture and spirituality of people who are not like them. That devaluation has been the impetus for genocide, the murder of peoples, cultures, and identities, the stripping of families from one another, and the stripping of their land and other natural resources. It has caused the spirituality of our faith traditions to be whitewashed, along with the people of color who birthed them.

It is essential that spiritual directors make space for the remembrance of those who came before us and for the spiritual wisdom that lay dormant in the souls of those who seek out our hospitality. It is important that we help lead the way to internal freedom in the same way Harriet Tubman led the way to physical freedom during enslavement. Black liberation theologian James Cone talked about finding the *imago Dei* (the image of God) in blackness. In the devaluing of our bodies, we have struggled to value and to love ourselves, to see ourselves, our blackness in the image of God, but Cone reminds us that in our families, in our communities there is often love, creativity, and "nephresh," which from the Hebrew at its fullest means soul. This soul allows us to see the *imago Dei* in blackness, just as Jesus displayed the *imago Dei* in his own brutalized body. Though there may be moments when we need to isolate ourselves from others, solitude is not the fullness of life God has in mind. We are called to a loving communion that mirrors the Trinity, which in itself symbolizes very diverse aspects of that Mystery we call God.

We are called to remember God declaring humankind as "like us" and "good" and Jesus's internal freedom found in that kin-dom, his image being seen as the son of God. We are being called to follow one who showed us the *imago Dei* and how to live it in a way that makes God's kin-dom real. Our devaluing of others to elevate ourselves is ancient. It is part of the human condition. More than reformation, we need to embrace our evolution where everyone and every part of creation is valued equally and allowed to fulfill its part in the image of God. May it be so!

Notes

1. Alice McDowell, "The Three Dimensions of Spiritual Direction," in *The Christian Ministry of Spiritual Direction*, edited by David L. Fleming (St. Louis: Review for Religious), 95.
2. Howard Thurman, *Meditations of the Heart* (Boston: Beacon Press, 1981), 15.
3. Howard Thurman, *Jesus and the Disinherited* (Boston: Beacon Press, 1976).
4. Ibid., 13.
5. Ibid., 16.
6. Ibid.
7. Ibid., 20.
8. Ibid., 22–23.
9. Howard Thurman, "The Sound of the Genuine," commencement address, Spelman College, Atlanta, 1980, available at https://www.uindy.edu/eip/files/reflection4.pdf, from the Crossings Project at the University of Indianapolis.
10. Thurman, *Jesus and the Disinherited*, 39.
11. Ibid., 42, 43.
12. Ibid., 45.
13. Bessel van der Kolk, *The Body Keeps the Score: Brain, Mind, and Body in Healing Trauma* (New York: Viking Press 2015), 27, 30.
14. Thurman, *Jesus and the Disinherited*, 56.
15. Ibid., 62–71.
16. Ibid., 68–73.
17. Ibid., 75.
18. Ibid., 75–78.
19. Ibid., 79, 81, 82.
20. Ibid., 81.
21. Howard Thurman, *A Strange Freedom* (Beacon Press: Boston 1998), 181.
22. "Baby Suggs and the Clearing," https://youtu.be/om4c8bALlec.
23. Thurman, *Jesus and the Disinherited*, 91.
24. Ibid., 97.

9

Social Trauma and Public Spirituality
A Womanist Relational Ethic of Spiritual Practice

Phillis Isabella Sheppard

TRAINING PRINCIPLE | HEALING

In this chapter, we turn our attention to spiritual direction as one relationship within the complex of supports needed for healing from the impact of trauma. Phillis Isabella Sheppard "situates trauma as a force, not an event, operative between the individual and the social and public milieu, on the psyche and in group processes, and permeating through the social structures that shape public and private life." She states, "The trauma that black and brown people carry, extends, and is preceded by, events beyond the individual, and it is handed down in memories, narratives, stories, warnings, and reenactments in public, fantasies, and the most intimate of relationships, and even in the spaces we consider sacred." The wounds we carry go with us wherever we go and impact every aspect of life as well as our relationship with God or whoever the Divine is for us. This carrying is "sometimes known and sometimes not conscious or acknowledged" but still has real consequences.

The author, in acknowledging the pervasiveness of trauma as a "force" within the lives of black and brown people across generations, identifies that the only possible remedy or intervention must be relational. She states, "The legacy and vestiges of trauma inculcate themselves in the psychic and social spaces and relationships,

For my ancestor warriors and first teachers: Hattie Booker Peterson, Lois Peterson Quillian, Luvi Camp Sheppard, Ernestine Winona Quillian Sheppard. I give thanks.

including those spaces designated as sacred and spiritual." "Social and public trauma . . . erupts in and from an intertwined relational, social, and political domain. Trauma's trajectory of impact is, ultimately, relational." Trauma manifests itself in massacres, assassinations, and sexual violence; in lynching, murder, and exploitation; in racism, sexism, segregation, and marginalization; in bullying, brainwashing, and colonization of the brain. The author suggests that "social trauma," because it is ultimately relational, "demands a relational ethic on which to build spiritual practices and practices of care that disrupt the impact of trauma in all domains in which it operates."

The chapter lays out for us the development of a womanist relational ethic that is foundational to the design and implementation of a retreat environment and appropriate for fostering collective and individual spiritual care for participants experiencing social trauma. The aspects of the retreat design are explained, and an example format is provided as one that may be particularly useful in group spiritual direction.

Trauma, in the lives of black and brown people, is seldom distinct and unrelated to the social and public contexts in which they live. When we discuss trauma and spiritual responses to it, we must take up the ways in which society and systemic forces are sources and sites of trauma. Any consideration of spiritual guidance must also be affected by social and public practices. In fact, there is an overreliance on the inner experience of the individual and, often, a decontextualized discourse on trauma and spirituality. I seek to situate trauma as a force, not an event, operative between the individual and the social and public milieu, on the psyche and in group processes, and permeating the social structures that shape public and private life.

This means that all trauma is social phenomena experienced in relational contexts with implications for the person and the group, regardless of where trauma seems to originate. For example, sexual trauma, such as what gave rise to Tarana Burke, a black woman and activist from Harlem, starting the "Me Too" movement, may seem to some to be new when viewed through a decontextualized

and ahistorical lens. Part of the trauma of sexualized violence per-
sistently directed toward black women is the long history of such
trauma. In actuality, sexualized violence exists in domestic and intimate partner relations, as an underlying threat in labor and work,
and cultural depictions of black, especially women and girls', sexuality. In her now classic article, "Rape and the Inner Lives of Black
Women in the Middle West," Darlene Clarke Hines argued that the
rape and sexual violation of black women was systemic and struc-
turally "institutionalized. . . . [I]t has always involved the patriarchal notions of black women being, at best, not entirely unwilling
accomplices, if not inviting sexual assault."[1] In 1936, Jessie Daniel
Ames included the psychological dimension when she argued that
white women had so often heard that black women were at fault
for the sexual violence white men directed toward them that "we
[white women]have believed . . . that not only was there no such
thing as a chaste Negro woman . . . a Negro woman could not be
assaulted, that it was never against her will."[2] The trauma of sexual
violence is punctuated by the history of race and gender, in which
a black woman's life is expected to include the experience of sexualized violence and, in many cases, renders her silent about such
violence, because, as one patient reported to me, "I don't want to
just be a statistic." Silence and its oppression seemed a more bear-
able alternative especially since it allowed her to project a picture
of strength and invulnerability. As a mother, she expected and even
demanded the same from her daughters.[3] These expectations and
silences infiltrate familial relationships at the root, and it is only
through the hard work of telling the stories that we have been
taught to silence that the transgenerational power of secrecy begins
to be disrupted. In spiritual guidance, we have to name that which
is bearing down on the chest, choking back truth and horror. The
myth of the strong black woman is a myth gone awry.

An example of the traumatizing exploitation of the "strong Black
woman" myth is captured poignantly in the experience of two black
women sitting in a café having a conversation about racism. One
of the women, Zoé Samudzi, tweeted their experience, and April
Hathcock reported on her blog:

A couple months ago Zoé, a beautiful Black woman

with a lot of powerful things to share, tweeted a story about having a conversation with another Black woman about racism in different national contexts. It was a life-giving session of shared truths and traumas, as often happens when women of color are blessed to be in honest communion with one another.

After their trauma-baring and sharing talk, a white man sitting nearby turned to them to thank them for their words and to let them know that he had been listening and that, as a doctoral student studying issues of race, he now felt he had a lot of great material to think about for his dissertation.[4]

Their stories of racism, pain, and perseverance as doctoral students themselves was, without permission or even acknowledgment of their agency, appropriated for "his work" and use. He felt entitled to listen in on a conversation that was not his to hear; he felt entitled to their conversation and felt entitled to evaluate it as "great material." Their raw and undisguised communication was subjected to his unacknowledged sexualized colonization. The exploitation of black women's bodies, minds, spiritualities, and lives contributes to their exhaustion, anger, and rage. Such exploitation is integral to any social-activism work in which many of us are involved because it is—contrary to popular parlance of "micro"—a major aggression that occurs repetitively on a daily basis. These events take a toll on the psyche, on relationships, and in public spaces.

The trauma that black and brown people carry, extends, and is preceded by, events beyond the individual, and it is handed down in memories, narratives, stories, warnings, and reenactments in public, fantasies, and the most intimate of relationships, and even in the spaces we consider sacred. In other words, the legacy and vestiges of trauma inculcate themselves into psychic and social spaces and relationships. These spaces include those that have been designated as sacred and spiritual.

Massacres, Assassinations, and Sexuality:
Trauma in LGBTQ Communities

In June 2016, many who identify as Lesbian, Gay, Bisexual, Trans, and/or Queer awakened to the unfolding horror story of the Pulse massacre in Florida. For those of us who identify as black, brown, or People of Color, LGBTQ feelings of anger, powerlessness, and near despair shook us to the core. It would magnify the harm, including the spiritual harm, to ignore the full weight of the trauma that this violence inflicted. In her reflection on the meaning of the Pulse club for the spirituality of the Orlando LGBTQ community, Cecilia Aldarondo wrote "Sanctuary after Pulse," in which she argued that the massacre was directed against black and brown people, specifically Latinx. More forcefully than most, she connected the massacre to an attack on their spirituality and sacred spaces; the implications for mental health, cultural, and spiritual needs are clear and profound:

> The overwhelming majority of people who died were Latinx. If you look at the list of the dead—it's blatant. Sotomayor. Gonzalez-Cruz. Torres. Flores. Velazquez. Rivera. Why should this matter? Because for queer people of color, the need for sanctuary is that much greater.[5]

Aldarondo stated what so many of the shock news announcements blasting across social media failed to notice or to notice enough—Pulse and clubs like it are places of sacred refuge for those seeking community and respite from a homophobic society; they are a place to be. The gathering together, being recognized, the dancing, the care and care-taking of one another, the resources shared just because you are a part of the community and show up cannot be underestimated. The massacre was an attack not only on brown and black people "worshiping," but it was an attack on the culture and idea that LGBTQ people have spiritual practices specific to them.

> Every town, every city has its Pulse, its UC, its Bachelor. These are spaces of refuge, of safety, of

> sanctuary. Traditionally, "sanctuary" was a religious
> word, meaning a sacred space in a church where fu-
> gitives from danger would be protected. . . . A sanc-
> tuary, above all, offered refuge, comfort, a place to
> rest. . . . But for many queer people, "sanctuary" in
> the religious sense has never existed. . . . For many,
> clubs like Pulse have provided that sanctuary.[6]

And in the early-morning hours of a Sunday, a sacrilegious violent act destroyed this sacred gathering space.[7] An African American man, Keinon Carter, who survived the Pulse massacre, stated he is trying to find how his life can be a life in and for community. His is a deeply spiritual question. It emerges from a fulcrum of sexuality, violence, and spirituality. Are we prepared as spiritual guides to walk the path with him?[8] Are we prepared to walk this path with and in community?

In attempts to ignite the spirits, ancestors, and the sacredness of life, many people gathered to protest and mourn the massacre. Almost simultaneously, common public space became sacred holy spaces near the club. People congregated, cried, sang, and prayed. One artist from Illinois, Greg Zanis, created forty-nine crosses, each with the name of a person murdered by the gunman. White crosses with red hearts lined the street, as did the mourners. I was there among the many and stopped before each cross to pray a litany for each one named. This public gathering revealed emerging needs for public sacred ritual that is as much for the dead as it is for the mourning. Malidoma Patrice Somé has pointed out that we need communal/community rituals, "because our soul communicates things to us that the body translates as need, or want, or absence. So, we enter ritual to respond to the call of the soul."[9] Care of the call of the soul continues in Orlando. The mantra "One Orlando" to communicate the collective sense that Orlando was attacked, while it diminished the ethnic-racial target of the massacre, was an attempt to be(come) the community they needed. In Orlando, public remembering continues among brown and black LGBTQ groups as well as throughout the city. The spiritual dimension is embedded in acts of remembering, in religious services, and in the refusal to accede to fear. This path is not an individual path. As a pastoral theologian, invited to come and offer spiritual care, my role was to be with the community, families, and individuals and to challenge the places that brown and black LGBTQ voices were absent in local response. My role was also to remain present in person and, once I returned home, to continue to remember in word and prayer, but also to see the connections with brown and black LGBTQ beyond the United States.

Brazil: A Black Lesbian Activist, Marielle Franco, Was Assassinated.

On March 14, 2018, less than two years after the Pulse massacre, Marielle Franco, a Black lesbian Brazilian activist who fought for the rights of "Rio's black, LGBTQ and favela communities, lay slumped on the backseat of a white Chevrolet . . ."[10] Franco was murdered, along with her driver, Anderson Gomes. Franco was targeted and shot four times in the head after leaving a political debate in Rio. The impact on the black/LGBTQ community in Rio is heard in the litany of voices who gathered after learning of her murder:

> Camila Pontes, 30: "I feel lost, without hope," she said. "It is a very tough blow for anyone who fights for justice, for freedom, for equality."

> "She was a symbol of the politics we believe in." said student Jefferson Barbosa, 21. "I have never been so scared," he said. "People are shocked with what happened. They did this to Mari, one of the most popular lawmakers in Rio. *What will stop them from doing this to others?*"[11]

> Marinete da Silva, Franco's mother, is left with soul-wrenching questions and laments because, every day, "I still have no answers."[12]

> Franco's fiancé Mônica Benício's grief continues unabated since she learned of Franco's murder, "I ran at her shouting: 'Where's Marielle? Where's Marielle?' " "I screamed and I shouted. . . . It was like

I was having a nightmare and would wake up at any moment."[13]

Those who knew of Marielle Franco's work for justice among the most marginalized mourned and protested her murder. Almost immediately they suspected what the police responsible for investigating could not fathom: her murder was not random but in retaliation for justice commitments, her outspoken support of the black LGBTQ community of which she was a member, her fearlessness in pointing the finger at police brutality. Franco was committed to "the survival of a whole people," and she threatened the powers of oppression. She was murdered because of it, and her communities had to mourn and protest simultaneously. Finally, after eight months of investigation and wide social protest, public grief, and global outrage, the investigators "discovered" what the family and friends knew.

> The Rio de Janeiro secretary of public security, General Richard Nunes, also confirmed that the police suspect that militia groups committed the crime. He also said that it's "likely" that there are politicians involved in Franco's assassination. The councilwoman was a human rights activist and advocated for the rights of people of color and in impoverished conditions.[14]

Social and public trauma erupts in and from an intertwined relational, social, and political domain. Trauma's trajectory of impact is, ultimately, relational. As such, social trauma demands a relational ethic on which to build spiritual practices and practices of care that disrupt the impact of trauma in all domains in which it operates. In the remainder of this chapter, I first develop the contours of a womanist relational ethic. Next, using a "case study" approach to two retreats and presentations, I discuss how the womanist relational ethic was operative in the design and implementation of the retreats, and how the different aspects of the retreats performed the work of spiritual care and guidance collectively and individually for the participants. Finally, I discuss why this kind of spiritual work is necessary for working with black retreatants during this contemporary moment in the U.S. context.

Womanist Relational Ethic

A womanist relational ethic is an ethic that emerges from a critical reflection on the black experience and, specifically, beginning with black and brown women's life. As a practical theologian, I take seriously Alice Walker's four-part definition of womanist and have long noted that a womanist relational ethic is infused throughout: In definition one, the relational ethic is expressed in the mother-daughter exchange, "From the black folk expression of mothers to female children, 'you acting womanish,' i.e., like a woman . . . acting grown up. Being grown up. Responsible. In charge. . . ."[15] We hear it especially in definition two, which includes:

> A woman who loves other women, sexually and/ or non-sexually. Appreciates and prefers women's culture, women's emotional flexibility. Sometimes loves individual men, sexually and/or nonsexual . . . committed to the survival of a whole people . . . not a separatist, except periodically, for health.[16]

In definition three, we hear the self-communal that is infused through the relational-spiritual domain, "Loves music. Loves dance. Loves the moon. Loves the Spirit. Loves love and food and roundness. Loves the struggle. Loves the folk. Loves herself. *Regardless*."[17] Walker's definition of womanist captures the cultural, social, self, spiritual, historical, political, and activist: "Traditionally capable as in: 'mama, I'm walking to Canada and I'm taking you and bunch of other slaves with me.'"[18] And in definition four, Walker names the importance of black women's cultural and social location, particularity in relation to white women's experience: "womanist is to feminist as purple is to lavender."[19]

Taking a relational ethic seriously makes demands on the tasks, aims, and activities of a womanist responding to spirituality in light of trauma. Womanist pastoral theologian Carolyn Mc-Crary gets at the relational-ethical dimension when she discusses interdependence as communal responsibility to each other and each person's responsibility to the community's survival and well-being—emotionally, "economically, physically and spiritual development of the group as a whole."[20] A slight revision of my discussion of the dimensions of a womanist practical theology of trauma may be instructive for this discussion.

1. Trauma and mourning processes are religious experiences occurring in the intrapsychic and social dimension of experience;
2. Experiences of race, gender, sexuality, and religion are integral to the formation of the self and group affiliations;
3. It is necessary to understand religion and religious experience—whether rejected, adopted, or disavowed—as part and parcel of a process of mourning cultural and personal traumas and disappointments.
4. Spiritual guidance (practical theology) must listen to the critical perspectives heard in the stories of those who have abandoned religion and religious institutions, and must contextualize, communally and historically, any effort to understand and respond;
5. Spiritual guidance (practical theology) emerging from the reality of black women's experiences must, then, become embodied and embodied in practices of transformation.[21]

The emphasis is on the relational ethic in embodied practices of transformation. A relational ethic of spiritual care and guidance is counter to many of the values pervading the contemporary cultural milieu. Without a relational ethic undergirding our work, we can actually reproduce trauma and suffering, but we also replicate the social structures of traumata. A womanist relational ethic of spiritual care and guidance has a trajectory that is disruptive of sociocultural ways of being. Sometimes these ways of being have been passed down to us unquestioned. We take them in as how it is, is supposed to be, and will be—and because these ways of being may not be conscious to us as ideas or values that we have accepted or agreed to, we may also be unconscious of their effect on our spirituality and sense of well-being. We may also resist efforts to make them conscious or to do the spiritual, relational, and public work to change. Spiritual guidance is hard work for those who accompany and for those who long to end their suffering and suffering in the world.

Integration

Womanist Relational Ethic in Spiritual Care with Black Pastors: An Advent Retreat

Opening: African Drummers Djembe in Paris Subway

> Claiming the space sacred and remembering the ancestors:

> We are here with four candles before us. This first week of advent we light one candle. Remember: We begin by lighting one candle, and so, we have just a little light to guide our way. Let us claim this sacred space with the burning of the sage and the remembering of the ancestors (as I make a full circle around the room carrying the burning sage).

Music: "Glory to God"
(*Handel's Messiah: A Soulful Celebration*)

Advent Reflection 1: Howard Thurman

> When the song of the angels is stilled,
> when the star in the sky is gone,
> when the kings and princes are home,
> when the shepherds are back with their flocks,
> the work of Christmas begins:
> to find the lost,
> to heal the broken,
> to feed the hungry,
> to release the prisoner,

to rebuild the nations,
to bring peace among the people,
to make music in the heart.[22]

SHARED RESPONSES: Who is lost, and who are you to find? Who is hungry and imprisoned in your world?

Let us name names and call forth for their healing.

RESPONSE: African Drummers Djembe in Paris Subway

RESPONSE: What are we called to in our lives?

ALL: To find the lost, to heal the broken, to feed the hungry, to release the prisoner, to rebuild the nations, to bring peace among the people, to make music in the heart.

Written Reflection

1. Reflect on your life as an instrument of God. What kind of instrument would you be? A flute, a piano, a trumpet, a sax, a drum, a violin, a clarinet? What draws you to see yourself this way?
2. What kind of music is God playing in your life now? A golden oldie, a spirited march, a dissonant piece, a dirge, a lullaby, a rock song, hip-hop, rap, a ballad?
3. What song title sums up the way God has been a part of your life?[23]

We bring into this space tonight all that we are aware of going on in the world and at our borders. We are staring into an abyss.

We must ask ourselves what will we do as a nation to end this violence.

What will we collectively do? What will we collectively demand?

How will our prayers and lament become more than cycles of ritual?

Our nation needs healing and justice . . .

there is blood on the hands of those that preach guns and hatred . . .

we the people must use every resource and power we have

to undo this love of guns and violence . . .

we the people must stand up.

What must we stand up to and hear tonight?

Music: "People Get Ready," Sung by Aretha Franklin

Responsive Reading: Joel 1:1–3

Listen to this, you elders!
Pay attention, all who dwell in the land!
Has anything like this ever happened in your
    lifetime,
or in the lifetime of your ancestors?
Report it to your children.
Have your children report it to their children,
and their children to the next generation.

Silence

Let us pray the news.

National News

November 25, 2018, in response to "U.S. Agents Fire Tear Gas at Migrants Attempting to Cross U.S.-Mexico Border in Tijuana" (*Huffington Post* headline)

ALL: This is Advent? What is happening? Why is it happening?

Communal sharing of our responses to

- What is happening?
- Why is it happening?

- How is it happening?

Reading 1: Reflection on Joel in Light of the News

Be ashamed,
because we sit
silent with pursed lips of stifled groans.
Howl, Wail, and Cry
all vicarious mourners
Watching as the people are rejected
to perish from hunger, violence, and
terror while air is sucked from their lungs
and inconsolable children are gathered in their
parents' arms.

ALL: What are we waiting for?

All that we declare as good and whole
before our congregations, in our prayers,
in loud declarations, and melodious
statements—they are withering before our eyes
Our altars' bread broken in memory of what—
it molds and holy drink is no more sweet
bitter and dank it flows through our innards.
There is no sackcloth strong enough to hold
our lament and mourning
and our offerings cause laughter
our tears melt before they water our lashes,
they are waste

ALL: What are we waiting for?

What shall we do? What can we do? What must we
    do?
Call for the elders, listen to the young,
gather the people, head into the streets
face the bloodied faces, and hate-filled news;
cry out for justice; create holy sanctuaries;
encircle the cities, shout down the politicians, pray
the news, make pilgrimages to end the reign of
    horror

Repent in action.

ALL: What are we waiting for?

Silence

Writing Meditation: What Are We Waiting For?

ALL: Sharing from your writing: one- to two-word responses (three times)

Walking meditation: Concluding with sharing one or two words in responses written on flip charts

Reflection Questions

The season is Advent, and the news is breaking our hearts.

What are we waiting for?

In meditation, spend time with this question, "What are we waiting for?"

Still silent, we capture in large print the collective responses. We circle the room and read what each has written in response to the meditation.

Reading the News 2: A Response to "Trump Defends Use of 'Very Safe' Tear Gas on Migrant Children" (*Chicago Tribune*, November 28, 2018)

Reading II: Reflection on Joel in Light of the News

Pray the news? How?
They who lead, fail us
While they drink the blood of the young
and shout victory, victory, victory!

We should be alarmed!
Wake up and sound the drums!

ALL: Make a noise! Make a noise, make a noise, make a noise!

Call for the ancestors' courage to envelop us;

We are asking, can these dry bones live and
struggle with us?

Blow the horns, improvise, create!
Sound the alarm my people; we the people must
    rise up,
there is no hiding place on some far-off holy hill

ALL: Make a noise! Make a noise! Make a noise!

We must stand and tremble together
moving into place to stop the days of evil that sur-
    round us
the day of demand is at hand
the shadows and moonless nights
are here;
the days are without clouds
as horror rains down upon the children

Ferguson, Washington, Guatemalan Children at the Border

ALL: We have been told what is right, true, and
just!

ALL: Make a noise! Make a noise! Make a noise!

Drumming Meditation

Reflection Questions

- The season is Advent, and the news is breaking our
  hearts.
- What are we waiting for?
- In meditation, spend time with this question,
  "What are we waiting for?"

*Still silent, we capture our collective responses on
large print. We circle the room and read what each
has written in response to the meditation.*

Communal Sharing

What will we hold onto that we did not bring with
us?

Local News 2, City/Local: Oversight Board

> The headlines read: "Nashville Amendment 1 for
>   Police Oversight Board Passes Overwhelmingly"
> There is no coming warrior, we are the warriors
>   of this day. The ancient of days? We know not
>   what such words mean.
> Look, look, look and see: a field of bodies falling all
>   around us ablaze with the fire of hate, chok-
>   ing on polluted air in a desert waste, this place
>   where injustice lives unabated.
>
> ALL: Make a noise! Make a noise, make a noise,
> make a noise!

Music: "People Get Ready, There's a Train a-Comin'"
(Aretha Franklin)

Response

1. Nashvillians voted overwhelmingly to amend the
   city's governing document by creating a new citizen-
   led panel to oversee the actions of police, the culmination of a decades-long push from black leaders in the
   city.
2. The victory for supporters of Amendment 1 to the
   Metro Charter came despite facing a massive fund-
   raising disadvantage against the Nashville Fraternal
   Order of Police, which bankrolled efforts to defeat the
   measure.
3. The amendment passed by a margin of 59 percent to
   41 percent—134,135 votes to 94,055—with all precincts
   reporting (from the *Tennessean,* November 6, 2018).
4. A coalition of social-justice activists called Community
   Oversight Now led the push for the new panel as a way
   to create a check over alleged claims of racial bias and
   other controversial actions of police.
5. They've argued that the word of a police officer is too
   often taken for granted in disputes with the public.
6. But many police officers pushed back in a contentious

local campaign that collided with high turnout in the statewide elections for U.S. Senate and governor.

7. "This victory is the outgrowth of a people's movement—the transformative energy of hundreds of volunteers and everyday people representing diverse racial and ethnic groups, faith traditions, young and old," the group said.[24]

Communal sharing of our responses to

- What is happening?
- Why is it happening?
- How is it happening?

Music: Hallelujah

Praying the News 3: Congregational News

What are your headlines this Advent season?

Reflect on your congregation. Write down some thoughts:

- What has been the congregation's vocation? Write this out.
- What has been the congregation's vocation in light of "the news"?
- What is the good news, bad news? What news are you changing?

ALL: Make a noise! Make a noise, make a noise, make a noise!

Share your news of your congregation. Large-group sharing:

- What is happening with us here at the retreat?
- Why is it happening?
- How is it happening?

SHARED RESPONSES:

- What will we hold onto that we did not bring with us?

- What will we leave here when we leave?

CLOSING: Claiming the sacred space and remembering the ancestors

We are here with four candles before us. This is the first week of Advent that we light one candle. Remember: We began by lighting one candle, and so, we have just a little light to guide our way. And so, we remember to give thanks for the wisdom of the ancestors.

What was the spiritual-guidance work I was doing throughout the retreat? This retreat was an Advent retreat for pastors to reflect on the vocation of the congregation in light of justice struggles in the world and in their local community, Nashville, Tennessee.

My aims were:

1. To have them deepen the group's cohesiveness so that they would be able to rely on each other for spiritual care and congregational vocational discernment in their congregation and broader community.
2. To have individuals and the group wrestle with the trauma many were experiencing (as were their congregants) because of the current political climate. Prior discussions, in the nonretreat setting, sacrificed mourning and sadness for anger. The retreat was to widen the emotional and spiritual space. One way we worked to bring this about was to remind (re-member) the ancestors' experiences and to connect to the biblical narrative.

- Another aim not represented in the material above was to stop in the middle of a reflection, because I sensed a great deal of unspoken pain. I reported to the group what I was sensing, and this opened up painful emotions regarding their personal vocational discernments in their contexts.

- This contributed to the group's cohesiveness, trust, and sense of community—not just a "group feeling," but they began to identify with the collective aims of the program more explicitly.
- This also released into the space important topics related to class, gender, race, and sexuality as well as feelings of loss related to the need for new spiritual language, songs, ritual, and meaningful ways of being community.

3. To work with the group to move from interior experience to social/public experience by having them write on large paper. The aim here was to make public intense emotional responses, to help the group see the amount of shared experience they held, and to bring these responses into their understanding of spiritual practice (rather than sequestering them from full awareness).

4. To bolster the group and individuals' sense of agency about how much of their own experience they would share, and what they would do with work of the retreat. We worked on this by naming, without judgment or response, what each would take from the retreat and what each would leave in the retreat space.

5. During the retreat portion, when people could say what they would take and leave, three pastors requested to use portions of the retreat for their Sunday service; some stated that they were now able to write or revise their upcoming sermons. One said, "Dr. Sheppard, this was hard, hard, hard. I didn't know it, but this is what I needed." We were all exhausted after this retreat. Not all can be captured in my reflections, but suffice it to say, the spiritual care and the fruits of it are future tense. We will know how deep and how transformative our time was when we meet again.

In Practice: Public Spiritual Care
for "Womanist Wednesday" Program
with an Online Church

Stop, Listen, and Breathe: The Holiday Season and Self-Care

Many of us carry memories, and probably a lot of unacknowledged fantasies, about the season spanning Advent and Christmas.[25] Advent, the season of holy waiting, is anything but holy. Unfortunately, the season of Advent-Christmas has become, for many, less about the spirit of the season and more about the pressure to perform Christmas. Bright lights are displayed everywhere. Selecting the perfect gift, for everyone in your life, is more burden than gift-giving pleasure.

The pressures are often internal and external and, when combined, can have us holding our breaths just waiting for the season to be over. Though we may recognize that feeling exhausted, and even disheartened, are not what we want for ourselves or loved ones, we do not know how to get out of it. The consumer culture in which we live lurches into hyperdrive just before Thanksgiving. We are inundated with messages to create the most idealized season. The images we see often display "perfect families" in which the season is a lovefest free of real-life family dynamics. The gift-giving is extraordinary. We are encouraged to spend more than we can afford. We take on a greater share of the work involved in celebrations, and we are expected to take on still more. We are told we are the glue that holds it all together. And, we believe it. So, we resist asking for help. We really believe we can and must do it all.

There is often a gulf between the images the media projects of what the holidays are "supposed" to be and the reality of our particular lives. Among the work, frustrations, and, sometimes, despondency, we often lose sight of what we need spiritually, physically, and emotionally during this season. In fact, we forget about ourselves.

This season, disrupt the tradition of exhaustion and replace it with a holy season. This Womanist Wednesday program had three intentions: (1) to reclaim the spiritual dimension of the holiday season through self-care practices; (2) to recognize that self-care is a yearlong process that sustains us in our spiritual practices; and

(3) to help us recognize when we are in need of care from others and ways to receive such care.

The holiday season is seldom a stress-free environment for anyone. However, for some of us, the stress and even unhappiness are complicated or made more intense during the period leading up to Thanksgiving past Christmas. This is, in part, because in our experience this is not a true holy or holiday time.

Sometimes, we try to use this season to make up or repair past holiday seasons. Often this may be out of awareness; we barely notice what we are doing. But we want to make it extra special. We want to give and buy generously because we did not experience such generosity. If we fall into this category, we tend to overspend, extend ourselves beyond what is good and necessary, and place expectations on the holiday that cannot fully be met. The problem with this is that it actually re-creates earlier disappointment rather than modulate or even work through it.

The day is not actually our day; it is like Groundhog Day—it repeats the past when what is needed is to face the past and, in some cases, mourn the disappointments. Another reason this season can be stressful is because our sense of self or belonging, which may be fine or acceptable during the rest of the year, is suddenly under the stress of holiday cheer. The media tell us to ignore the reality of the struggles happening in our lives and in our world; we may feel torn, feel like we are negative people. We ask, "Why can't we just try to get into the spirit of Christmas that Wall Street is offering?" Something in us recognizes that we cannot, because "Wall Street" is not the reality of our life. And yet it pulls with its bright lights and commercials calling us into the vortex of capitalism and consumerism that we likely cannot afford; spiritually, it is an image to which we cannot afford to succumb. I shared with them the Joel reading from the pastors' retreat.

Our skirting of the feelings of the past means that this season loses its capacity to help us do spiritual work. Advent is a season of waiting, but we cannot wait, because the past tells us that waiting is for naught. If we resist or run from the past, run from the season of waiting, bury our feelings, and, instead, throw ourselves into activity, we do not know where the source or place of waiting resides. This makes for a spiritless season. And a season where, in all our business of performing the holidays, we forget about ourselves and what should sustain us through the Advent season.

> Stop your racing mind. Take a minute and sit with me. Plant your feet.
>
> Listen to yourself. Have you stopped your lists of things to do or the shopping you hope to complete? What are the tasks on the front burner bearing down on you? Listen.
>
> I have three questions tonight:
>
> - What are you waiting for this season?
> - How are you waiting this season?
> - And with whom are you waiting with this season?
>
> Let's breathe together: inhale, exhale.
>
> As I read the questions, what did you notice? In your body, in your thoughts, and your emotions?
>
> Breathe. Inhale, exhale.
>
> What can we do to have an Advent worthy of our faith? Worthy of our time? Worthy of our hopes? As black women, as a black community, we have to develop practices where we stop, listen, and breathe.[26]

Self-Care

Choose a day within the coming weekend. Choose a two-hour window of time. Find a time and a place without interruption. This plan can be incorporated as a group practice as well.

- Stop: Ritually clear the space. You may burn sage or cedar, candles, remember the ancestors who have spoken into your life, offer a libation to them.
- Stop: Sit in a comfortable position.
- Stop: Sit for thirty minutes of silence. Notice what

thoughts, feelings, and images emerge. Allow them to arise freely and leave freely.

Listen: What have been the places, activities, times, people, spiritual practices, and so on that have renewed me in this season, this past week, past six months, the past year? Allow ten to fifteen minutes to reflect on this question. Then, jot down notes.

Listen: What happens to me when I am overly stressed, overwhelmed, or burdened? What places, activities, times, and people are a part of me feeling this way? Allow ten to fifteen minutes to reflect on this question. Then, jot down notes.

Listen: What happens to my relationships when I am overly stressed, overwhelmed, or burdened in ministry? Allow ten to fifteen minutes to reflect on this question. Then, jot down notes.

Breathe: What kinds of self-care processes will I incorporate into my life on a

- Breathe: weekly basis

  _____

- Breathe: monthly basis

  _____

- Breathe: yearly basis

  _____

This is not a "job." Think realistically and practically. Stop, listen, and breathe is a way of life, not something that becomes drudgery or another job or chore.

Stop, listen, breathe needs to become a practice, and this means tending to yourself, being accountable with yourself and others.

Who in your life (nonfamily member) can you share this plan with to help you care for yourself, your relationships, and your ministry?

Can you commit to reviewing this form?

A week _____ month _____ year _____

Conclusion

In spiritual guidance, we direct our efforts toward loosening the grip of trauma and the nightmarish daily trauma-inducing assaults on black and brown lives. This aim or intention emerges from a womanist relational ethic of the practice of spiritual guidance. As trauma is a social-relational phenomenon, as spiritual guides we are compelled to foster communal spiritual practices undergirded by a relational ethic, and the power and harm that social trauma inflicts require us to enter the crucible of lived experiences. If our spiritual practice of guidance and direction does not link our suffering and healing to the suffering in the world around us, we have only substituted cheap and temporary relief for deep healing and transformation. As spiritual guides, we cannot afford to engage in ineffectual dangerous talk, because spiritual practices, including those of silence, meditation, prayer, and stillness—seemingly harmless—have the efficacy to make a mark on the world and on those in our care. To engage in the work of spiritual direction without knowledge of the "powers and principalities" operative in lives of individuals and communities is to let loose a storm of evil, or to be taken up in it, by participating in its havoc. In other words, we must enter the abyss of trauma prepared to guide those who seek us out to resist and climb out of its clutches. Entering the abyss unprepared and without support, without the experience of having done one's own deep work, without the accompaniment of the ancestor teachers' teachings, and without the infusion of the Spirit's wisdom—that is, to enter alone—is dangerous for the spiritual guide and those in the midst of transformative spiritual processes. Trauma must be understood as social, public, and relational in its focus, its aim, and its practices—as must be our guidance.

Notes

1. Darlene Clark Hines, "Rape and the Inner Lives of Black Women in the Middle West: Preliminary Thoughts on the Culture of Dissemblance," *Signs: The Journal of Women, Culture, and Society* 14 (Summer 1989): 2–20.
2. Quoted in Jacquelyn Dowd Hall, "'The Mind That Burns in Each Body': Women, Rape, and Racial Violence," in *Powers of Desire: The Politics of Sexuality*, edited by Ann Snitow, Christine Stansell, and Sharon Thompson (New York: Monthly Review Press, 1983), 331.

3. See Chanequa Walker Barnes, *Too Heavy a Yoke: Black Women and the Burden of Strength* (Eugene, OR: Cascade Books, 2014); and Shawn Arango Ricks, "Normalized Chaos: Black Feminism, Womanism and (Re)Definitions of Trauma and Healing," *Meridians: Feminisms, Race, Transnationalism* 16, no. 2 (2018): 343–50, for a useful discussion of the "The Black Woman" image and how it diminishes black women's well-being.

4. April Hathcock, "My Trauma Is Not Your Thought Experiment: On Oppressive Empathy," At the Intersection (blog), June 15, 2018, https://aprilhathcock .wordpress.com/2018/06/15/my-trauma-is-not-your-thought-experiment-on -oppressive-empathy/. The referenced tweet can be found at https://twitter .com/ztsamudzi/status/982638118250532864.

5. Cecilia Aldarondo, "Sanctuary after Pulse: We Cannot Let the Orlando Shooter Win," The Daily Beast, last modified July 12, 2017, http://www.thedaily beast.com/sanctuary-after-pulse-we-cannot-let-the-orlando-shooter-win. Emphasis added.

6. Ibid.

7. Ibid. Aldarondo also noted the mental-health implications: "Seventy percent of anti-LGBT murder victims in the U.S. are people of color. LGBT people of color are more likely to live in poverty. The risk of youth suicide is higher. They are more likely to get kicked out of their homes."

8. Lupe Llerenas, "How 'Pulse' Club Shooting Survivor Keinon Carter Is Turning Tragedy to Triumph," Live Civil, June 16, 2017, http://livingcivil.com/how -pulse-club-shooting-survivor-keinon-carter-is-turning-tragedy-to-triumph/.

9. Malidoma Patrice Somé, *Ritual: Power, Healing, and Community. The African Teachings of the Dagara* (New York: Penguin, 1997), 25.

10. Tom Phillips, " 'I'm Waiting for Her to Come Back': Marielle Franco's Fiancée on Life a Month after Rio Councillor's Murder," *The Guardian*, April 13, 2018, https://www.theguardian.com/world/2018/apr/13/marielle-franco-fiancee -rio-brazil-monica-benicio.

11. Dom Phillips, "Protests Held Across Brazil after Rio Councillor Shot Dead," *The Guardian*, March 15, 2018, https://www.theguardian.com/world/2018/mar /15/marielle-franco-shot-dead-targeted-killing-rio. Emphasis added.

12. Marinete da Silva, "My Daughter Was a Rising Politician in Brazil: Six Months after Her Murder, Why Are Her Killers Still Free?" *Time*, September 14, 2018, http://time.com/5395074/mother-brazilian-activist-murdered/.

13. Ibid.

14. "Rio Police Identifies Suspects of Marielle Franco's Assassination," *Folha de São Paulo*, November 23, 2018, translated by Natasha Madov, https://www1 .folha.uol.com.br/internacional/en/brazil/2018/11/rio-police-identifies -suspects-of-marielle-francos-assassination.shtml.

15. Alice Walker, "Womanist," in *In Search of Our Mothers' Gardens: Womanist Prose* (London: Women's Press, 1987), xi.

16. Ibid.

17. Ibid.

18. Ibid.

19. Ibid.

20. Carolyn McCrary, "Interdependence as a Normative Value in Pastoral

Counseling with African Americans," *Journal of the Interdenominational Theological Center* 18, nos. 1–2 (1990–91): 118.

21. Phillis Isabella Sheppard, *Self, Culture, and Others in Womanist Practical Theology* (New York: Palgrave Macmillan, 2011).

22. Howard Thurman, "The Work of Christmas," in *The Mood of Christmas* (Richmond, IN: Friends United Press, 2001).

23. Laura Kelly Fanucci, *Called to Life Participant Guide: A Program of the Collegeville Institute Seminars* (Collegeville, MN: Collegeville Institute, 2016), https:// collegevilleinstitute.org/wp-content/uploads/2016/02/CI_Called_to_Life _Participants_print.pdf.

24. From the *Tennessean*, November 6, 2018.

25. See "The Gathering: A Womanist Church," https://www.thegathering experience.com.

26. Phillis Isabella Sheppard, "Stop, Listen, and Breathe: A Womanist Self-Care Plan," presented at a Womanist Wednesday program for The Gathering: A Womanist Church in Dallas. I am a ministry partner and attend virtually. This was a Zoom/Facebook presentation open to the public.

Part IV: Professional Matters

Spiritual direction or spiritual companioning is an ancient practice. In the Christian context, it belongs to and finds it roots in the list of charisms, gifts of the Spirit, written about in the letters of Saint Paul (see Romans, Corinthians, and Ephesians). Today, spiritual direction and accompaniment has grown into a ministry and for some a full-time profession. In the past twenty-five years, we have seen the growth of the number of contexts for employing spiritual directors on full-time staffs at churches, retreat centers, schools and training centers, holistic rehabilitation centers, and private practice.

This section attempts to highlight this shift in the last twenty-five years, yielding a spectrum of contexts to consider as one discerns how to make a response to a vocational call (a spiritual impulse), a professional career (human education and training), or somewhere in between.

It is important to acknowledge the tragedy that rests in seeking comfort, guidance, and spiritual care from a stressed-out, wounded spiritual caregiver. Negligence of spiritual self-care for the director impacts not only the director, but also those whom they guide and companion. Fittingly, chapter 10 addresses self-care, a look to the care of the earthen vessels that we are in order to optimize the spiritual director's ability to listen and respond well to those whom we accompany even as we listen and learn from our life's suffering, pain, and woundedness.

In chapter 11, the author addresses the process of "becoming" a spiritual director. Though there are, in every age, many and varied ways to live out the vocation of spiritual director, the author takes us on a personal journey, from the training stage to building a "full-time practice as a business." The twelfth and final chapter addresses a most critical component of spiritual direction that begins as a requirement in training and serves as the sustaining element in the professional practice of spiritual direction. Supervision is presented as both the final principle and lasting fundamental. These three final chapters are instructive and push us to consider the many facets of this ministry to be considered, spiritually, humanly, and professionally.

10

A Feast of Losses
Being Present While Experiencing Pain

Maisie Sparks

TRAINING PRINCIPLE | SELF-CARE
*"Good self-care for spiritual directors is essential for both the main-
tenance of our own well-being and for the breadth and depth of holy
listening that we offer to our directees."[1] Self-care is not only a requirement for the ministry of spiritual direction, but is in fact a good
witness to the spiritual director's authenticity and good stewardship[2]
of personal life gifts and resources. These are the gifts that God has
given us to be placed at the service of those we companion. Usually,
a well-rounded self-care program includes time for personal prayer
and reflection, meditation on sacred texts, regular health and well-
ness checks, adequate time for recreation, your own time for personal
spiritual direction, regular supervision, and fun and relaxation with
friends. In addition, adequate rest should be one of the top priorities,
along with learning and setting personal limits (saying "no" when you
need to say no) and taking advantage of ongoing professional-development opportunities. Good self-care optimizes our ability to listen
and respond well to those we accompany even when we have experienced difficult life issues (our own experience of loss, hurt, or abandon-
ment) within the same time frame we are offering spiritual direction.*

*Maisie Sparks challenges us to reflect together on a particular
aspect of self-care: "practices that can help awaken us to God's presence during hard times." What do we discover about God, ourselves,
and others from these unsought and uncharted journeys? The invitation to "awaken to God's great love in the midst of great loss" comes*

to us in four stories of great loss that uncovered God's great love in the midst of pain and suffering. Through the lives of "four friends" we enter reverently, respectfully into aspects of self-care and soul care that not only sustain but push us to embrace personal transformation where we didn't expect to find it.

❁

> . . . the LORD gave, and the LORD hath taken
> away; blessed be the name of the LORD.
>
> Job 1:21 KJV

Experiencing loss is one of the most painful things we must endure on this road called life. Someone we love dies; our job gets outsourced; hearts, kidneys, and other body parts fail us; good desires go unmet; and marriages shatter. These realities don't just happen to those who seek spiritual direction, they also happen to spiritual directors—men and women who know their Enneagram number, the stage of faith they are currently traversing, and the appropriate Ignatian principle to apply when discerning life's next big decision.

Does all this knowledge make a difference when we, spiritual directors, find that we must withstand the vicissitudes of life? How do we care for our own souls then? Are we able to discern God's Presence in the hard times when it's our lives that have been broken open as opposed to the lives of the ones who are seated in front of us? Like many spiritual directors, my go-to question when I'm listening to people share a painful loss in their lives is, "Where is God in this?" I might ask a few clarifying questions that make a deeper dive into the person's soul possible. But I also know that sometimes the moment is too deep for words. Holy silence provides the space to fathom the depths of a soul in hope that rock bottom truly is the firmest place on which to stand.

Parker Palmer, in his book *On the Brink of Everything: Grace, Gravity, and Getting Old*, writes that he finds his spiritual path in the god-awful mess of life.

> The spiritual journey is an endless process of engaging life as it is, stripping away our illusions about

ourselves, our world, and the relationship of the two, moving closer to reality as we do. That process begins with losing the illusion that spirituality will float us above the daily fray.[3]

One of the first times I went to see my spiritual director, I took the risk of telling her about some of the god-awful messiness in my family of origin. She wasn't one who spoke much, but when she did, I listened. After my rather lengthy discourse, all she said was, "Everyone's life is messy." Her words were both disappointing and profound. I had hoped that my desire to become a spiritual director myself would somehow transport me to a spiritual haven where I'd live life above the daily fray. God, I was to discover, was to be found in the very life I had lived and was currently living. I would have to find God's kingdom on earth before I could enjoy it in heaven.

In the poem "The Layers," Stanley Kunitz, a poet laureate of the United States, reflected on the meaning of his life, not merely the chronology of its events. A line in the poem included the phrase "feast of losses," which I co-opted and used as part of the title for this chapter. The moment I read them, the three words struck me as an invitation. They became my writing assignment: to feast on what I've lost. Really? How does one do that? Loss means something's gone; there's nothing there. What's there to feast on? Perhaps the feast is served up as we chew on the bitter morsels of our lives until we can "taste and see that God is good." We feast, when we, like Jacob of Old Testament fame, experience an awakening and realize that surely God was in that place and we had not realized the fullness of that truth.

Are there practices that can help to awaken us to God's presence during hard times? What do we discover about God, ourselves, and others from these unsought and uncharted journeys? How are our lives transformed for the good? I shared these questions with four spiritual directors that I know. Over the years, I had heard bits and pieces of their stories and asked if they would share with me—for publication—a piece of their journey that was particularly hard to swallow. They all agreed. None asked for anonymity, but I conferred it anyway because their stories sometimes involved other people's stories. I was humbled and grateful that they allowed me to mine the practices that helped them find meaning while they experienced pain and loss. I edited their reflections, which they reviewed and approved for publication. I share a story of loss as well. Each reflection has been given a pseudonym in the title to help you, the reader, move from one of the reflections to the next.

A little about the five of us. Our faith traditions fall under the very broad spectrum of Christianity, with exploration and study into other religious traditions. We are human, we have suffered loss, and we are spiritual directors. The Franciscan priest and spiritual writer Richard Rohr once proposed that people are awakened by experiences of great suffering or great love. Modifying that thought, one of the spiritual directors interviewed remarked, "My great suffering revealed the Great Love." May we all find that to be so. And may these stories invite you to savor that same Great Love, feast on the losses that you have experienced, and discover even more deeply that God is a very present help—precisely when we are experiencing god-awful loss.

Nadine: Find Rest

December ended with the loss of my sister. January started with the loss of my brother. My mom, who had been living near my sister, came to live with my husband and me the first week of May. She died in my home the day before Mother's Day. I keep a ten-year journal. My practice is to record one special event from each day in it. There are six months of blank pages.

Before my siblings died, I had planned a retreat with a girlfriend of mine. We go away once a year to dig into the Word and share what God is teaching us and what we are contemplating for our futures. With these back-to-back losses, I wasn't going to go, but my husband and son encouraged me to attend. Over that weekend, I was able to cry, act out, and do whatever I needed to do. That time with my friend was divine, holy time. It helped me to catch my breath for a moment. The ministry of friends is one of the greatest gifts we have.

One day when I was taking a walk with another friend, she gently asked me, "Have you ever thought about taking a break from offering spiritual direction?" Being a number two on the Enneagram, which describes me as a helper, motivated by a need to help others, it never occurred to me to stop caring for others. But the wisdom of her words hit me. Of course, I could take a break.

I took to knitting. I started knitting together squares for a blanket. I would sit in total silence and knit. In that space, I was still and quiet. I just drank in the silence. That's what my soul needed. And that was where my spirit was at rest. One day, there came a point when I rolled up the ball of yarn and stopped. But for a while, my hands needed to be doing something so that my mind could be still.

I read the Psalms, especially Psalm 46:10, "Be still, and know that I am God" (KJV). I would hold that scripture close. Also, the first verse in that same psalm, "God is our refuge and strength." That was one of the very first verses I memorized when I came to know Jesus. It has always been a bedrock for me. God was my refuge. I would sit with that thought.

My mom had a saying, "Yesterday left last night." I've taken that as my banner. I'm learning from the past, but I'm not to dwell on the past. I live in today—this moment. I'm to passionately pursue God as God passionately pursues me. I know that sounds super-spiritual, but it's how I'm to live. When the losses start to dominate my thinking, I return my thoughts to what I'm pursuing.

With each loss, my world turned upside down, then right-side up and then down again, and then again. That magnified for me just how brief life is. It highlighted the wisdom of living in the present. I'm a planner and organizer; I always want to know what is to be done next. I found in these losses a need to hold everything loosely. Life can change on a dime. Yet God is faithful every step of the way. That was the consolation in my desolation.

I was surprised that I didn't feel angry with God. As a spiritual director, I've heard many directees share their anger toward God for various kinds of losses. Somehow, for me this was more a matter of trust. Even though my family, except for my husband and son, was gone, I felt that I was being protected. I kept seeing where God was showing up; I still felt God's love and care. Friends would send me a text with the perfect words at the perfect time. There was one friend in particular who was so supportive. She consistently reached out to me and would go out of her way to do things for me. God used people to love me.

In light of the extraordinary losses of that year, I found that my physical being was in need of restoration. My body had been keeping score and was speaking loudly and clearly for help. Even though I seemed to be holding things together, my physical self had taken a hit. I began to give more focused attention to that part of me. I started to get massages and experienced release and relief from the tensions within me. Our bodies, souls, and spirits cry out to be in alignment. There was a wholistic awareness that was crucial to my journey with grief.

Rest, though, is more than physical. I think there is still a deeper rest that God is inviting me into. During my morning time, I often offer this question to God: "I know you're calling me to rest, but I don't know what that means. Can you give me a clue?" Part of the answer is peace, part is trust, but there is something more. I'm waiting and open to God's response. I know that God gives us rest, so I don't have to work for it. God will give me the rest that I need.

Carla: Listen to Your Heart

A few years ago, I found out that during my heart transplant some years ago, a little piece of my old heart was left in so that the doctors would have something to attach the new heart to. That little piece still had some electrical impulses that we discovered were affecting my new heart. The medical answer was a pacemaker. Another surgical operation. How did I cope? The only way that I had come to know. I started writing to my heart, listening for the God within who can help you get through anything. Anyone can have a conversation with their heart. The challenge is listening and following what you hear.

My letters to my heart began as what I thought was some kind of New Age psychobabble from my therapist to help me get over the fact that I had needed that heart transplant nearly twenty-five years ago. Soon I discovered that this exercise was more than a coping mechanism; it was a path to both healing and enlightenment. An openness to this kind of self-discovery had been with me all my life.

As a child, I enjoyed just sitting outside and listening to the wind, but it was in college that I started to practice a deeper kind of listening. My roommate had taken a class from a Buddhist scholar. That professor and my roommate became friends, and she taught us how to meditate using a Tibetan chant. The practice opened me up to a world I had never known, and I started to read widely about spirituality. After leaving that university, I went on to another one, and new friends asked if I'd read the book *A Course in Miracles*. I hadn't even heard of it, but not long after, walking through a bookstore, the book was right there on the counter waiting to be purchased by me. One of the things it emphasized was spending quiet time with God every day. So, I started practicing silence. I still spend about thirty minutes each morning in silence. I needed and need silence far more than I realize. I was a "Type A" crazy person. Driven. Competitive. I spent most of my career trying to win a Nobel Prize in psychology, even though one isn't awarded in that field. I had insane expectations for myself all my life. Yet, I also had this contemplative stream running deep inside me.

I was a spiritual companion long before I had the language to explain what I was doing. People always came to me with the question, "Do you have a minute, I'd like to talk to you." The question was asked so many times that I had started to consider transitioning from teaching at the university level to being part of a pastoral counseling team at a church. The thought, however, had to be put on hold a couple of times. Once was when I was experiencing a rejection episode. My transplanted heart wasn't getting along with my body. I had welcomed "Grace," the name I had given to my new heart, but I found that she was having trouble talking because hearts typically communicate through feelings. We both had learning to do.

Knowing that I would be in the hospital for some time while the doctors worked to get my heart and body in sync, I had brought several books with me that were on the syllabus of a pastoral-counseling course at a local seminary. In one of them, I read about an area of theology called spiritual direction that I had never heard about before. More curious than weak, I got out of bed, went down the hall, found a public computer, and searched the term "spiritual direction." I was amazed at the number of results. I knew that once I got over my health issue, I was going to pursue this field. And I thought it would be soon. My doctors brought me some good news: they were going to be able to save my heart. It was tempered with some bad news: they would have to kill my kidneys to do it. The medications required to save my heart were that strong. Six months later, I suffered renal failure and was on dialysis for about a year.

Despite that setback, while recuperating, I found a spiritual director. I also called fifteen girlfriends and asked them to meet with me for six consecutive Sunday evenings to discuss our spirituality. I wasn't a spiritual director yet, but I wanted to see if practicing some of the things I was learning would be helpful to other women, and whether I would enjoy doing something like this. I did! It was time for me to get into a spiritual-direction program. But first I needed that kidney transplant. There was no immediate kidney donor available, so I had to postpone entry to the program for a year. It was frustrating.

All my life I had tried to ignore my medical challenge and its disruptions. I was born with a genetic disorder. I was diagnosed with a heart murmur when I was nine months old. Under the care of a pediatric cardiologist throughout childhood, I had my first heart catheterization when I was eleven, another at sixteen. I couldn't play volleyball, which I enjoyed; nor could I engage in too much physical activity. When I was twenty, I had another catheterization and underwent open-heart surgery during my fourth year of graduate school. A genetic time bomb made my heart big and flabby and unable to pump blood throughout my body. Hence the need for the heart transplant; a kidney transplant; a valve replacement on the transplanted heart; a pacemaker. Why was I still alive? What was the point of living?

I was starting to view my life through the lens of spiritual direction. I felt that I was growing spiritually. Being involved in spiritual direction during the time of my kidney transplant helped to quell the craziness that lay within me. It was the vehicle that helped me to understand how all the pieces and distractions of my life fit together.

As I tended to my heart, over time I came to realize that neither my fear of death nor my distress about transplants was the real issue. It was my lack of control. Listening conversations helped me to see what had to be carted off with my old heart—resentment, jealousy, envy—and what I needed to make room for in my new heart—compassion, peace, and joy. When the pains and frustrations became unbearable, I heard Someone . . . a Presence . . . a Voice . . . God saying, "Focus on the quiet spot in your mind where you'll find some earthly peace."

Listening to my body and my heart is how I've come to notice where my joy comes from. Recently, a directee recommended a book for me to read. The recommendation caught my attention because it had to do with writing as a spiritual practice. My takeaway from its pages was that my calling is found in my joy. I pay attention now to where I find joy: a session that makes me a better person just by listening to someone else's soul; a retreat I offer where people experience the transforming power of silence. What I was seeking was lost to me in my ego-driven world. Listening to my heart helped me to acquire the wisdom needed to find the love that is manifested as overflowing peace and joy.

Beth: Keep Going

There's an adage that says, "When you're going through hell, just keep going." I had always attributed those words to Winston Churchill, Britain's prime minister during most of World War II. It certainly would have made sense for him to say these words of perseverance when his country was being blitzed by German bombers for nights on end. A little digging, however, revealed a different possibility. The saying could have been adapted from a 1943 story in the *Christian Science Sentinel*:

> Someone once asked a man how he was. He replied, "I'm going through hell!" Said his friend, "Well, keep on going. That is no place to stop!" If you seem to be going through the deep waters of physical anguish and cannot for the moment seem to gain the understanding which binds the strong man, keep on going—keep on clinging to Truth, and hear again the comforting, strengthening message, "My grace is sufficient for thee." God, divine Love, is eternally sustaining His child, and will "bind the power of pain" as surely as the summer sun will melt the stubborn frost.[4]

That story was written by John Randall Dunn, a Christian Science lecturer and editor, but he attributes the discourse to an unnamed man and his anonymous friend. While I don't know whom to attribute the saying to, I am grateful for its message. The two words—"keep going"—kept me going through a two-year divorce ordeal. Keep going to church. Keep going to see my therapist. Keep going to my spiritual-direction sessions. Keep going on retreats. Keep going daily to God's Word. Keep going to the fitness center. Keep going to graduation parties and fun-filled weddings. Keep going to funerals to comfort friends who mourn. Keep engaging with life.

A few days after being served divorce papers, I went to my church's weekly Bible class. Once there, I questioned whether this was the place to be. I was feeling emotional but wasn't quite sure what emotion I was feeling. The worship band started up, and they were doing a great job. I wasn't feeling it, though. I wanted something very different . . . something soulful. But I didn't believe that could happen here. This is a predominantly white church, and I am black. While the worship music is always technically excellent, I didn't want perfection, I wanted feeling—the raw feeling that gospel/jazz/blues singers bring to a song—the kind of spiritual musical expression I had grown up with in a black Pentecostal church. But these very fine worship singers would have to do. As I was accepting that reality, the worship leader announced that there would be a twist in the program: "We have a guest psalmist tonight. She has come with the guest speaker. We asked her to sing. We really haven't rehearsed. Pray for her. Pray for us as we offer you something."

This unscripted intro was so typical of my black church experience that I couldn't believe my ears. Here, we don't do things impromptu. Everything is planned to the tenth degree. To have someone—a black woman at that—just get up and sing was a major break with my experience of white-church protocol. But that is exactly what happened. A black gospel singer came to the mike and sang a blow-the-roof-off-the-church rendition of Richard Smallwood's "Total Praise." Overcome with emotion, I sat and cried. God had read my mind . . . and my heart.

In the weeks and months of the legal, financial, and emotional unraveling of my family, I kept going. At the beginning of the first year, before I knew what the year would hold, I had made a New Year's resolution to read *The Message*. I finished it in late October. Then I started reading a daily devotional. Reading became a source of direction and strength for me. At a church service, I heard a visiting minister speak about surviving the storms of life and got his book. I read it three times that first summer. His questions challenged me, like this one: "What if God doesn't choose to save us in spite of our failures, losses, and embarrassments, but precisely through them?"

I was asked to review a book about remarkable faith in allegedly unremarkable people. That meant I had to read the book. What an unexpected pleasure that became. Every chapter spoke clearly to keep going. When I finished it, I could honestly write:

> When we're at our wit's end, drained of every ounce of spiritual energy, this book invites us to reach out—just one more time—to our loving Father who delights in saving us . . . when it seems all hope is lost. . . . [T]hat is the moment unfailing faith connects us to a never-failing God.

Those were not just words for a book review; they also were words that strengthened my resolve to keep doing what I know to do.

I attended one-day retreats, weekend retreats, and a four-day retreat called the Great Banquet. I had gone on one of these Great Banquet–type retreats years ago, but I didn't realize that it was the same because the first one was called a Discipleship Walk. I was told that a person is supposed to attend only one of these retreats over the course of their lives. I received a special dispensation of grace. I needed both of them—especially the second time around. The great cloud of witnesses there was an encouragement for me to keep going.

I kept going to see my spiritual director and my therapist. What's interesting about seeing both a therapist and a spiritual director is that they say the same thing; they just use different language. And, it's not so much that they say anything. It's more that I had somewhere to be honest and not have to burden friends and family—too much—with the raw stuff of my soul, especially when it was still in very raw stages. They made themselves still enough for me to be able to drink from their quiet streams when my head was reeling from a painful loss and an uncertain future.

I kept volunteering to serve two-year olds while their moms attended a gathering for mothers of preschool children. For three hours every other week, I didn't have to think about myself because I was too busy keeping the runners in the room, picking up Cheerios before someone stepped on them, and reading stories with lots of energy and excitement.

I kept journaling. I did a lot of structured journaling based on a workbook about managing one's life during divorce. I made lists of things, like all the things I was losing in addition to my marriage. I listed my feelings and made a list of people to pray for besides myself. I also freestyled when I felt up to it. One particular journal entry changed the direction I was going in. I was spending a weekend with a friend who lives so far off the beaten path that my GPS couldn't find her home. On a quiet Saturday morning, I was reading my devotional and just sitting with the thoughts that emerged. A few times in my life, I've felt that I was being divinely invited to write something down. This was one of those moments. This is what I heard; this is what I wrote:

> You believe Wikipedia more than you believe My Word. You'll read something online, and you'll quote it, include it in a paper, and even change what you do because of what you've read. But when you read My Word, you don't believe it, you don't change your life because of it, you're afraid to share it with others in ways that will change their beliefs about Me. You know it. You write about it. But you don't believe it. You don't take Me at My Word. What do I have to say to express My love for you? This is what I keep telling you in My Word:
>
> - I will never leave you nor forsake you.
> - I will take care of you.
> - I love you.
>
> If you believe Me, then damn it act like it.

I stopped fighting the reality that I was being divorced. I stopped praying about restoration and started picturing transformation. My divorce was finalized in the next two months. I have kept going, moving toward a greater experience of these truths: I am God's beloved child, his grace is sufficient for me, and he will bind the power of pain as surely as the summer sun will melt the stubborn frost.

Allen: Give and Receive Grace

This is a gift. I remember saying those words as I walked out of my workplace for the final time. My twenty-year run with one organization had come to a halt. Plans for retirement would have to be pushed further into the future. This is a gift. The depth of that truth would be revealed over and over again during the next twenty-six months of unemployment.

As a spiritual director, I'm familiar with the abundant use of the word *gift* in our circles, and I have an understanding that all of life is "gift." Yet for me, the word *gift*, at that time, was more intellectual than experiential. The "gift" of this between-jobs season was to experience loss as a gift—to notice where my intellect became empowered by my heart, to take advantage of every opportunity to participate in the graces that were to save me.

This was such an amazing time, so very rich and full and yet tough. I had sleepless nights, calls for second interviews that provided false hope, and reality checks at the breakfast table dealing with the terror of not having a job and nowhere to go. I tried teaching at a community college, but they pulled me out of the classroom after six sessions, which was three sessions longer than I should have been there. It was devastating to have doors closed and opportunities lost. In my late fifties, people half my age had the cutting-edge computer skills. Over the last few years, I had focused on retiring, not finding a new job.

I had been a spiritual director for about ten years, and I also served as a facilitator for a spiritual-direction program. During that time, I'd seen students as well as my directees deconstruct and then reconstruct right before me. I had to do the same. Descent, I had recently heard a speaker say, is where we go and are uncomfortable, but it's there that we are transformed. It's not the ascending path, it's the descending one. That's where Christ went. It's there that we are stripped down and rebuilt into something closer to what God intended us to be.

I was asked to serve as a spiritual director to the staff at a homeless shelter. Because they see and handle so much misfortune on a daily basis, the program's director thought they could use the strengthening that spiritual direction can provide. There was no salary, but it was a gift to listen to those who wanted a space to cast their cares on God.

My son came back from an overseas military deployment and was in terrible emotional shape. He was having a hard time transitioning back into civilian life. It was a gift to have the time to be available to him. I went on trips with my mom, and we were able to enjoy some very memorable times. I got to be part of a morning men's group and had the opportunity to listen to men and see men cry in the presence of other men. We are connected to each other, not by our religious beliefs, but by our suffering. Everyone hurts. If we lean into our suffering, we learn compassion. Kindness is a very valuable thing.

Transformation happened as I led with my vulnerabilities and as I interacted with people without judgment. I was experiencing more deeply how the spiritual disciplines were really to change my life. I felt that I was becoming a more authentic person. I think that came from owning the good and bad that came to me. I brought the reality of failed job searches to my peer-supervision group. I received loving silence and space to cast my cares upon God. I found that I paused more when people had a question and that I didn't have to have a good counterpoint to everything that was said. Instead of doubling down with my own ideas, I wanted to know more about other people's positions. I thanked them for sharing their thoughts. I realized that certainty is a dangerous place to live.

This gift of time made long retreats possible, and they were especially welcomed when the job-search process drained me. Do you know that you can go insane looking for a job eight hours a day? Being able to walk a prairie wilderness, watch the clouds drift overhead, or see stars unhindered by city lights, was a balm. It didn't hurt that the retreat center gave me an "unemployment" discount. I ended up serving on its board for four years. I also served on the board of a spiritual-direction program. I made some great friends who were supportive and helped to ease my fears about being out of work.

Near the end of my second year of unemployment, I was offered a position that would start early the following January. My wife and I were plenty thankful during the Thanksgiving and Christmas holidays. It was the end of being in a dark room; the lights had finally been turned on. The two-year crucible of job loss left me with more compassion for others. I had a completely different attitude reentering the work force. I was more mindful; I spoke with less anger and offered constructive criticism as well as praise. Every day, I took a route to the new job that led me along a river walk. As I watched the construction that was going on in the city around me, I also reflected on all the little things that had been reconstructed in my life over the past two years. Now that I'm retired, I miss the gift of those morning and evening walks. I have found a new kind of freedom. It's a freedom that comes from knowing that my relationship with God is not transactional. It's not that God does a good thing, and I say, "thank you." Gratitude now comes just from having the relationship, nothing else.

Johnetta: Welcome the Unwanted

Grieving the loss of a desire that I had held since a little girl was hard. And I was not only grieving my loss, I also had taken on the grief of my husband and our daughter. We all wanted another child. Our daughter had been conceived through in vitro fertilization (IVF), a series of very complex procedures to fertilize a human egg. Now, in our second attempt to conceive a child, we were having one failed attempt after another. I experienced a very weird relationship with hope. On some days, I would be afraid to hope. And on other days, I'd cling to it as if it were all that I had. When I allowed my heart to hope, it felt like a very vulnerable place of waiting. I was waiting for my body to do what is needed for conception, but also waiting for God—the only One who can bring life—to do what only he can do. I welcomed my counselor's input and had often benefited from her physiological insights, but, in this season, I felt like I needed more than that. I needed God's perspective. I needed God's reassuring presence in the complexity of the emotional roller coaster I was on. I needed him to strengthen my heart to be able to hold hope while surrendering the outcome to him.

My journey with infertility had to do with trusting God and taking risks. It was about integrating medical expertise with God's desires for me. I needed someone to hold a space for me where I could express my fears, my doubts, my disappointment, and the unwanted questions I had about God's will and his work—and at times what seemed like lack of work—in my life. I needed a person who would have no other agenda than to help me stay connected with God in the midst of my turmoil. That's why I went to see a spiritual director. After the third cycle of IVF attempts, I realized how much the procedures were taking a toll on my body. I laid my desire to rest. I accepted that our family was complete. In that hard place of loss, with the companionship of my spiritual director, I was able to remain connected to God in my grief. What I experienced awakened in me a desire to become a spiritual director and offer this kind of space to others.

I've been a spiritual director for about four years now, and the lessons from that loss have been invaluable in holding space for directees as they grieved. What I did not anticipate is how many more seasons of deep grief were still ahead in my journey. Recently, my church family experienced a tsunami of devastating losses and disillusionment. I found myself in a fresh inner space of grieving again, but this time it was while I was to serve as a companion to others as they navigated similar grief. The importance of tending to my own heart became vital. Being in a very tender place of grief myself, I needed to prepare my own heart so that when I would meet with these directees, my emotions wouldn't hijack the listening I needed to do for them. I started to practice welcoming prayer. Welcoming prayer is not new. It's been around for a few centuries. It's a practice that helps to process unwanted and uncomfortable emotions. It allowed me to actually experience these emotions rather than just trying to toss them aside or suppress them. Instead, I welcomed them, I noticed them, I engaged them, I felt them, and I released them to God.

This prayer had three movements for me. First, I'd sink into what I was experiencing in my body. I'd focus on my emotions and feel its sensations. Was I holding the emotion in my face, my hands, my gut? Where was the energy of that emotion? I tried not to judge myself nor the emotion, nor try to control it. I just wanted to be present to it. Then I welcomed what I was experiencing. Instead of treating the emotion as an enemy, I welcomed it as a guest. It's not natural to welcome something that's unwanted, but such a posture removed the power of the unwanted emotion to control me. I'd say, "I welcome you sadness or anger or fear," or whatever the emotion was. And, I'd also welcome God's indwelling presence. I'd say, "God, you are in control; I am not. I trust you with this emotion." Finally, I'd release the emotion and any assumptions that accompanied it. Along with my unwanted emotion were often desires for security, approval, and control. All of them had to be given up to God.

There are many ways to release pain and losses to God. The welcoming-prayer practice has served me well in processing my loss. There's no cookie-cutter formula for cultivating our spirituality. All of us are on our own paths. I am grateful for my spiritual director, inner-circle friends, and peer group who listen with me. As we take care of our own souls, we are equipped to care for the souls of others.

Notes

1. Hannah Rowan, "Spiritual Directors and Self-Care," a research project for the Spiritual Directors' Training Programme of Spiritual Growth Ministries, 2012.
2. Parker J. Palmer, *Let Your Life Speak: Listening for the Voice of Vocation* (San Francisco: Jossey-Bass, 2000), 30-31.
3. Parker J. Palmer, *On the Brink of Everything: Grace, Gravity, and Getting Old* (Oakland, CA: Berrett-Koehler, 2018), 54.
4. "If You're Going Through Hell, Keep Going," December 10, 2018, https://quoteinvestigator.com/2014/09/14/keep-going/.

11

Getting My Side Hustle On
Developing a Spiritual-Direction Practice

Consuella L. Brown

TRAINING PRINCIPLE | VOCATION

"Vocation" is a word derived from the Latin "vocationem," literally "a calling, a being called." In common use today, vocation *is variously defined as "a calling or mission in life, finding the purpose of one's life, or an occupation or job one is particularly suited for." However, from its earliest use, the word carries the sense of an inner summons or divine impulse to respond to a particular course or direction in one's life. This is especially true of what we identify as ministry, ordination, or religious life. In a sense, vocation has to do with the meaning and purpose of one's entire life, as Kate Harris states in "The Heart of Vocation."*[1] *She states, "It is a word that seeks to account for everything: our entire life lived in response to God's call." As spiritual directors, it is a word we wrestle with both professionally and personally. What we do is caught up in listening for and to the divine impulse within the human life's journey. Spiritual direction is a work of helping the directee expose the sacred story of their everyday lives.*

According to Parker Palmer, "Vocation is not a goal to achieve but a gift to be received. It means accepting the treasure of your authentic self and the gifts already within you but that need unveiling, perhaps. It comes from a voice within calling you to become the person you were born to be, to fulfill the original selfhood given at birth by God." These words, taken from Palmer's Let Your Life Speak: Listening for the Voice of Vocation, *help us to put into perspective what we might understand or mean when we say that spiritual direction is a vocation, a calling. Spiritual direction in this sense is not just one other "helping relationship" in the cast of thousands of careers,[2] as in every other Christian ministry, and similarly in other faith traditions. Spiritual direction is rooted in God's call/the divine call first and then in human response.*

A spiritual director is a person who has been granted a sacred trust by God and by those we companion, to tend the holy and the sacred as revealed, discovered, or uncovered in the earthen vessels of human lives. Professionally, this requires training and ongoing supervision, ongoing honing of skills, and personal commitment to spiritual growth. By virtue of training and ongoing growth, the spiritual director's context for exercising this ministry may change from a training or teaching setting, to a church or retreat and workshop/conference setting, to a collaborative holistic rehabilitation setting, to private practice. We could go on and on. In each setting there are practical skills and professional ethics that will require refining and personal discernment of the rightness of fit for the spiritual director, colleagues, and those seeking accompaniment. In this sense, the spiritual director lives a life of discernment of being and yet becoming. Consuella Brown gives us a window into how this process unfolds for a neophyte spiritual director "becoming" in the context of building a spiritual-direction practice. This will be instructive for those who might need a reality check of the many moving parts of what it takes to start and run a business. For others, the chapter provides ready insights for searching out the many other contexts for discerning and responding to a call to be a spiritual director.

Fear and Becoming

The occasion of writing a chapter in a book on spiritual direction broadly and the topic of practice basics more specifically summons forth two interesting emotions: fear and audaciousness. As a nonprofit consultant, adjunct faculty, and executive coach, the only things I seem to write a lot of these days are comments on written assignments and grant proposals. The possibility of not having much to say that is meaningful to the rest of the world absolutely consumes my mind and heart. I fear not only the possibility of crafting text that has no relevance whatsoever, but I am also afraid that you, the reader, will color me an absolute impostor in the spiritual-director world. This is the place in the direction session where you would stop and say, say more about the fear please.

I remember plunking down my annual membership fee to Spiritual Directors International (SDI) and being both delighted and terrified to have my name and contact information included in the "Seek and Find Guide." Then the reality set in: what if someone actually called me? This nagging fear of being found and found out leads to my first big observation in this chapter on developing a spiritual-direction practice. My mom had always told me, from as far back as I could remember, that I had to work twice as hard to be just as good because the ground I walked on was never going to be level—even in the faith business. I imagine every newly trained spiritual director experiences some trepidation upon first beginning their practice, but I have to own the fact that, as a woman of color, I am often reticent to call myself an expert because of internalized racism and the world's tendency to render everyone but a person of color as proficient.

From a spiritual perspective, I believe we are all just light and energy. I almost always begin ventures, such as starting a spiritual-direction practice, in prayer and meditation. I also tap into a practice called visioning created by Dr. Michael Beckwith of Agape Church of Religious Science and Center of Truth. As explained in the center's manual, visioning is defined as "becoming a space of deep listening available to hear Spirit's highest vision/idea for any individual/project/organization."[3] Spirit's vision, I have found, is almost always bigger than anything that I can imagine by or for myself. Even in this beautiful space of being and hearing and receiving guidance about what I should embrace and release in order to realize Spirit's vision, my mortal ego and self almost always gets in the way.

Hence, the first lesson in building a spiritual practice is to believe that you are standing in divine light and are equipped and qualified to be a practicing spiritual director. There are lots of people who know much more about the history, techniques, and practice of spiritual direction than I do. Additionally, it took many years for me to embrace the fact that I was trained to be a spiritual director—I have the certificate on my office wall to prove it. The truth, the real added value for me, is that no one else leads a spiritual direction session quite as I do (not bragging, just noticing).

For me, it is important to explore how comfortable you are in exploring the roots of the discomfort and owning your own expertise and knowledge. Perhaps you would prefer to "practice" a little more before adding your name to the SDI "Seek and Find Guide"—or, in my case, taking your name out of the directory. Perhaps you did hang out your shingle and no one came. It sometimes happens and may have to do less with how you are perceived and more to do with marketing and creating a pipeline. Finally, perhaps you had a couple of sessions and the person stopped coming. What I have seen in my own practice and learned from speaking with other spiritual directors in peer supervision, is that this in fact might happen. My final observations about finding comfort in owning your particular gifts and skills is to be mindful of your own discernment process, spiritual health, and limitations.

Given the physical and emotional toll that unconscious bias and explicit racism have on individuals from the nondominant group, finding spiritual refuge can be literally life-saving. What I have personally found is that non-church-affiliated people of color have never heard about spiritual direction but seem completely open to it when I explain what it is and why it can add value to someone's life. If they are in Chicago, I can usually make a referral; unfortunately, the "Seek and Find Guide" does not provide information about a director's ethnicity, so I am sometimes reticent to refer them to this directory. I personally believe that it will be incumbent upon spiritual directors of color to bring more people of color and communities of color to the practice of spiritual direction.

When I completed my spiritual-director training, the first thing I did was to buy as many books as I could on the subject of spiritual direction. The fear of not being prepared enough and not being good enough ran deep. I wanted to be absolutely prepared in the event that someone phoned and wanted to interview me as a potential spiritual director. In those books, I found some really great ideas and suggestions that I still use in my practice today. One such gem was a chapter entitled "Becoming a Spiritual Director" in *The Practice of Spiritual Direction* by William A. Barry and William J. Connelly, which offers an interesting insight about the qualities that a spiritual director must possess, based on a study of the Roman Catholic priesthood. In addition to awareness of the Christian community, deep faith, a contemplative attitude, and trust, the authors have other suggestions about effective spiritual directors:

> The kind of men and women most likely to engender trust in others are those described in the same study as developed persons. They are not perfect, but they are relatively mature. They show signs of having engaged in life and with people. They are optimistic, but not naïve, good-humored, but not glad-handers. They have suffered, but have not been overcome by suffering. They have loved and been loved and know the struggle of trying to be a friend to another. They have friends for whom they care deeply. They have experienced failure and sinfulness—their own and others—but seem at ease with themselves in a way that indicates an experience of being saved and freed by a power greater than the power of failure and sin. They are relatively unafraid of life with all its light and darkness, all its mystery.[4]

As I read these descriptors, I found comfort and more courage to be my authentic self and to trust my skills. I did in fact possess the qualities to make a great spiritual director.

In April 2017, Anil Singh-Molares, executive director of SDI, penned a guest column on the organization's blog about the nature of a spiritual director. In addition to being inclusive and welcoming, in this piece Singh-Molares offers up additional observations about what makes a good spiritual director:

> Second, at their roots, spiritual directors are individuals committed to helping others seek and find connection with a higher power, however that power might be defined. This characteristic always

holds true, regardless of the particular spiritual configuration or orientation of the directors and seekers.

At a recent retreat that I had with the SDI Coordinating Council, we identified some other key factors to look for in authentic spiritual directors, namely that they be

- rooted in personal experience and display "depth."
- willing to follow universal ethical guidelines, summarized as "Do no harm."
- accountable in a community setting.
- committed to contemplative, compassionate listening, with respect for the agency of directees.
- supervised by other spiritual directors and accountable through that direct supervision.
- committed to ongoing education and learning.

I offer both "Becoming a Spiritual Director" and "What Makes a Good Spiritual Director?" for those of you who may still be in doubt about whether you are good enough to be in the spiritual-direction business. The first step in the development of your practice is to believe that you are already prepared enough to begin to fully live into this version of yourself. If all fails, play the song by India Arie titled "I Am Light" and be reminded that all is in divine order.

Audaciousness

Once I moved beyond the fear of not being ready or good enough to be a spiritual director, the next step in the unfolding of my particular spiritual-direction practice was remembering why I chose to become a spiritual director in the first place. In 2006, when I submitted my application to the Institute for Spiritual Leadership, I knew only two things. The first was that I was being called to do something bigger than myself. Second, I was looking for a structured opportunity to explore my own spirituality. In essence, I found myself needing to engage in what I have come to call "spiritual sense making."

My mother, a devout Christian, raised me in the Baptist church until I was twelve years old. While I could sing both the A/B music selections with great fluidity and recite certain scripture in the Bible, the concept of a heaven and hell or accepting Jesus Christ as my personal savior just never quite stuck for me. Perhaps it was because I subconsciously knew that I would travel the world and encounter many non-Christians throughout my life. In my teens, my father, a devout Muslim, tried to get me to adopt the teachings of the Nation of Islam, the Koran, and Elijah Mohammed, but that did not stick either. It was no surprise to anyone but my parents that, in my early twenties, I found peace in chanting. For a decade, I was a practicing Nichiren Buddhist until I realized that my soul ached for the Divine Spirit. I now like to call myself a humanist with Buddhist tendencies.

When I walked into the spiritual-director training for the first time, I was convinced that I was going to be escorted out immediately if the staff and my peers realized that I was not a Christian. Fortunately for me, I was taught how to be a spiritual director by mostly former Catholic nuns and priests that were more concerned about my ability to listen, process, reflect, and discern than what my religious beliefs were. I feel like I am still a bit of an anomaly in the spiritual-director world. I, like one in four Americans, call myself spiritual but not religious.[5]

Becoming a Full-Fledged Spiritual Director

After meditating a lot and going back to my oracle cards, I finally decided that I was going to try out this being a "real" spiritual-director thing. My goal, primarily, was to see if others would benefit from everything that I had learned over the past two years. I also wondered, in my heart, if maybe I could assist someone else to find their own path back to their true north. In addition to getting listed in the SDI directory, my first act of becoming a full-fledged spiritual director was to order business cards. I do not know why I thought that by putting a name and title on a card that it would make it so, but I did. The irony of course was that I chose super unappealing cards. This in part was because the cards were free and in part because I could remain partially noncommittal to this new identity.

The next step that I took in becoming a full-fledged spiritual director was to figure out if I needed to purchase liability insurance. In truth, I was not sure why I thought I needed insurance, except for the fact that we live in a litigious nation and there seems to be insurance for just about everything. I called around to those who had a spiritual-direction practice up and running and to those who were newly minted. There was no consistent answer, so I made the personal decision not to purchase liability insurance at that time.

If you decide to pursue liability insurance, there is a possibility that you could get a discounted student or SDI member rate from the American Professional Agency, Inc., by following instructions outlined on the SDI website. The organization also offers the following guidance about liability insurance that you should also take under advisement before you make your final decision:

> Spiritual Directors International does not underwrite insurance nor does SDI have an opinion as to whether liability insurance is needed or appropriate for individual members. As an educational not-for-profit that supports the global ministry and service of spiritual direction, SDI provides information about liability insurance for those who request it. Each spiritual director needs to determine with the guidance of his or her own legal and insurance advisors whether liability insurance is advisable.[6]

As with everything written about thus far in this chapter, taking a moment to pray, meditate, ponder, or intuit what your personal needs are related to liability insurance is very much encouraged.

In the Beginning: Covenant Making/Ethical Guide

When I am wearing my executive-coach hat, I develop a written contract with my clients that spells out what executive coaching is, services that will be rendered, length of each session, cost for each session, and how payments will be made. I end the contract with specific information about confidentiality. I read the entire contract to the client, stopping after each section to ensure that the client with whom I am working is able to ask questions and fully digest what our working relationship will entail. I also make sure to have two copies on hand. We sign both copies, and I hand one copy of the executed contract back to the client for their records. Engaging in a contractual agreement or covenant with a spiritual directee is an advisable best practice. Contacting an administrator or faculty at the institution where you trained to be a spiritual director may be the easiest route for finding a contract template. A quick search on the internet will also yield several examples of templates that are easily customizable to suit your unique practice needs.

My spiritual-direction practice has never been teeming with directees. At most I am working with one or two individuals in a year. I do not record my sessions with a directee, nor do I prepare case notes for peer supervision. As a result, I do not yet use an engagement letter in my spiritual-direction practice. I typically start the director and directee relationship with a call to get a feel for what the person is looking for in a director and in direction. I also disclose at that time that I am not a Christian. In our initial meeting, I use the first thirty minutes to walk the directee through what I call the basics. It includes the following elements: my working definition of what spiritual direction is and is not (two to three minutes); my training and style (five minutes); my own faith trajectory (two to three minutes); what I get out of spiritual direction (two minutes); ethics and confidentiality (five to seven minutes); and payment (one to two minutes). I then use the remaining ten minutes getting appropriate contact information and a better understanding of what has drawn the directee to direction.

I keep a direction journal, in which I capture contact information shared in the first session and any other notes that I think will be relevant in future sessions. I bring it to every session but never open it unless it is necessary to do so. After the initial intake process, I proceed with an abbreviated session and a reminder that spiritual-direction sessions will be for sixty minutes on a monthly basis, unless other arrangements are needed. I also make it a point to always leave room at the end of each session to check in about whether there is interest or need for another session.

In many ways this introductory process encapsulates the key components of the covenant outlined in SDI's "Guidelines for

Ethical Conduct," which I highly recommend sharing with all new directees. Copies of this document can be purchased directly from the SDI website.

Do No Harm

Striving to do no harm should be the prevailing goal of any spiritual-direction practice. While it is easy to say the words "do no harm," the reality of what this looks like on a practical level in spiritual direction is harder to define. In truth, I am not sure that I know the answer to this question. Of course, the most obvious place to explore how not to cause harm in a spiritual-direction practice would be to revisit SDI's "Guidelines for Ethical Conduct (Revised Edition)." In this document, SDI outlines specific action steps and recommendations in the areas of personal spirituality, formation, supervision, personal responsibilities, and limitations. Maria Tattu Bowen in her *Presence* article "Do No Harm: A Case for Professional Boundaries and Supervision in Spiritual Direction" argues:

> Amidst spiritual direction's regenerative chaos, creating and maintaining clear professional boundaries and receiving regular supervision allow us to negotiate the spiritual direction relationship safely. Underestimating our need for these proactive measures is tantamount to underestimating the powerful processes at work in spiritual direction.[7]

I remember on long trips back and forth to monthly spiritual-director training sessions, one of my classmates and I would spend many hours mapping out sustainable business models for a vibrant spiritual-direction practice. She was planning to retire shortly after completing the program and had hoped to earn some supplemental income. I, on the other hand, was in my early forties and was not yet planning to exit the labor market.

We knew spiritual direction could be healing and transformative, and we wanted to offer this gift to African Americans living on the south and west side of Chicago. The business model we ultimately settled upon was weekly group spiritual direction that was to be offered to parishioners at a demographically changing Lutheran church. The plan was that we would offer group spiritual direction for free one day a week at the church, and, in exchange, we would make ourselves available for paid individual spiritual-direction sessions for anyone who was interested. We had hoped that by using donated space and by taking advantage of free marketing—word of mouth—we could keep our fees and overhead low.

We spent hours prepping for our meeting with the pastor from the Lutheran church. We had a one-page business plan and a rather lengthy PowerPoint presentation that laid out, in great detail, the services we were planning to bring to members of the congregation and the surrounding community. As three of us colleagues practiced our presentation, we hit a major snag that prohibited us from moving forward as a group. Two of us felt that we needed to embed conversations around race and racial equity into the group-direction process. The remaining partner argued that spiritual direction was not about guiding but about listening. It was this bump in the road that not only derailed our work together, but ultimately shaped how I come to the phrase "do no harm," particularly as it relates to people of color and other marginalized individuals.

Before there was a Spiritual Directors of Color Network, the one resource that I leaned on heavily, and still do, to make sense of what it meant to be a spiritual director who also happened to be African American, female, lesbian, non-Christian and totally committed to social justice was a book, *Still Listening: New Horizons in Spiritual Direction,* edited by Norvene Vest. It was published in 2000; yet, its relevance to the world we inhabit in 2019 cannot be denied. In this collection of essays, Juan Reed wrote a chapter, "Can I Get a Witness? Spiritual Direction with the Marginalized," in which he argues that the lives of marginalized people in direction tend to be either foreign or romanticized by those in the dominant culture.[8] He further cautions spiritual directors from bearing false witness and notes, "Too often marginalized people, some who have experienced trauma, but all who have experienced not being listened to and not being seen, have this experience repeated in the present by spiritual directors who are blind and deaf to their experience."[9] Reed's observations ring as true today as they did almost twenty years ago. Despite some people's perceptions that we were headed to a postracial America after the election and reelection of the forty-fourth president, the reality is that we are more fractured as country than we have ever been in this twenty-first century.

Sadly, when looking at Federal Bureau of Investigation hate-crime data over a five-year period, it would appear that the number of reported hate crimes is increasing. Even in this multicultural United States, in 2017 the hate-crime offenses tended to be motivated by race, ethnicity, and ancestry (59.5 percent), religious bias (20.7 percent), and sexual-orientation bias (16 percent). In an era of nationalism, violence, widespread economic disparities, opioid addiction, and a resurgent and growing #MeToo movement, the need for spiritual refuge is increasingly more important as well as the need to see and hear each other more intently and intentionally. As I think about a spiritual-direction practice where no harm is done, I think about a practice that includes accessing professional-development opportunities that help me better understand how trauma, microaggressions, oppression, and privilege manifest spiritually in marginalized communities currently. I am also trying to listen differently as a director by increasing my vocabulary and understanding of evolving concepts related to race, gender, sexuality, and social justice. For instance, when engaging new clients, I am asking them about their preferred gender pronouns, how they identify themselves, and how they express and experience their own spirituality (not religion or faith).

Harm reduction, for me, is not only about ethical and professional considerations and boundaries. It is also about seeing and acknowledging the trauma and harm that directees experience on a daily and personal basis and allowing this to manifest in their sessions. This I refer to as "Thelma and Louise" moments. It is in those instances when you are holding your directee's metaphorical hand and agreeing to walk right up to the ledge, jump, and trust in the Divine Spirit that all will be well in the end.

Spiritual Direction versus Counseling

When a potential client calls me, more often than not I hear, "If I participate in spiritual direction, I find I do not have to go to therapy." While this might be the case, I am always the first to remind the caller that spiritual directors are not therapists and spiritual direction is not therapy. The experience of being accompanied might be therapeutic for some, but I was always taught that my responsibility to the directee is to be clear about what spiritual direction is and is not. When I was being trained to be a spiritual director, I was told on several occasions that if the line between counseling and spiritual direction was crossed, I should always stop and suggest that the directed might be better served by working directly with a licensed social worker, therapist, or psychiatrist. One of the most effective resources I have found on the internet regarding the difference between spiritual direction and counseling is a list of definitions from Covenant Church in West Lafayette, Indiana. In a very simple way they note that "the counselor can help untangle and make better sense of our emotions. The spiritual director can help us focus on where and how God has worked or may be working in our lives right now."[10]

Sometimes I have been concerned about whether I have crossed that line between direction and therapy. I find it impossible to accompany someone on their spiritual journey or path and not be moved in some way or another. This is essentially why I do this work. Yet, there have been those "matching pictures" moments when the directee's trauma has triggered my own, and I was somehow moving away from spiritual-direction mode. I find myself using completely different guiding questions than those I have been taught to use. I also find that instead of repeating back to the directee what they are telling me, I am using words like "you must have felt," or "It must have made you react like . . ." In some cases, I have completely begun to check out of my body. This is one of those do-no-harm moments known as transference. I try to get myself back into the session and the session back on track as quickly as possible.

The first step in this process, for me anyway, is to invite the directee to pause for a moment, take in a few breaths, wiggle their toes, and begin to feel their feet in their socks or shoes. I do this with them, and, when it feels appropriate, I ask their permission to continue. When the session is over, I make it a point to write my own reflection question(s) about that which was triggered in the journal I bring to all of my spiritual-direction sessions. Self-care is really important to me as a spiritual director, so, depending on what has surfaced during a particularly hard session, I will either take my reflection question to peer supervision, my spiritual director, or my therapist, if I am working with one at the time.

The bigger red flags are easier to spot when thinking about counseling versus spiritual direction; however, in those moments when I need to affirm that a recommendation to see a therapist would likely be in the best interest of the directee, I often rely on the American Psychological Association Post-traumatic Stress Disorder Guidelines. They say simply, "Two general guidelines can be helpful when considering whether you or someone you love could benefit from therapy. First, is the problem distressing? And second, is it interfering with some aspect of life?"[11] Additionally, if a directee is threatening to harm him or herself it might be necessary to encourage them to seek medical attention immediately.

I do not usually make a referral to a therapist. Instead, I suggest that the directee check with their health-insurance providers to find out if there is a list of preferred or in-network therapists. If this is not plausible, I suggest they reach out to one of three agencies for possible referrals: the National Alliance on Mental Illness, Mental Health America, or the Depression and Bipolar Support Alliance. It is important in developing a spiritual-direction practice to establish a plan for the less common but significant challenges that organically arise.

Mandatory Reporting

Whenever I ride the local commuter trains from my house to downtown Chicago, inevitably during the trip an announcement will come over the speaker system: "If you see something, say something." Should you do this if you are a spiritual director? The short answer is yes, if it is possible and appropriate to do so. There is always a possibility during one of your sessions that your directee might report instances of domestic violence, suicidal ideation, child abuse and neglect, or sexual assault. If you have a signed covenant or agreement, your next steps may already be outlined and have been discussed with your directee. If this not the case, a conversation about mandatory reporting and confidentiality should take place early on in the director/directee relationship. To know what is legal and correct to tell your directee about the role and responsibilities of a spiritual director, SDI provides the following advice:

> SDI does not provide specific information about mandatory reporting and confidentiality regulations because laws vary from country to country and state to state. The best course of action is to consult a local attorney if you are concerned about the legal ramifications around mandatory reporting and confidentiality.

It is prudent to assume, and wise to inform spiritual directees, that all information shared in a spiritual-direction relationship is subject to subpoena in the United States.

In addition to consulting an attorney, you might also be able to access the laws regarding mandatory reporting and confidentiality requirements in your state by going to the U.S. Department of Health and Human Services' Child Welfare Information Gateway webpage. The information is dated but is a good starting point. For instance, I was able to confirm that, in Illinois, spiritual directors do not appear on the list of mandatory reporters. On the other hand, members of the clergy in Illinois are legally responsible to report child abuse and neglect; however, they are allowed to maintain a certain level of confidentiality if ever called to testify in court. In my handy journal, I also keep a few helpful hotline numbers to offer or use in the event that a directee may need them.

Matters of Compensation

My own spiritual-direction practice has not been as robust as I had initially hoped. The major challenge for me has been space. I live with two cats and have found more people allergic to cats than not. I either travel to the directee's home or office, speak with them over the phone, or meet them at a quiet coffee shop. The benefit to this particular approach is that I have limited overhead and don't have to feel pressured to keep my office neat and tidy, but it also means that I am traveling, and sometimes the directee is distracted. The other challenge in my practice is that, for most of the past decade, I have not asked for money for this work; thus, I have been compensated in the form of baked goods, knitted scarves, fruit, and homemade CDs. People are often curious about why spiritual direction has not become my primary side hustle, to which I often reply that spiritual transformation is priceless.

As hard as it feels at times for me to ask people to pay, in whatever form that takes, for something that helps them grow spiritually, it is absolutely necessary. As a spiritual director, I paid for training and am providing my time and an invaluable service. For these reasons alone, it is reasonable to ask for compensation. In addition, the exchange of money for services allows for the relationship between the director and the directee to remain professional and for a mechanism to hold the other accountable. Regarding the amount you should charge directees, here are three ways this range might be determined: (1) ask your peers what they charge and what the going rate is for these services in your city; (2) look on the websites of local centers that offer spiritual direction as a service to see what they are charging for each session; or (3) calculate your annual expenses to run your spiritual-direction practice and amortize over a twelve-month period across your client base.

Final Thoughts

In summary, I offer the following thoughts for those of you who are still thinking about building either a full-time spiritual-direction practice or a side hustle. There are many moving pieces when starting and managing a business. Seeking guidance from the Divine Spirit before embarking on this important journey is always recommended. Trust the guidance you receive and breathe. This has always been for me about ministry and living into God's vision for my life. I cannot imagine trying to be a spiritual director and leading with my ego. As with most moments of healing, I often grow stronger in my own spiritual practice when I am walking with another. Once I accepted the call and honored that I was good enough and had the necessary tools, I was able to move forward with my spiritual-direction practice.

Remember that you are good enough, and that the time is always right. Do no harm and look to your inner moral compass to know exactly how that looks for you. It helps to follow the ethical guidelines put forth by Spiritual Directors International. Even if you are listed in the SDI directory, it is likely that there is going to be additional need to advertise. Business cards are a first step in the marketing process. Having a website and social-media presence are helpful as well. Adding a line about being a spiritual director in your e-mail signature, biography, and LinkedIn profile has always been a conversation starter for me. Finally, being a guest speaker or panelist on the topic also provides an opportunity to market your services.

There are several ways to get your side hustle on. You could work with clients in your home or theirs or in a neutral donated or paid space. You could also choose to work with clients over the phone or virtually via Skype or Zoom. Alternatively, you could offer services through a retreat center or seminary. Additionally, there is the possibility of offering group supervision or bundling spiritual direction with other healing modalities.

Notes

1. Kate Harris, "The Heart of Vocation," The Washington Institute for Faith, Vocation, and Culture, April 23, 2013, http://www.washingtoninst.org/4262 /the-heart-of-vocation/.
2. David L. Fleming, ed., *The Christian Ministry of Spiritual Direction* (St. Louis: Review for Religious, 1988), 5.
3. *Visioning: Agape Church of Religious Science and Center of Truth Manual*, 7.
4. William A. Barry and William J. Connelly, "Becoming a Spiritual Director," in *The Practice of Spiritual Direction* (San Francisco: Harper & Row, 1982), 124–25.
5. The United States Department of Justice, Federal Bureau of Investigation, "2017 Hate Crimes Statistics," FBI: UCR, November 30, 2018, https://ucr.fbi .gov/hate-crime/2017/resource-pages/hate-crime-summary.
6. https://www.sdiworld.org/membership/benefits-of-membership. Accessed August 12, 2019.
7. Maria Tattu Bowen, "Do No Harm: A Case for Professional Boundaries and Supervision in Spiritual Direction," *Presence: An International Journal of Spiritual Direction* 23, no. 3 (2017): 29–37.
8. Juan Reed, "Can I Get A Witness? Spiritual Direction with the Marginalized," in *Still Listening: New Horizons in Spiritual Direction*, edited by Norvene Vest (Harrisburg, PA: Morehouse, 2000), 94.
9. Ibid., 100.
10. Covenant Church, "Other Resources," accessed August 12, 2019, https://

www.covenantepc.org/resources/. See the back of the book for a comparison chart among the caring professions.

11. American Psychological Association, Clinical Practice Guidelines for the Treatment of Post-traumatic Stress Disorder, "How Do I Know if I Need Therapy?" https://www.apa.org/ptsd-guideline/patients-and-families/seeking-therapy.pdf, accessed October 1, 2019.

12

Final Principle and Lasting Fundamental
Supervision as Pathway to Wholeness

Daeseop Daniel Yi

> With a focus on the present, supervision for spiritual
> directors provides a flexible and hospitable space for
> the director to discern, through education, consultation
> and inner reflection, together with their supervisor(s),
> areas for growth and areas for celebration in themselves
> and in their practice of spiritual direction.
>
> Ineda P. Adesanya

TRAINING PRINCIPLE | SUPERVISION
*No text on spiritual direction, or any other caring profession, is complete
without acknowledging the place of supervision within the discipline.
There are a couple of comprehensive books dedicated to the subject of supervision in the practice of spiritual direction that may be consulted for a
laser focus on the subject.*[1] Kaleidoscope *has pulled together the breadth
of necessary principles, skills, and qualities that must be sustained for
an effective and fruitful practice of spiritual direction. This chapter
focuses on the final principle: the fundamental role and importance of
supervision in fostering wholeness in the spiritual director. It gives clear
examples of how supervision contributes to the process of becoming and
remaining whole in an art that requires one to give all of oneself in the
care of another. The author sets the tone of supervision in such a way
that one can begin to envision its lasting and sustaining efficacy.*

❀

Why Supervision?

Supervision helps transform our head knowledge into specific living knowledge. Thus, it is the most important part of any training program. Furthermore, it is the key to the continuing growth of spiritual directors after their initial training. I will explain my rationale for this claim and illustrate with specific cases.

The most important component of a training program leading to a formal spiritual-direction credential is supervision, because supervision helps us transform what we have only learned and known cognitively, and that may lack clarity, into specific living knowledge. In the process of completing the intense classes and practices in the program, we begin working with people in spiritual direction. We need to take our written summaries and transcripts of particular cases to our supervisor to explore and reflect upon those times when we felt overwhelmed, stuck, or distracted, or when we felt particular joy, peace, or excitement. The process of supervision leads us to grow in our awareness of ourselves, in our ability to be present with our directees, and our capacity to offer them the space to encounter themselves, others, God, and the world. Maureen Conroy emphasizes the importance of supervision, writing that "the overall goal of supervision is to help spiritual directors to grow in self-awareness and interior freedom in order to stay with directees' experiences and to be attentive to God during direction sessions."[2] Supervision is the key to unlocking the treasures of experiential learning that are necessary for spiritual directors.

Growth in self-awareness and interior freedom is needed not only during the training period but also after completing the program, when we are actively engaging as spiritual directors. I have observed, as a spiritual director and supervisor, that after finishing their training, many people drop the process of becoming a spiritual director and do not go further. I believe that this cessation in growth in the practice of spiritual direction flows from ending supervision. Directors in training grow in their awareness of themselves while in their programs, but once the program and its accompanying supervision concludes, they naturally stop growing, because the impetus to keep growing has ended. Therefore, I conclude that ongoing monthly or bi-monthly supervision is at the heart of the lifelong process of becoming a spiritual director and continuing to grow in this role.

Supervision has played a decisive role in my becoming a spiritual leader, being a supervisor, and giving spiritual direction and supervision. It is now a key element in my transformation to becoming whole. When I first came to the United States from Korea and was trained in a spiritual-direction program,[3] it was difficult for me to understand English well, and it was also challenging to receive supervision in English. I almost wanted to give up. I had a strong desire to quit, but my supervisor supported me and encouraged me to stay in the program. That is why I was able to finish the training. After that, I worked in a Korean immigrant church and offered spiritual direction, but it seemed that I did not do much different from what I had done before in my work in other churches. However, I had actually changed a great deal in ways that helped me be more present and contemplative with my congregants.

Then, I took part in a peer-supervision group with experienced spiritual directors, and this experience gave me a new opening to spiritual direction. I became better able to deepen and to see myself through sharing and dealing with my own and others' issues in the group. My specific questions, at that time, had to do with (a) how to charge money for a session; (b) why I could not finish sessions within one hour; (c) my motivation to give the directee a solution instead of being present; (d) understanding the fundamental differences between counseling and spiritual direction; (e) uncovering what was blocking my heart from being present; (f) knowing why I was hurt when a directee stopped coming; and more. These at first seemed to be practical issues that could be easily fixed, but I realized that there was a "hidden wholeness" beneath the surface that I needed to address. In particular, facing my fears and even embracing them helped me to be my authentic self and to bring my whole self to what I was doing in my ministry of spiritual direction.

After becoming a group facilitator in the Diploma in the Art of Spiritual Direction program at San Francisco Theological Seminary, I began deepening my understanding of the essential qualities and skills of a spiritual director in classes and group practices. I have had valuable experiences of genuine growth, understanding myself better, and dealing with my fear of rejection, my altruism, and my various forms of ignorance. Each year, this experience has sharpened my contemplative listening heart as well as various listening skills. When I was trained as a supervisor,[4] I became acquainted with the essence of in-depth spiritual direction. As a supervisor, I was able to experience the process of growth through serving my supervisees, discovering even more profound meanings of spiritual direction and new aspects of myself.

Now, I am receiving supervision from my supervisor from time to time and from my regular peer group, and together these two forms of supervision promote my ongoing growth in self-awareness. Because of these experiences, I have become a more fully undivided human being and a more effective spiritual director in dealing with the various issues that have arisen in the sessions. My point is not that all spiritual directors should be like me, but rather that, by benefiting from various supervision experiences, I have become not perfect—but more whole. That is, I have become more free, authentic, and real by acknowledging my whole self in practicing spiritual direction and even in living my life. I would have otherwise become stuck and would have practiced spiritual direction by mixing with it many other good things, eventually giving it up by relying on skills only and by not involving my whole being.

What Is Supervision?

According to the *Cambridge English Dictionary*, supervision is "the act of watching a person or activity and making certain that everything is done correctly, safely, etc." This definition indicates that supervision happens when a more experienced person provides others with safe and correct knowledge or skills to resolve issues and dilemmas they confront in their workplaces. However, in spiritual direction, as James Neafsey notes, the prefix "super" means not only "over and above" but also "beyond" or to an especially high degree. His suggestion of an alternate meaning of supervision involves "seeing beyond ordinary appearance or seeing with a high degree of vision."[5] Thus, the primary focus of supervision of spiritual directors is not correcting the performance or providing knowledge or skills but helping directors discover their unique image of God and affirming their gifts of grace and their strengths—that is "seeing beyond." At the same time, supervision helps directors to integrate their weaknesses and the shadows of their gifts.[6]

Through the process of supervision, spiritual directors may increase their self-knowledge and enable the practice of spiritual direction in a deeper way. As Conroy observes, cultivating directors' self-awareness and interior freedom so they can be with their directees' experiences is a unique component of the supervision of spiritual directors. Elizabeth Liebert writes that "supervision, then, though it may (and frequently does) touch on matters of skill, or the directors' own hidden blocks, does so primarily in service to this primary end, recognizing and responding to the Holy Mystery we Christians call God."[7] Here, she mentions not only directors' self-awareness and skills but also the process of recognizing and responding to the Holy Mystery in supervision. Thus, she emphasizes that supervision contains a contemplative aspect and that it involves discerning the interior movements of directors.

Similarly, my own definition of supervision is that the supervisor is present with the spiritual directors in order that they may become more aware of themselves (their true identity, strengths, and weaknesses) and be more fully present with directees (by creating a safe and sacred space in which directees can fully explore the movements of God's presence and follow them more freely) through contemplative listening, asking questions, and responding to the stories expressed in the session and in their life. In other words, supervision is about the why and the what—spiritual directors grow in self-awareness and freedom, becoming more whole and better able to be themselves and to be more fully present with their directees. Subsequently, the director can create a more sacred and safer space in which directees can be themselves and be aware of God's presence and follow the movements of God. Supervision is also about the how—about the supervisor being fully present with the director, listening contemplatively, asking open, honest questions, and using various responding skills as the director's experiences arise throughout the session.

As an example, I want to share my experiences of self-awareness and freedom in a supervision session with a supervisor that allowed me to be more fully present with my directee. This is a self-supervision piece that I wrote and later brought to my supervisor.[8]

> *What I did:* My directee has a niece who has schizophrenia. She maintains a distance from her niece because she thinks that her niece doesn't meet God and glorify God. She does not know how to treat her niece. I suggested that she change her position from that of an aunt to a mother. Once she imagined her niece was her daughter, her perspective changed so that she could be with her niece and love her as she is.
>
> *Why I did it:* I wanted her to experience God's love for her niece, so I encouraged her to think of herself in the role of being her mother.
>
> *What happened:* She realized that she had misunderstood the gospel by believing that a disabled person can't glorify God unless the person is healed. Because of this session, she was able to understand her disabled niece in a new way from the perspective of God's heart.[9]
>
> *What I learned about myself:* I wanted to guide her into a deeper way of understanding and loving a disabled person as God loves that person, but I noticed that I had a limitation in doing so. I wanted to know more deeply, for example, about a theology for disabled people so that I would be able to deal with the topic more confidently.
>
> *What I learned about spiritual direction:* I had this thought in my mind: "Oh, I don't know about this topic. How am I going to help her? If I knew about some passages related to loving disabled people in the Bible or was familiar with a theology for them, I would be able to guide her in a better way." However, regardless of my thoughts or fear of my lack

of knowledge, the presence of the Spirit was fully there and so I was able to help my directee to be awakened and to see her niece with God's heart and in a different, more holistic way. In spite of my not having specific knowledge, the Spirit led her to go deeper to see the real truth.

I brought this self-supervisory material to my supervisor. During the supervision session, thanks to my supervisor's help, I had in my mind an image of myself mining for gold in my work as a spiritual director. As a miner, I was not able to see the whole gold mine, but the headlamp on my helmet shined a light where I was working. I was able to do my work there without any trouble. What I realized then was that the spiritual director has boundaries, just as the miner sees only a limited area. But, as a spiritual director, I don't have to know and see everything to do my work. All I need to know is the territory that is in front of me here and now. I felt relief and freedom when I discovered this truth about being a spiritual director; despite my limited knowledge and experience, I can be with my directees.

I noticed that I was afraid that if I didn't know something fully, I might be criticized or rejected by others. This fear came to me when I stayed in the ego level of myself. Through supervision, I became grounded in my true self and aware of why I had this fear and what the fear was about. I gained the freedom to be courageous with the directee, even though I didn't know everything about her situation, because I knew that the Spirit was with me. I realized further that, as a spiritual director, having a beginner's mind, which is an "I don't know everything" mind not an "I should know almost everything" mind, is important for me in this spiritual journey, since it gives me the space to trust the Holy Spirit and let the Holy Spirit lead both my directees and me. Without needing to know everything, I can be fully present with directees. This is an example of how I have gained greater self-awareness and freedom through supervision and how this allows me to be fully present with directees no matter what issues they bring to me.

Integration

What Is the Process of Supervision?

What is the specific process of supervision? How does a spiritual director become more aware of him or herself and experience freedom more deeply during the supervision session? What does a supervisor do to help the spiritual director see more deeply his or her interior space and experiences as a director? Although all sessions are unique, I would like to use part of an actual contemplative reflection form[10] to describe how self-awareness and freedom unfold in an actual supervision session. The supervisee, Mary,[11] has been training in the Diploma in the Art of Spiritual Direction program for two years. She has brought her reflections and a focus question to her supervision session based on the contemplative reflection form. The sentences in italics are the instructions on the form:

> 1. *Notice your interior movements and settle on an experience to take to supervision. As you reflect, do any emotions, body reactions, intuitions, etc., arise in you? Describe what you notice about yourself*: I [Mary] feel a little bit disappointed in my presence with my directee and my presence with the Spirit today. I believe I "got caught up in my own material" at several points during our visit, which inhibited my ability to "dig deeper" with the directee. I noticed a narrowing feeling instead of an expansive feeling during several points of spiritual direction, an indication that my own material, not the Spirit, was leading the way. This happened in particular when the directee was speaking about systemic injustice, vocation, and money. I believe that my disappointment in the quality of my presence may have to do with my own inner disposition at that time. I met with this directee the day before I was leaving for a trip to see my family, and, more generally, my husband and I have been thinking through moving/changing jobs. I also missed several of my

yoga classes this week, which I know has negative implications for my openheartedness. So, my poor presence with my directee and with the Spirit is an indicator of the way in which my Inner Teacher is inviting me to attend to Her. I have a desire for more silence and more spaciousness in my own heart and life, especially as there are many possible changes on the horizon.

2. Articulate a focus drawn from what you described above. What one aspect of your experience as a spiritual director would you like to explore in supervision? I would like to explore the opportunities for spaciousness in my own heart and in the time with my directee. Where could the conversation have opened up and where can I practice spaciousness?

Before the supervision session, Mary had prayerfully reflected after her direction session. For example, she identified her specific feelings, noticed areas of unfreedom that prevented her from being present with her directee's experiences, and savored God's presence during the session. She had felt disappointed during the direction session. She noticed a disconnected feeling instead of feeling involved in the directee's experience. She was able to name what lay underneath those dissonant feelings: a sense of scarcity, of not getting enough. She experienced for a moment a lack of God's presence when the directee mentioned that her soon-to-be spouse had a large salary. Mary is good at being aware of herself and articulating her inner movements clearly. From this reflection, she created a focus to explore during the supervision session.

At the beginning of the supervision session, I clarified with Mary her real focus. Even though she wanted to explore opportunities for spaciousness, I noticed that she was hooked by a feeling she experienced when her directee mentioned that her fiancé was earning lots of money. I asked her to choose between two options, to explore either opportunities for spaciousness or her "hooked" feelings, as we went forward. She chose her "hooked" feelings, her disappointment and even anger. First, I let her explore her feelings and the reasons underlying those feelings. After listening to her describe her feelings, I then asked her about her emotional reactions as the directee shared her experience: "What went on inside of you when your directee mentioned money? Could you elaborate on the anger you felt?" She was able to talk about how she was not jealous of the money but of the spaciousness of time money allows. She was also able to feel empowered to act on the desire she has to create more spaciousness in her own life.

I invited her to focus on her own financial situation to get to the root of the matter. This is an excerpt from part of the supervision session dialogue.

> SUPERVISOR: *Can you say more about your finances?*
>
> MARY: *I have student loans that stress me out, but I am not special among millennials in that regard. And we have bills to pay—a mortgage, a car payment—but we try to do things as reasonably as possible; we live somewhere affordable, and we don't buy fancy things. We don't want things. Right now, our health insurance is connected to my job, but we can change that next year. In reality, my spouse and I are fine financially. All things considered, we are very well off in relation to the rest of the world, as we do not live paycheck to paycheck. It's just that I am working so much now. My job does not feel like it's sustaining my spirit.*
>
> SUPERVISOR: *There are two types of freedom I am hearing: financial freedom and freedom of time.*
>
> MARY: *Yes, that's right. What I am jealous of is freedom of time. I have been feeling that way for a long time; since starting this job. I do not like coming home and feeling too tired to do anything because I worked all day. I just want a small house with a garden, to be closer to my family, and to live in warmer weather. I want meaningful work with flexible hours. I want the opportunity to have a child in a somewhat sane way. I want enough space in my life to do the things I love*

like art and making dinner for my friends and being involved in community projects.

SUPERVISOR: *This sounds like the abundant life! Is there a time when you lived abundantly but did not have much money?*

MARY: *After college and in grad school, I had about five dollars in my bank account and worried about paying bills all the time and hoped my car wouldn't break down, but there was definitely a sense of abundance. Hanging out with friends, making food together, asking the big questions, healing, figuring out who I was. I had a lot of part-time jobs and loved divinity school and being a student.*

SUPERVISOR: *So abundance must come from . . .*

MARY: *Oh, the Spirit. It's a gift from the Cosmos.*

SUPERVISOR: *Having experienced the Spirit as the real source of abundant life, how does that affect your feelings of not being enough or of wanting to get more in this capitalist society?*

MARY: *There is a lightness and a sense of gratitude. I feel proud of the steps my spouse and I are mindfully taking for me to have more restful and creative time in my schedule. . . . I am feeling affirmation about taking these steps. I am thinking about all the experience I have from being with dying people—I see people die with a scarcity mentality—I want to connect with the spirit of gratitude and full-heartedness that I see in people I admire.*

Before closing the supervision session, I helped Mary to reflect on any clear insight or deeper understanding she had gained related to her focus question. I asked her, "Where or how did you grow in greater interior freedom and self-awareness through this supervision session?"

Mary told me, "You and I talked about unhooking our hearts

from the lie that capitalism tells us—that we don't have enough. I was able to see that the jealousy of the free time my directee would have because her partner makes a lot of money was me leaning into the lie that I don't have enough, instead of leaning into the generosity of the Spirit." She continued by saying that

> the supervision session helped me define what the abundant life is—one deeply grounded in the qualities of the Holy Spirit, a gift from the Cosmos, and a disposition of the Spirit. It also helped me to connect with the ways I have lived a life full of abundance in the past, the ways in which I am currently living a life of abundance, and the desire that I have to cultivate an abundant life in the future. I felt a grateful heart for the ways in which I have been able to connect with the qualities of the Spirit—relationship, liberation, intimacy, joy—in my own life.

Finally, I encouraged her to leave with a specific realization that will enable her to be present with her directee in a more contemplative way by asking, "How do you hope to stay with the same issues when the directee brings them up again?"

She answered, "Instead of being hooked, I would be thankful to be reminded of my own abundant life full of relationships, meaningful work, and everyday beauty. So, my response could be to say, 'That's good for you,' and then keep moving on."

The supervision process in the above session can be summarized as follows, based on Conroy's outline of the process. Supervision assists the spiritual director to (1) notice their initial reaction (for example, "I feel a little bit disappointed"); (2) explore deeper feelings and attitudes that lie beneath a reaction ("I got caught up in my own material"; "It is the mirror of the *scarcity*, a lie that capitalism tells us"); (3) uncover and embrace experiential reasons underneath the feelings ("Her partner makes a lot of money was me leaning into the lie that I don't have enough, instead of leaning into the generosity of the Spirit"); (4) grow in self-awareness and freedom ("I felt a grateful heart for the ways in which I have been able to connect with the qualities of the Spirit—relationship, liberation, intimacy, joy—in my own life"); (5) recognize differences in oneself that result from sharing difficult emotions ("I am grateful for the abundance of today—laughing with nurses in the break room, eating homemade soup with my spouse, sitting on the back stoop with my cat, catching up with an old friend on the phone"); and (6) apply insights and learning gained from supervision to specific direction sessions ("I would be thankful to be reminded of my own abundant life full of relationships, meaningful work, and everyday beauty").[12]

In this process, when Mary was able to connect with the Spirit and her true self, she could clearly identify the gifts in her life and see others and the world in a new way. She was better able to be present with the directee and enjoy the fullness of her own life.

Becoming a Whole Person

In the case described above, through supervision the supervisee experienced self-awareness and freedom when she became aware of her belief and the reasons beneath her feelings. She then connected with the Spirit. I noticed that Mary experienced a wholeness that came when she gained an integrated awareness that was connected to herself (intrapersonal with the Spirit), others (interpersonal with her spouse and family and her coworkers), systems and structures (systematic and structural capitalism), and nature (her experience with environment when she went out into nature).[13] As Parker Palmer notes, "Wholeness does not mean perfection: it means embracing brokenness as an integral part of life."[14] The journey toward wholeness involves the integration of thought and affection and the nonthematic and Mystery dimensions that empower spiritual directors to order every arena of their lives (encounters with self, others, systems and structures, nature) as authentic persons. Supervision of spiritual directors consistently helps spiritual directors remember who they are in God and assists them in living out this truthful, authentic identity as whole persons in their spiritual-direction ministry and in each arena of their life. Therefore, supervision is not just about developing the skills of spiritual directors but about their being whole persons in God who are becoming aware of how their various thoughts, feelings, and nonthematic dimensions affect their spiritual-direction sessions and their connections with other people, society, and nature.

Becoming a whole person is a process, but it is not simple or linear. We may step on and off the path of becoming a whole person many times, and we may even sometimes feel we are going back to the beginning. Thus, becoming more self-aware and authentic requires community and support. Having an individual supervisor is ideal, but, if not, we need accountability, perhaps with a peer group of directors, as well as connection with the Spirit. A supportive community can provide encouragement to help us take authentic action and live the truths we discover as spiritual directors. A peer-supervision group that has only inexperienced spiritual directors should invite an experienced spiritual director or supervisor to guide them. The benefits of peer-group supervision include being encouraged and nourished by the various gifts and valuable feedback that individual supervision cannot offer.[15] Fellowship and feeling oneness with others in the joys and struggles of spiritual direction give us the strength to keep moving on even though we may be discouraged while practicing spiritual direction.

Also, a good way to connect with the Spirit on an ongoing basis in order to be self-aware is to keep a self-supervision journal. Journaling after spiritual-direction sessions can help us recognize specific feelings, feel more deeply and notice and savor God's presence, and gain understanding or insights into our areas of unfreedom.[16] Out of the journaling, we can bring some of these unfree areas to the group and explore them. Within a supportive community with other spiritual directors, we can keep reintegrating the pieces we have lost, become unaware of, or failed to act on; this is part of the process of becoming whole as a spiritual director.

I have explored why supervision is essential, what supervision is, and how supervision is offered and have discussed an actual supervision case. Ultimately, I have contended that the spiritual director needs a supportive community, a peer-supervision group, because supervision is one of the critical ways for the director to keep growing and deepening, both as a whole person and as a director. The reason that supervision is necessary for spiritual directors is that it is crucial in transforming abstract head knowledge into specific living knowledge that can be put to use for the directees' benefit. At the same time, supervision enables spiritual directors to increase in self-awareness and freedom, which allows them to create a safer space and to be more fully present with their directees. The specific process of supervision involves the spiritual director noticing initial reactions after a spiritual session, exploring and uncovering deeper feelings, and embracing the reasons underneath those feelings with a supervisor. After growing in self-awareness and freedom, the spiritual director can apply those insights to subsequent direction sessions. In this way, supervision is an essential process of becoming aware of the inner movements that influence spiritual-direction sessions. In the end, I hope that all spiritual directors who are in an official training program will continue to receive supervision after the program ends for the purpose of becoming a whole person as a spiritual director. This is an ongoing, never-ending process of moving toward wholeness.

Notes

1. Mary Rose Bumpus and Rebecca Bradburn Langer, eds., *Supervision of Spiritual Directors: Engaging in Holy Mystery* (Harrisburg, PA: Morehouse, 2005); and Maureen Conroy, *Looking into the Well: Supervision of Spiritual Directors* (Chicago: Loyola University Press, 1995).
2. Conroy, *Looking Into the Well*, 9.
3. I was trained at the Mercy Center Burlingame in 2005.
4. I was trained in the Together in the Mystery program in 2014.
5. James Neafsey, "Seeing Beyond: A Contemplative Approach to the Supervision Relationship," in Bumpus and Langer, *Supervision of Spiritual Directors*, 18.
6. Ibid., 25.
7. Elizabeth Liebert, "Supervision as Widening the Horizons," in Bumpus and Langer, *Supervision of Spiritual Directors*, 129.
8. This self-supervision write-up is based on one of the models of supervision that I learned from Lucy Abbott Tucker in her 2018 supervision workshop.
9. I want to introduce Susan Phillips's compassionate perspective to those who are interested in doing spiritual direction with disabled persons. She says that "to see the whole person, the visible frailties as well as the vital spirit, is our commission and blessing." Susan S. Phillips, "Regarding the Spiritual Direction of Disabled Persons," in Bumpus and Langer, *Supervision of Spiritual Directors*, 178.
10. The supervision process should invite the director into their own contemplative reflection process. Such a process can be deepened by supervision-reporting forms that point to these aspects, such as the contemplative-reflection and dialogue forms used at San Francisco Theological Seminary. This form was developed by instructors in the Diploma in the Art of Spiritual Direction

program at SFTS. The complete contemplative-reflection form and dialogue form can be found in Bumpus and Langer, *Supervision of Spiritual Directors*, 181–91.

11. I have changed the directee's name to preserve confidentiality.

12. Conroy, *Looking Into the Well*, 41. I usually keep in mind the seven phases of supervision in Conroy's book and roughly follow them. If you want to learn more about the phases, including specific questions by the supervisor appropriate for each phase, see pages 121–31 of Conroy's book.

13. Liebert, "Supervision as Widening the Horizons," 131. The four arenas come from the Experience Circle (see the "Resources" section at the back of this volume).

14. Parker J. Palmer, *A Hidden Wholeness: The Journey Toward an Undivided Life. Welcoming the Soul and Weaving Community in a Wounded World* (San Francisco: Jossey-Bass, 2008), 5.

15. I suggest the following two different peer-supervision models for those who want to explore what such a group might look like: Rose Mary Dougherty, "One Form of Group Supervision for Spiritual Directors," *Journal of Supervision and Training in Ministry* 18 (1997): 115–28; and Susan S. Jorgensen, "Peer Supervision: One Model," *Presence: The Journal of Spiritual Directors International* 2, no. 1 (January, 1996): 23–37.

16. If you want to know more about this type of journaling, see David McCormack, "The Transformative Power of Journaling: Reflective Practice as Self-Supervision," in *The Soul of Supervision: Integrating Practice and Theory*, edited by Margaret Benefiel and Geraldine Holton (Harrisburg, PA: Morehouse, 2010), 25–37.

Afterword

Cultural sensitivity and understanding is and has always been of critical importance in working with and relating to individuals and groups at a spiritual level. Unfortunately, this has not always been recognized and affirmed. Yet, as the Christian churches and other religious entities more and more become locations where persons of color congregate, it is imperative that those engaged in spiritual direction become familiar and comfortable with these cultures including their history, traditions, experiences (especially of marginalization and oppression), race, ethnicity, gender/sexuality, and even class. Knowledge of and familiarity with these aspects are of critical importance, both for the directee who is seeking to become closer to God and to understand their calling and to the director who has to be aware of and comfortable with not only their own cultural context but also aware of that of the directee if they are to be able to speak, pray, guide, comfort, share, and walk with them.

This collection of essays, ably compiled and edited by Ineda Adesanya, presents an ideal introduction into the ways in which spiritual directors can learn of and work with persons of color who are exploring their own spirituality and calling. The authors are all persons of color who are experienced in the field of spiritual direction and members of the Spiritual Directors of Color Network. In their work with persons of color, they have realized the need for guidance in how one relates to and works with a directee from a race or ethnicity other than their own. They have also personally experienced the difficulties that emerge when a director attempts to work with a directee in ways that do not take account the directee's cultural context.

Thus, the authors seek to reveal, from their own experience, how to learn to walk with persons unlike themselves. Chapters include the history of spiritual direction, the importance of discernment, the presence of spirit, creating authentic sacred space, listening, and trauma and healing among others. It provides excellent background especially for those unfamiliar with other traditions and cultures. An important aspect of most of the articles is the personal stories of the writers. As Naisa Wong states in chapter eight: "I believe it is in our stories where we are able to find connections and restoration and even a genuine experience of the Divine."

Diana L. Hayes, JD, PhD, STD

Resources

One challenge that resonates across the hundreds of spiritual-direction training programs is the lack of diversity in resources. The following organizational, literary, and practical resources have been included here because of their unique benefits and twenty-first-century offerings for, by, or about people and spiritual directors of color. The contents in these resources, therefore, are more far-reaching in terms of culture, tradition, and orientation.

Organizational Resources

Spiritual Directors of Color Network, Ltd. The Spiritual Directors of Color (SDC) Network, Ltd., is a nonprofit incorporated in Maryland and headquartered just outside of Washington, DC. We can be contacted through https://sdcnetwork.org/sdc-network/, or at https://www.facebook.com/groups/SDCNetwork/. As children of God and members of the human family, we seek to use our collective gifts as spiritual directors of color to bring love and healing to all seekers. We are a community that fully embraces the lived experiences of people of color but is welcoming to all people regardless of race. We strive to be a group that celebrates the richness of diverse cultures, faith traditions, and spiritual practices. We look for opportunities to serve, support, educate, train, nurture, reclaim, and unite those who are seeking God through contemplative practices such as the ministry and practice of spiritual direction. Our primary mission is to:

1. create a space for Divine Presence and Mystery;

2. reclaim as people of color our ancient traditions of contemplative practice that includes the practice and ministry of spiritual direction;
3. support spiritual directors in their work with diverse populations;
4. lift up and transmit the unique traditions of our various heritages;
5. build a bridge within the broader international spiritual-direction community; and
6. offer spiritual support in a culturally affirming context.

Mystic Soul Project. The Mystic Soul Project is a 501(c)3 which creates spaces that center the voices, teaching, practices, and wisdom of People of Color at the intersections of mysticism, activism, and healing. This mission is inclusive and centering of the margins of the margins—which includes centering queer and trans voices of color as well as being intentional about being inclusive across the spectrum of spiritualities. Programming from MSP includes Mystic Soul Conference (annually), the Mystic Soul Podcast (www.mysticsoulpodcast.com), along with other educational, spiritual practice, and community-building webinar series). To learn more about the Mystic Soul Project, visit www.mysticsoulproject.com, @mysticsoulproj on Twitter, and the Mystic Soul Project Facebook page. You can contact MSP by e-mail at info@mysticsoulproject.com.

The Chaplaincy Institute. In the provision of spiritual care, it is imperative that the care provider do no harm. Doing no harm becomes more likely when the spiritual-care provider has a basic knowledge of interreligious and interfaith traditions and orientations. Honoring the sacred connection of all, the Chaplaincy Institute (ChI) was envisioned by clergy from a variety of faith traditions who saw a need for deeper interfaith dialogue, and for building bridges of understanding across religious divides to bring peace and understanding to today's world. An interfaith seminary and community, ChI employs a spiritual-care approach to healing and transformation in the service of human, social, and environmental restorative justice. In addition to its core interfaith chaplaincy curriculum, ChI offers a solid formation program in interfaith spiritual direction. This program is designed for those who feel called to a private practice in personal, one-on-one, or group spiritual direction, and who anticipate working with clients from a variety of faith traditions. The program is also suited to other helping professionals who want to add a spiritual-guidance perspective to their current work (such as psychotherapists, health practitioners, ministers, and chaplains). Diversity scholarships may be available for spiritual-direction students of color. For more information, visit https://chaplaincyinstitute.org/ or follow https://www.facebook.com/ChaplaincyInst/.

Sojourners. Sojourners are Christians who follow Jesus, but who also sojourn with others in different faith traditions and all those who are on a spiritual journey. They are evangelicals, Catholics, Pentecostals, and Protestants; progressives and conservatives; blacks, whites, Latinos, and Asians; women and men; young and old. They reach into traditional churches but also out to those who can't fit into them. Together they seek to discover the intersection of faith, politics, and culture. They invite you to join, to connect, and to act. "We are a committed group of Christians who work together to live a gospel life that integrates spiritual renewal and social justice. . . . We seek to inspire hope and build a movement to transform individuals, communities, the church and the world." https://sojo.net/.

Literary Resources

Bryant-Johnson, Sherry, Rosalie Norman-McNaney, and Therese Taylor-Stinson, eds. *Embodied Spirits: Stories of Spiritual Directors of Color.* New York: Morehouse Publishing, 2014.

Holmes, Barbara A. *Joy Unspeakable: Contemplative Practices of the Black Church.* 2nd edition. Minneapolis: Fortress Press, 2017.

Hopkins, Dwight N., ed. *Looking Back, Moving Forward: Wisdom from the Sankofa Institute for African American Pastoral Leadership.* Valley Forge, PA: Judson Press, 2018.

Jones, Kirk Byron. *Addicted to Hurry: Spiritual Strategies for Slowing Down.* Valley Forge, PA: Judson Press, 2003.

———. *Rest in the Storm: Self-Care Strategies for Clergy and Other Caregivers.* Valley Forge, PA: Judson Press, 2001.

Kellemen, Robert, and Karole A. Edwards. *Beyond the Suffering: Embracing the Legacy of African American Soul Care and Spiritual Direction.* Grand Rapids: Baker Books, 2007.

Mabry, John R. *Noticing the Divine: An Introduction to Interfaith Spiritual Guidance.* New York: Morehouse Publishing, 2006.

Park, Jung Eun Sophia. *Border-Crossing Spirituality: Transformation in the Borderland.* Eugene, OR: Pickwick Publications, 2016.

Taylor-Stinson, Therese, ed. *Ain't Gonna Let Nobody Turn Me Around: Stories of Contemplation and Justice.* New York: Church Publishing, 2017.

Vest, Norvene, ed. *Still Listening: New Horizons in Spiritual Direction.* New York: Morehouse Publishing, 2000.

Weems, Renita J. *Listening for God: A Minister's Journey through Silence and Doubt.* Touchstone ed. New York: Simon & Schuster, 2000.

Practical Resources

Comparison of Three Helping Professions: Similarities, Differences, Overlaps

	Pastoral Care	Spiritual Direction	Counseling/Therapy
Role	Pastor, priest, minister, deacon, etc.	Spiritual director, spiritual companion	Counselor, therapist, psychologist
Setting	Congregation or other public ministerial setting (e.g., hospital chaplaincy); "called" by a community or ecclesiastical body to provide ministry for the congregation/community. Pastoral care takes place within both public and private/confidential encounters. (Pastors are also called to preach, teach, administrate the sacraments, and provide organizational leadership for the congregation/community.)	Invited by an individual or group to accompany him/her/them in paying attention and responding to the movement of God in oneself, others, systems, and creation. Private and confidential encounters.	Works with individuals or groups to promote emotional and mental health, alleviate crisis, and deepen self-awareness. People seek out counselors, may be referred for counseling, or even required to be in therapy. Private and confidential encounters.

The table is a work in progress by Maria Bowen, Sam Hamilton-Poore, Jen Herrmann, and Lewis Rambo. © Diploma in the Art of Spiritual Direction, San Francisco Theological Seminary, 2011. It has been included here with permission.

	Pastoral Care	Spiritual Direction	Counseling/Therapy
Provided By	Trained clergy—or trained, designated laity.	Someone with gifts, skills, and sensibilities for compassionate, contemplative listening—may or may not be trained; may be clergy or laity.	Someone professionally trained and certified in mental health and wellness, with various degree options (e.g., LCSW, PhD, PsyD) and licensed by the state.
Co-creates Relationship With	Congregation, congregational leadership and members.	With each directee, individually; or with small group.	With each patient, individually; or with small group.
Training	Three to four years of graduate study (usually including internship); training in biblical studies, theology, preaching, worship, pastoral care, etc.	Varies widely in depth and breadth. Ideally a spiritual director has special received training, formation, and supervision in listening for the presence and movement of the Holy in their own and other lives, the life of the church, etc. Versed in biblical-theological and contemplative traditions of the church; familiar with contemporary psychology, etc.	Trained in human developmental sciences, psychology, social work, mental health and wellness. "Pastoral counselors" would also be trained in most of the same areas as "pastors" (i.e., have an M.Div. or equivalent).

	Pastoral Care	Spiritual Direction	Counseling/Therapy
Listening Approach and Ministerial "Tools"	Active listening, rites, rituals, prayer, worship. *Liturgical/theological*	Contemplative listening to the movement of God in self, others, systems, and creation. Teaching of contemplative practices and awareness. Holding space for transformation. *Contemplative/discernment*	Various types of listening, depending on skills and type of training—i.e., cognitive-behavioral, psychoanalysis, art therapy, etc. *Analytical/diagnosis*
Accountability	Congregation, congregational leadership, ecclesiastical authority (e.g., presbytery, synod, bishop, diocese).	Directee, supervisor(s)—perhaps to the same authorities as pastor and counselor. Codes of ethics from organizations such as Spiritual Directors International.	Professional associations which certify/credential counselors.
Payment	Ordained pastors receive a salary, benefits, etc. from the communities they serve.	A spiritual director may charge a fee or request an honorarium, depending on how they support themselves. Many spiritual directors are not exclusively spiritual directors—they may work as pastors, counselors, teachers, artists, cooks, doctors, nurses, etc.	Ordinarily paid per hour/per session. Insurance may help defray the patient's expense.

The Experience Circle

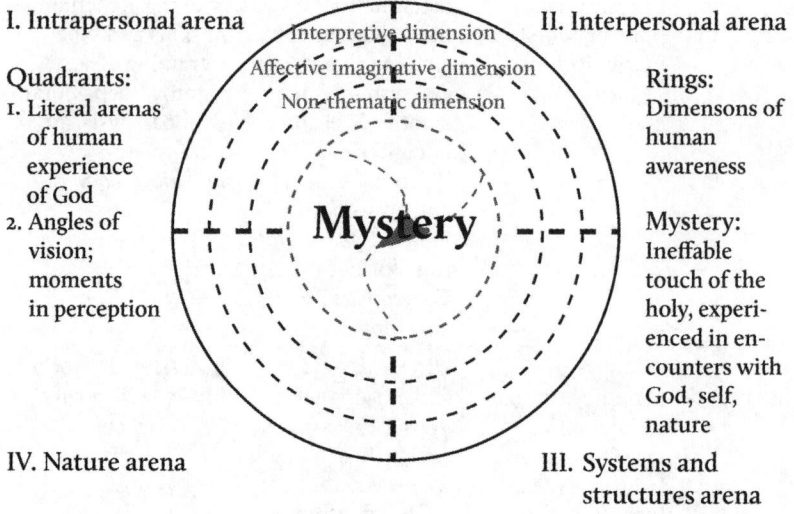

I. Intrapersonal arena

Quadrants:
1. Literal arenas of human experience of God
2. Angles of vision; moments in perception

Interpretive dimension
Affective imaginative dimension
Non-thematic dimension

Mystery

II. Interpersonal arena

Rings:
Dimensons of human awareness

Mystery:
Ineffable touch of the holy, experienced in encounters with God, self, nature

IV. Nature arena

III. Systems and structures arena

Revised June 2004, E. Liebert and N. Weins St. John, SFTS

A Toolkit for Working Spiritual Directors

SD On-The-Go Bag

Greetings Friends and Colleagues,

I am quite excited to share with you one of my most valuable tools as a working spiritual director (SD), my SD On-The-Go Bag! I first developed this tool while in training at the San Francisco Theological Seminary. As it was, my very first directee was most comfortable meeting with me at her country club. Two of my first directees were seminary students who could not easily make it to my church in the inner city where I had appropriate spaces for this spiritual practice. Instead, we met in the library study room, a coffee shop, or went for walks. Soon I had a directee who was homebound. What could have been perceived as challenges rather presented the opportunity for me to "get prepared"!

I had been divinely called to "help others to live less stressful and more abundant lives by yielding to the Holy Spirit who lives within." I interpreted the art of spiritual direction as a direct response to this call and was convinced that it would all work out. My life has never been less than full. Interculturally married for thirty years, my husband and I have four children who have always kept us "on our toes." Upon entering seminary full-time and beginning my SD training program, I was still running a small land-development firm part-time. Currently, I remain in seminary earning a PhD; I serve through the Allen Temple Baptist Church as Associate Minister of Spiritual Life; lead small SD groups; work part-time with a team of campus pastors for the Pacific Lutheran Theological Seminary; teach spiritual direction and other spiritual practices; and I manage my private spiritual direction practice, WJoy—A Spiritual Care Ministry.

In each of these settings, I am regularly afforded the opportunity to offer spiritual care, including spiritual direction. Creativity beckons. I have most treasured my SD On-The-Go Bag! Keeping it well-stocked and always in my vehicle for easy access has made my living into my call so much more fruitful and less stressful. Here are the basic contents:

    a.   Brochures, business cards

b. Leaflets on SD
c. Covenants
d. Receipt book
e. Candles (real and faux); lighter
f. Bowl, rocks, shells (representative of divine creation)
g. Singing bowl
h. Tablecloth
i. Blanket/throw
j. Pens/small writing tablets
k. Tissue
l. Portable clock
m. A small Bluetooth speaker

Note: I also keep my smartphone well-stocked with instrumental, meditation music, and other soothing sounds, gospel or spirituals, prayers, poems, and other inspirational readings.

Peace to you as you walk alongside others to less stressful, more abundant lives following the direction of the Holy Spirit.

REV. INEDA ADESANYA

Bibliography

Barnes, Chanequa Walker. *Too Heavy a Yoke: Black Women and the Burden of Strength.* Eugene, OR: Cascade Books, 2014.

Barry, W. A., and W. J. Connolly, W.J. *The Practice of Spiritual Direction.* San Francisco: Harper & Row, 1982.

Barton, Ruth Haley. *Pursuing God's Will Together: A Discernment Practice for Leadership Groups.* Downers Grove, IL: InterVarsity Press, 2012.

———. *Sacred Rhythms: Arranging Our Lives for Spiritual Transformation.* Downers Grove, IL: InterVarsity Press, 2006.

Bidwell, Duane. *Short-Term Spiritual Guidance.* Minneapolis: Fortress Press, 2004.

Bourgeault, Cynthia. *Centering Prayer and Inner Awakening.* Lanham, MD: Cowley, 2004.

Bowen, Maria Tattu. "Do No Harm: A Case for Professional Boundaries and Supervision in Spiritual Direction." *Presence: An International Journal of Spiritual Direction* 23, no. 3 (2017): 29–37.

Brown, Judy. *The Sea Accepts All Rivers and Other Poems.* Bloomington, IN: Trafford, 2016.

Brown, Lerita Coleman. "An Ordinary Mystic: Contemplation, Inner Authority, and Spiritual Direction in the Life and Work of Howard Thurman." *Presence* 18, no. 1 (March 2012).

Bumpus, Mary Rose, and Rebecca Bradburn Langer, eds. *Supervision of Spiritual Directors: Engaging in Holy Mystery.* Harrisburg, PA: Morehouse, 2005.

Choi, Hee An. *A Postcolonial Self: Korean Immigrant Theology and Church.* Albany: State University of New York, 2015.

Coady, Mary Frances. "Nouwen Finds Rest at Daybreak." *Catholic New Times,* November 23, 1986.

Collegeville Institute. Communities of Calling. https://collegevilleinstitute .org/?s=advent.

Cone, James H. *The Spirituals and the Blues.* Maryknoll, NY: Orbis Books, 1992.

Conroy, Maureen. *Looking Into the Well: Supervision of Spiritual Directors.* Chicago: Loyola University Press, 1995.

Dougherty, Rosemary. *Discernment: A Path to Spiritual Awakening.* Mahwah, NJ: Paulist Press, 2009.

———. "One Form of Group Supervision for Spiritual Directors." *Journal of Supervision and Training in Ministry* 18 (1997): 115–28.

Dunne, John S. *The Way of All the Earth: Experiments in Truth and Religion*. New York: Macmillan, 1973.

Fleming, David L., ed. *The Christian Ministry of Spiritual Direction*. St. Louis: Review for Religious, 1988.

Fryling, Alice. *Seeking God Together: An Introduction to Group Spiritual Direction*. Downers Grove, IL: InterVarsity Press, 2009.

Gallagher, Timothy. *The Discernment of Spirits: An Ignatian Guide for Everyday Living*. New York: Crossroad, 2005.

———. *The Examen Prayer: Ignatian Wisdom for Our Lives Today*. New York: Crossroad, 2006.

The Gathering: A Womanist Church. "The Gathering: A Womanist Church." Accessed August 12, 2019. https://www.thegatheringexperience.com.

Green, Richard. "A Covenant for Spiritual Direction." High Desert Direction—The Spiritual Formation Ministry of Dr. Richard Green and the Christian Formation and Direction Ministry Contact Site. Accessed August 12, 2019. http://www.highdesertdirection.com/articles-more -information/a-covenant-for-spiritual-direction/.

Guenther, Margaret. *Holy Listening: The Art of Spiritual Direction*. New York: Cowley, 1992.

Hall, Jacquelyn Dowd. "'The Mind That Burns in Each Body': Women, Rape, and Racial Violence." In *Powers of Desire: The Politics of Sexuality*, edited by Ann Snitow, Christine Stansell, and Sharon Thompson. New York: Monthly Review Press, 1983.

Harris, Kate. "The Heart of Vocation." The Washington Institute for Faith, Vocation, and Culture, April 23, 2013. http://www.washingtoninst.org/4262 /the-heart-of-vocation/.

Hathcock, April. "My Trauma is Not Your Thought Experiment: On Oppressive Empathy." At the Intersection (blog), June 15, 2018. https://april-hathcock.wordpress.com/2018/06/15/my-trauma-is-not-your-thought -experiment-on-oppressive-empathy/.

Hay, Leslie A. *Hospitality: The Heart of Spiritual Direction*. Harrisburg, PA: Morehouse, 2006.

Hegewisch, Ariane, and Emma Williams-Baron. "The Gender Wage Gap: 2017 Earnings Differences by Race and Ethnicity." Institute for Women's Policy Research, March 7, 2018. https://iwpr.org/publications/gender-wage -gap-2017-race-ethnicity/.

Hines, Darlene Clark. "Rape and the Inner Lives of Black Women in the Middle West: Preliminary Thoughts on the Culture of Dissemblance." *Signs: The Journal of Women, Culture, and Society* 14 (Summer 1989): 2–20.

Hoover, Conrad C. "Going Deep to the Truth: Thomas Merton and Spiritual Direction in a Cross-Cultural Context." In Rakoczy, *Common Journey, Different Paths*, 67–74.

Hull, Akasha Gloria. *Soul Talk: The New Spirituality of African American Women*. Rochester, VT: Inner Traditions, 2001.

Jalāl al-Dīn Rūmī, and Coleman Barks. *The Essential Rumi*. San Francisco, CA: Harper, 1995.

Jorgensen, Susan S. "Peer Supervision: One Model." *Presence: The Journal of Spiritual Directors International* 2, no. 1 (January 1996): 23–37.

Keating, Thomas. *The Human Condition*. Mahwah, NJ: Paulist Press, 1999.
———. *Open Mind, Open Heart*. New York: Continuum, 2006.
Liebert, Elizabeth. "Supervision as Widening the Horizons." In Bumpus and Langer, *Supervision of Spiritual Directors*, 125–45.
Mabry, John. *Noticing the Divine: An Introduction to Interfaith Spiritual Guidance*. New York: Morehouse, 2006.
Martin, José Manuel. *Principles and Practice of Spiritual Direction in the Catholic Church: A Collection of Readings*. Lexington, KY: CreateSpace, 2017.
McCormack, David. "The Transformative Power of Journaling: Reflective Practice as Self-Supervision." In *The Soul of Supervision: Integrating Practice and Theory*, edited by Margaret Benefiel and Geraldine Holton, 25–37. Harrisburg, PA: Morehouse, 2010.
McCrary, Carolyn. "Interdependence as a Normative Value in Pastoral Counseling with African Americans." *Journal of the Interdenominational Theological Center* 18, nos. 1–2 (1990–91).
Merton, Thomas. "A Prayer of Thomas Merton." In *Thoughts in Solitude*. New York: Farrar, Straus & Giroux, 1958.
———. *Spiritual Direction and Meditation*. Collegeville, MN: Liturgical Press, 1960.
Migliore, Daniel. *Faith Seeking Understanding: An Introduction to Christian Theology*. Grand Rapids: Eerdmans, 2004.
Mogabgab, John. *A Spirituality of Living: Henri Nouwen*. Nashville: Upper Room Books, 2011.
Moltmann, Jürgen. *The Source of Life*. Minneapolis: Fortress Press, 1997.
Moon, Gary W., and David G. Benner. *Spiritual Direction and the Care of Souls: A Guide to Christian Approaches and Practices*. Downers Grove, IL: IVP Academic, 2004.
Morrison, Toni. *Beloved*. New York: Vintage, 2004.
Mulholland, M. Robert. *Invitation to a Journey: A Road Map for Spiritual Formation*. Downers Grove, IL: InterVarsity Press, 2016.
Neafsey, James. "Seeing Beyond: A Contemplative Approach to the Supervision Relationship." In Bumpus and Langer, *Supervision of Spiritual Directors*, 17–31.
Nouwen, Henri J. M. *Discernment: Reading the Signs of Daily Life*. New York: HarperOne, 2013.
———. *Reaching Out: The Three Movements of the Spiritual Life*. Garden City, NY: Image, 1986.
———. *Spiritual Direction: Wisdom for the Long Walk of Faith*. New York: HarperOne, 2006.
O'Reilley, Mary Rose. "Deep Listening: An Experimental Friendship." *Friends Journal*, November 1, 1994.
Palmer, Parker J. *A Hidden Wholeness: The Journey toward an Undivided Life—Welcoming the Soul and Weaving Community in a Wounded World*. San Francisco: Jossey-Bass, 2008.
———. *On the Brink of Everything: Grace, Gravity, and Getting Old*. Oakland, CA: Berrett-Koehler, 2018.
Phillips, Susan S. "Regarding the Spiritual Direction of Disabled Persons." In Bumpus and Langer, *Supervision of Spiritual Directors*, 165–79.

Rakoczy, Susan. "Unity, Diversity, and Uniqueness: Foundations of Cross-Cultural Spiritual Direction." In Rakoczy, *Common Journey, Different Paths*, 9–23.

———, ed. *Common Journey, Different Paths: Spiritual Direction in Cross-Cultural Perspective*. Maryknoll, NY: Orbis Books, 1992.

Reed, Juan. "Can I Get A Witness? Spiritual Direction with the Marginalized." In Vest, *Still Listening*, 93–104.

Reininger, Gustave. *The Diversity of Centering Prayer*. New York: Continuum, 1999.

Ricks, Shawn Arango. *Meridians: Feminisms, Race, Transnationalism* 16, no. 2 (2018): 343–50.

Rosenberg, Marshall B. *Nonviolent Communication: A Language of Compassion*. Del Mar, CA: Puddledancer Press, 1999.

Saint Gregory the Great, "Contemplative Outreach," https://www.contemplative outreach.org/christian-contemplative-tradition, accessed January 21, 2019.

Sheppard, Phillis Isabella. *Self, Culture, and Others in Womanist Practical Theology*. New York: Palgrave Macmillan, 2011.

Singh-Morales, Anil. "What Makes A Great Spiritual Director." SDI: The Home of Spiritual Companionship, July 20, 2017. https://www.sdiworld .org/blog/what-makes-good-spiritual-director.

Somé, Malidoma Patrice. *Ritual: Power, Healing, and Community. The African Teachings of the Dagara*. New York: Penguin, 1997.

Spiritual Directors International. "Frequently Asked Questions: Spiritual Directors." Accessed August 12, 2019. https://www.sdiworld.org /spiritual-directors/frequently-asked-questions.

———. "Guidelines for Ethical Conduct: Revised Edition." Bellevue, WA: Spiritual Directors International, 2016.

———. "Sample Agreement Template for Spiritual Direction." Accessed August 12, 2019. https://www.sdiworld.org/sites/default/files/find-a-spiritual -director/2012.11.21%20Sample%20Engagement%20Agreement.pdf.

Stairs, Jean. *Listening for the Soul: Pastoral Care and Spiritual Direction*. Minneapolis: Fortress Press, 2000.

Thibodeaux, Mark A. *Reimagining the Ignatian Examen: Fresh Ways to Pray from Your Day*. Chicago: Loyola University Press, 2015.

Thurman, Howard. *The Centering Moment*. Richmond, IN: Friends United Press, 2007.

———. *Deep Is the Hunger: Meditations for Apostles of Sensitiveness*. Richmond, VA: Friends United Press, 1951.

———. "Give Me the Listening Ear." In *Meditations of the Heart*. Boston: Beacon Press, 1953.

———. *Jesus and the Disinherited*. Boston: Beacon Press, 1976.

———. *Meditations of the Heart*. Boston: Beacon Press, 1999.

———. "The Sound of the Genuine." Commencement address, Spelman College, Atlanta, 1980.

———. "What Shall I Do with My Life?" In *A Strange Freedom: The Best of Howard Thurman on Religious Experience and Public Life*, edited by Walter Earl Fluker and Catherine Tumber. Boston: Beacon Press, 1998.

———. "The Work of Christmas." In *The Mood of Christmas*. Richmond, IN: Friends United Press, 2001.

United Church of Religious Science. *Visioning Workbook*, 2005. http://ggcsl .org/resources/pdf/The_Visioning_Manual.pdf.

van der Kolk, Bessel. *The Body Keeps the Score: Brain, Mind, and Body in Healing Trauma*. New York: Viking Press, 2015.

Vest, Norvene. "Wary Seekers: Spiritual Direction with Church Dropouts." In Vest, *Still Listening*, 49–62.

———, ed. *Still Listening: New Horizons in Spiritual Direction*. Harrisburg, PA: Morehouse, 2000.

Walker, Alice. "Womanist." In *In Search of Our Mothers' Gardens: Womanist Prose*. London: Women's Press, 1987.

West, Ruth T. "The Power of Three Voices." Placing My Stone on Awesomeness, August 10, 2017, https://ruthtwest.wixsite.com.

Williams, Mary. "The Examen Journal: Finding God Everyday." YouTube, March 25, 2015, https://www.youtube.com/watch?v=om4c8bALIec&feat ure=youtu.be.

About the Authors

Each of the contributing authors of Kaleidoscope is a member of the Spiritual Directors of Color Network, Ltd. They represent the following faith traditions: Christian (Protestant); American Baptist and Presbyterian (USA); Word-Based Christian (South Africa); Roman Catholic; Humanist with Buddhist Affinities; Interfaith; Contemplative/Evangelical Covenant Church; Apostolic Pentecostal. They have diverse training in spiritual direction from the following programs:

1. Christos Center for Spiritual Formation, Minnesota
2. Institute for Spiritual Leadership, Illinois
3. Mercy Center, Burlingame, California
4. Oasis Ministries for Spiritual Development, Camp Hill, Pennsylvania
5. Pecos Benedictine School of Spiritual Direction, New Mexico
6. Roman Catholic Seminary, South Africa
7. San Francisco Theological Seminary, Diploma in the Art of Spiritual Direction
8. Shalem Institute for Spiritual Formation, Washington, DC

Reverend **Ineda Pearl Adesanya** is an ordained American Baptist minister serving as Associate Minister of Spiritual Life for the historic Allen Temple Baptist Church. She is a founding board member of the Spiritual Directors of Color Network, Ltd. Ineda received both her Master of Divinity and Diploma in the Art of Spiritual Direction from San Francisco Theological Seminary (SFTS). She earned a Master of Arts in Religion and Psychology from the

Graduate Theological Union in Berkeley, California, where she is currently earning a PhD. Ineda holds a Bachelor of Arts from the University of California at Berkeley. Ineda provides spiritual direction, leads contemplative retreats, hosts an annual Spirituality and Hermeneutics Forum, and authors a weekly blog. She teaches courses in spiritual direction at The Interfaith Chaplaincy Institute in Berkeley, California. Ineda extends her practice part-time in pastoral counseling, spiritual direction, and supervision for the Pacific Lutheran Theological Seminary, SFTS, and in private practice.

Reverend **Gibbon Bogatsu**, B.Th., is an author and a speaker from Johannesburg, South Africa. He was ordained in 1988 as a Roman Catholic priest and transitioned into a Christian Word-Based Ministry in 1995 to establish Healthy Marriage Services Apostolate. He also cofounded Global Christian Unity Trust with his wife, the Reverend Duduzile Bogatsu, in 2012. Gibbon works primarily as a spiritual life coach, skills facilitator, and motivational speaker and has a passion for uniting Christians across mainline churches and evangelical born-again churches as a global Christian speaker.

Consuella L. Brown is a spiritual director, social-justice advocate, and recovering philanthropoid. She currently moonlights as an executive coach, not-for-profit consultant, and adjunct faculty member at Loyola University Chicago's School of Social Work and Dominican University's Masters of Arts in Conflict Resolution program. Consuella is a graduate of Scripps College, Illinois State University, and the former Institute for Spiritual Leadership in Chicago.

Diana L. Hayes is Emerita Professor of Systematic Theology at Georgetown University. She holds the Juris Doctor (Law), PhD (Religious Studies), and Doctor of Sacred Theology degrees (STD) and is the first African American woman to earn the Pontifical Doctorate from The Catholic University of Louvain (Belgium). Dr. Hayes's most recent publication is *No Crystal Stair: Womanist Spirituality.*

Maurice J. Nutt, C.Ss.R., D.Min., is a Roman Catholic priest in the Redemptorist community and holds a Doctor of Ministry degree in preaching from Aquinas Institute of Theology. He is a former director of the Institute for Black Catholic Studies at Xavier University of Louisiana. Maurice is the Diocesan Liaison for the cause for canonization of his mentor, Sister Thea Bowman, F.S.P.A., of the Diocese of Jackson and the convener of the Black Catholic Theological Symposium.

Reverend Dr. **Paula Owens Parker** is a Presbyterian minister, adjunct professor, and interim director of the Katie Geneva Cannon Center of Womanist Leadership at Union Presbyterian Seminary, Richmond, Virgina. She is the author of *Roots Matter: Healing History, Honoring Heritage, Renewing Hope.* Paula is a graduate of Union Presbyterian Seminary; San Francisco Theological Seminary; the School of Spiritual Direction at Pecos Benedictine Monastery, Pecos, New Mexico; and the School of Healing Prayer at Christian Healing Ministries, Jacksonville, Florida. Paula's faith and spiritual formation continues to be shaped by Baptist, Catholic, Episcopal, and Presbyterian faith traditions, each bringing their unique interpretation and practice of Christianity.

Phillis Isabella Sheppard is Associate Professor of Religion, Psychology, and Culture at the Divinity School/Graduate Department of Religion of Vanderbilt University. She is the author of the groundbreaking *Self, Culture, and Others in Womanist Practical Theology* (Palgrave Macmillan, 2011), and her current book project, *Tilling Sacred Ground: Interiority, Black Women, and Public Religion,* takes as its focus the intersection of black women's interiority, the sociality of race, gender, sexuality, and the public expression of religion. Phillis is a psychoanalyst and pastoral psychotherapist and has maintained a clinical practice for more than twenty-five years. She earned the PhD from Chicago Theological Seminary, and the Master of Arts from Colgate Rochester Divinity School. She is a graduate of the Chicago Institute for Psychoanalysis and the Center for Religion and Psychotherapy.

Maisie Sparks is a writer, editor, and communications consultant. A journalism graduate of the University of Illinois, she is the editorial director of The Sparks Group, a marketing and communications firm she founded nearly twenty-five years ago. In 2007,

Maisie received certification in the art of spiritual direction from the Christos Center for Spiritual Formation and, three years later, earned a master's degree in Family Ministry and Spiritual Formation from Dominican University. Maisie facilitates contemplative retreats and has spoken on Christian spirituality and faith formation at conferences and retreats nationally and internationally. She is the author of *151 Things God Can't Do; Holy Shakespeare; Christmas Quiet*; and other titles.

Therese Taylor-Stinson is the founding managing member of the Spiritual Directors of Color Network, Ltd., an elder-advisor for the Mystic Soul Project, and an ordained deacon and ruling elder in the Presbyterian Church (USA), serving a term as Moderator for National Capital Presbytery from 2015–2017. In 2018, as an author-editor, Therese won an Indie Author Legacy Award as Author of the Year in the area of social awareness for her solo edited work *Ain't Gonna Let Nobody Turn Me Around: Stories of Contemplation and Justice*, and was recognized by Grace and Race, Inc., as a Collaborative Bridge Builder. Therese has been a spiritual director in private practice for more than thirteen years. She is a graduate of the Shalem Institute for Spiritual Formation, where she is a member of the Shalem Society for Contemplative Leadership, and she also serves on Spiritual Directors International's editorial-review panel for its premier journal *Presence*.

Addie Lorraine Walker, SSND, PhD, serves full-time on the faculty of Oblate School of Theology as Associate Professor of Pastoral Theology. She is founder and director of the Sankofa Institute for African American Pastoral Leadership. Currently, she teaches graduate courses that include "Introduction to Black Church Studies," "African/African American Spirituality," "Reconciliation and Healing in the Black Church Community," and "Spirituality and Culture."

Ruth Takiko West is an ordained Presbyterian Church (USA) Minister of the Word and Sacrament. In addition to a Master of Divinity, Ruth holds an MBA, Diploma in the Art of Spiritual Direction, and a Certificate in Trauma and Spiritual Care. She is currently

Program Manager for Advanced Pastoral Studies at San Francisco Theological Seminary, which facilitates the Doctor of Ministry program, and has also worked on the Committee for Preparation in Ministry (CPM) and the Presbytery Engagement Team (PET) for the San Francisco Presbytery. Ruth's passion is to provide spiritual care especially to individuals and groups in transition. As a spiritual director and chaplain, she has developed, prepared, and presented spiritual, devotional, and meditational practices and provided spiritual direction and chaplaincy for groups and individuals in church, workshop, and retreat settings.

Naisa Wong is a proud member of the Spiritual Directors of Color Network, the Director's Guild of America, Stage Directors and Choreographers Society, and Literary Managers and Dramaturgs of the Americas. She is a featured spiritual director with Gravity Center: A Center for Contemplative Activism (www.gravitycenter .com). Naisa's continuing mission is to support and guide individuals and groups toward discovering and living out their most creative and authentic selves. She has her graduate training in spiritual direction and certifications in trauma care. Naisa has had the great honor of supporting several organizations using her creative care skills including Sojourners, Travis Air Force Base, Catholic Charities of San Francisco, New College Berkeley, and San Francisco Theological Seminary.

Reverend **Betty Wright-Riggins** is an ordained American Baptist minister. She is a spiritual director and certified grief recovery specialist in private practice. Betty is a visiting instructor at Oasis Ministries for Spiritual Direction, where she lectures on African American spirituality and is the Princeton Theological Seminary cohort leader for students seeking certification in spiritual direction. She is an adjunct instructor of spiritual formation at Palmer Theological Seminary. She has pastored and is a sought-after spiritual-formation retreat leader, conference speaker, and preacher.

Reverend Dr. **Daeseop Daniel Yi**, PhD, Korean Student Advisor and Affiliate Faculty in Spirituality at San Francisco Theological Seminary, is dedicated to understanding how humans can be their authentic selves and live their lives fully through various contemplative practices. Yi earned a PhD in Christian Spirituality from the Graduate Theological Union. He has been on the staff of SFTS's Diploma in the Art of Spiritual Direction program since 2008. He has also worked for many years as a pastor and chief of staff at a local church and in a campus ministry for young adults. He is interested in living "in between" so that he can be a bridge between the United States and Korea and be creative in both cultures.